THE BEDFORD SERIES IN HISTORY AND CULTURE

The Harlem Renaissance

A Brief History with Documents

Related Titles in

THE BEDFORD SERIES IN HISTORY AND CULTURE

Advisory Editors: Lynn Hunt, *University of California, Los Angeles*
David W. Blight, *Yale University*
Bonnie G. Smith, *Rutgers University*
Natalie Zemon Davis, *Princeton University*
Ernest R. May, *Harvard University*

THE INTERESTING NARRATIVE OF THE LIFE OF OLAUDAH EQUIANO WRITTEN BY HIMSELF *with Related Documents, Second Edition*
Edited with an Introduction by Robert J. Allison, *Suffolk University*

Crosscurrents in the Black Atlantic, 1770–1965: A Brief History with Documents
David Northrup, *Boston College*

NARRATIVE OF THE LIFE OF FREDERICK DOUGLASS, AN AMERICAN SLAVE, WRITTEN BY HIMSELF *with Related Documents, Second Edition*
Edited with an Introduction by David W. Blight, *Yale University*

UP FROM SLAVERY *by Booker T. Washington with Related Documents*
Edited with an Introduction by W. Fitzhugh Brundage, *University of North Carolina at Chapel Hill*

PLESSY V. FERGUSON: *A Brief History with Documents*
Edited with an Introduction by Brook Thomas, *University of California, Irvine*

THE SOULS OF BLACK FOLK *by W. E. B. Du Bois*
Edited with an Introduction by David W. Blight, *Yale University*, and Robert Gooding-Williams, *Northwestern University*

SOUTHERN HORRORS *and Other Writings: The Anti-Lynching Campaign of Ida B. Wells, 1892–1900*
Edited with an Introduction by Jacqueline Jones Royster, *Ohio State University*

Black Protest and the Great Migration: A Brief History with Documents
Eric Arnesen, *University of Illinois at Chicago*

BROWN V. BOARD OF EDUCATION: *A Brief History with Documents*
Waldo E. Martin Jr., *University of California, Berkeley*

Martin Luther King Jr., Malcolm X, and the Civil Rights Struggle of the 1950s and 1960s: A Brief History with Documents
David Howard-Pitney, *De Anza College*

THE BEDFORD SERIES IN HISTORY AND CULTURE

The Harlem Renaissance

A Brief History with Documents

Jeffrey B. Ferguson

Amherst College

BEDFORD/ST. MARTIN'S Boston ♦ New York

For Bedford/St. Martin's

Executive Editor for History: Mary V. Dougherty
Director of Development for History: Jane Knetzger
Developmental Editor: Ann Hofstra Grogg
Editorial Assistant: Laurel Damashek
Production Supervisor: Jennifer Peterson
Executive Marketing Manager: Jenna Bookin Barry
Project Management: Books By Design, Inc.
Text Design: Claire Seng-Niemoeller
Index: Books By Design, Inc.
Cover Design: Liz Tardiff
Cover Art: *Interpretation of Harlem Jazz*, ca. 1925, by Winold Reiss (1886–1953), 20 × 15″, ink and watercolor on paper. Private collection. Image provided by The Reiss Partnership.
Composition: Stratford/TexTech
Printing and Binding: RR Donnelley & Sons Company

President: Joan E. Feinberg
Editorial Director: Denise B. Wydra
Director of Marketing: Karen Melton Soeltz
Director of Editing, Design, and Production: Marcia Cohen
Manager, Publishing Services: Emily Berleth

Library of Congress Control Number: 2007933166

Manufactured in the United States of America.

2 1 0 9 8 7
f e d c b a

For information, write: Bedford / St. Martin's, 75 Arlington Street, Boston, MA 02116 (617-399-4000)

ISBN-10: 0-312-41075-1
ISBN-13: 978-0-312-41075-9

Acknowledgments

Acknowledgments and copyrights are continued at the back of the book on pages 193–94, which constitute an extension of the copyright page.

Foreword

The Bedford Series in History and Culture is designed so that readers can study the past as historians do.

The historian's first task is finding the evidence. Documents, letters, memoirs, interviews, pictures, movies, novels, or poems can provide facts and clues. Then the historian questions and compares the sources. There is more to do than in a courtroom, for hearsay evidence is welcome, and the historian is usually looking for answers beyond act and motive. Different views of an event may be as important as a single verdict. How a story is told may yield as much information as what it says.

Along the way the historian seeks help from other historians and perhaps from specialists in other disciplines. Finally, it is time to write, to decide on an interpretation and how to arrange the evidence for readers.

Each book in this series contains an important historical document or group of documents, each document a witness from the past and open to interpretation in different ways. The documents are combined with some element of historical narrative—an introduction or a biographical essay, for example—that provides students with an analysis of the primary source material and important background information about the world in which it was produced.

Each book in the series focuses on a specific topic within a specific historical period. Each provides a basis for lively thought and discussion about several aspects of the topic and the historian's role. Each is short enough (and inexpensive enough) to be a reasonable one-week assignment in a college course. Whether as classroom or personal reading, each book in the series provides firsthand experience of the challenge—and fun—of discovering, recreating, and interpreting the past.

Lynn Hunt
David W. Blight
Bonnie G. Smith
Natalie Zemon Davis
Ernest R. May

Preface

Today, academic and public discussion of African Americans focuses on culture, but this has not always been true. Nor has African American culture always borne the connotations of liberation, resistance, and connection with Africa that appear in our time to be its most salient attributes. Although it is possible to see these qualities at work from the earliest days of slavery, they did not come together in an enduring constellation of associations until the Harlem Renaissance, a black cultural movement occurring between the world wars and centered in New York City, but with national and international reach. Through an unprecedented outpouring of plays, novels, poetry, music, and visual art by such black artists as Langston Hughes, Zora Neale Hurston, Louis Armstrong, and Aaron Douglas, the writers and thinkers of the Harlem Renaissance collectively asserted the idea of a "New Negro" who protested vocally against racism and expressed identity on his or her own terms.

Born in an era marked by race riots, a resurgence of the Ku Klux Klan, and new brands of scientific racism, the New Negro of the Harlem Renaissance embraced black beauty, African roots, and African American folk wisdom while projecting urban sophistication, celebrating the social and biological mixing of the races, and holding out for democratic practices that reflected democratic ideals. Such a complicated agenda contained many possibilities for debate and conflict: Who was the New Negro? How should this New Negro express himself or herself? What role should whites play in the new movement? What should black art have to do with black politics? The artists and thinkers of the Harlem Renaissance shaped such questions, but they did not provide final answers. Yet, because their debates remain our own in so many ways, their art still moves us to think more deeply about the role of racial identity in the past, present, and future.

With a representative sample of Harlem Renaissance art, this volume introduces students to its most important artists, enduring themes, historical origins, legacies, and debates. As it delineates the special role of the imagination in the events of the period, the introduction explains the larger meaning of the Harlem Renaissance as a braiding of history, memory, and myth—as a layering of the official historical record, the unofficial popular account of the racial past, and the broad frameworks, or narratives, that guide thinking about the ultimate meaning of American life. Moving from the origins of the Harlem Renaissance in the black migration of the World War I era, the introduction recounts the rise of Harlem as an important center of African American life, the cultural events that prepared the way for the Harlem Renaissance, its major thematic thrusts, its main controversies, its demise, and its legacy.

The organization of the documents follows that of the introduction. The first section is largely chronological; the second is thematic, with investigations into internationalism and Africa, black folk culture, jazz and the blues, gender, racial intermixture, and the literature of "passing." The third section addresses debates over the practice of black art, the existence of black culture, the role of white patrons, black ownership of artistic institutions, and the legacy of the Harlem Renaissance. Document headnotes give background information on authors, contextualize the main themes, and ask questions that encourage critical reading. A glossary of major figures and publications provides an easy reference tool, and a chronology helps students put selections and events in sequence. A list of thought-provoking questions stimulates class discussion, and a selected bibliography helps guide further exploration. These student aids are designed to facilitate study of the Harlem Renaissance in both history and literature classes.

ACKNOWLEDGMENTS

I want to express my gratitude to those who have helped to make this volume possible. Bedford Series editor and my close friend David W. Blight advised me at every stage. My editor, Ann Hofstra Grogg, was tough and gentle, prodding and supportive, at just the right times. I appreciate the feedback I received from the reviewers who read an earlier draft: Ruth Feingold, St. Mary's College of Maryland; Ron Keller, Lincoln College; Natalie Ring, University of Texas at Dallas; Werner Sollors, Harvard University; and Bruce Tyler, University of

Louisville; as well as two reviewers who preferred to remain anonymous. My colleague Hilary Moss deserves special mention for her willingness to listen and for her crucial advice. John Stauffer and Rosalina de la Carerra deserve the same, as do Uday Mehta; Phillip Cooper; Rowland Abiodun; my mother, Virginia Jones Poree; and my partner, Agustina Suryawan. Last, I would like to thank someone who will never read this acknowledgment, the late Nathan I. Huggins, who taught me to love the Harlem Renaissance and to wonder about many other matters that I am still striving to grasp.

Jeffrey B. Ferguson

Contents

Illustrations

THE BEDFORD SERIES IN HISTORY AND CULTURE

The Harlem Renaissance

A Brief History with Documents

PART ONE

Introduction: The Harlem Renaissance as History, Memory, and Myth

The Harlem Renaissance comes down to us today as a braiding of history, memory, and myth. Understood as history, it names a period falling between the early 1920s and the late 1930s when culture came to the forefront of the many-sided debate surrounding African American freedom. These years corresponded with an unprecedented artistic outpouring in the form of plays, novels, poetry, music, and visual art representing black life across many social categories—urban and rural, light skinned and dark, upper and lower class, male and female, heterosexual and homosexual. As the name indicates, the Harlem Renaissance found its physical and spiritual center in New York City, but its reach extended to Boston, Chicago, Philadelphia, Washington, London, Paris, Africa, and the Caribbean.

Conceived of as memory, or as a matter of lived rather than official history, the Harlem Renaissance represents one instance of the larger African American attempt to transform the backward-looking story of slavery and its aftermath into a forward-looking narrative of self-possession and possibility. Toward this end, African American journals and newspapers heralded the birth of a New Negro, who stood in stark contrast to his supposedly shuffling and submissive forebear.[1]

Rather than submit to racism, this new type of black American insisted on full social and political equality and expressed herself in her own terms, often celebrating features of black life that Western culture typically vilified: thus black became beautiful, Africa became an exalted place of origin, and the black voice became a source of cultural and political power. Because it succeeded so well in providing lasting examples of both power and beauty in the form of art, the Harlem Renaissance holds a rightful place in African American memory as a time when freedom began to feel free.

Regarded as memory, the Harlem Renaissance shades ever more into myth. In this broader guise, it reflects the centrality of rebirth in American national ideology. From the Puritan "City on a Hill," to the forging of frontier settlement, to the immigrant ordeal of assimilation, Americans have always believed in transformation and progress. In its attempt to start African American history over again in a time and place unmarked by slavery, the Harlem Renaissance adds a twist to this tradition. In rough agreement with American myths of renewal but against the grain of American racial practice, it represents an enduring hope: that the lowest and most rejected of outsiders, slaves and former slaves in a nation of free people, may rise up and claim their birthright.

Because it reflects the larger aspirations of Americans and African Americans, the Harlem Renaissance comes down to us today as a historical subject with strong contemporary resonance. Consider the aura of magic surrounding the Harlem Globetrotters and *Showtime at the Apollo*, or the attention given to former president Bill Clinton for locating his office in Harlem. Because Harlem is still regarded as *the* symbolic African American cultural space, the Harlem Renaissance is both an intriguing and a daunting subject for historians. A lightning rod for American and African American racial aspiration, it seems to defy dispassionate analysis, as those who would comment on the events and works of the period are inevitably drawn into the vortex of current political debates. Moreover, because the Harlem Renaissance involves so centrally what black Americans have thought about themselves, it requires sympathetic involvement for full understanding. Yet this very requirement, combined with the high-stakes possibility of racial self-creation and regeneration, has often made it more an object of vilification or celebration than a subject of critical analysis.

As a result, the scholarly debate on the Harlem Renaissance centers around a single rather un-nuanced question: Did it succeed or fail? In other words, did a truly self-aware and authentic mode of black expression arise in this era? Such a question leads to many others regarding origins, legacies, individual artists, the range of participants in the movement, and the proper standards for judging the art it produced. It will be best to approach these questions historically, first by asking how and why the Harlem Renaissance began.

THE NEW NEGRO

Like any complex historical event, the Harlem Renaissance has many roots, some of which coil deeply into the subsoil of American and African American history. Nevertheless, its immediate origins go back only a decade to the militant "New Negro" movement of the 1910s. In turning the combative political energies of this earlier movement toward a cultural application, the Harlem Renaissance gave the term *New Negro* a new set of connotations.

Originating in the early nineteenth century as a name for newly arrived slaves, the term *New Negro* took on a range of meanings by the early twentieth century that included both violent resistance to oppression and the conservative, anti-protest orientation of Booker T. Washington, the president of Tuskegee Institute and the dominant figure in black American politics from 1895 until his death in 1915. During these years, southern states—where 90 percent of the U.S. black population resided—sought increasingly to exclude blacks socially through segregation laws (Jim Crow), politically by preventing them from voting (disfranchisement), and economically by limiting them to small, heavily indebted cotton farms (sharecropping). Widespread racial violence against blacks by police forces and by ordinary citizens added an element of everyday terror to the litany of racial oppression. Rather than fight for political and social rights under such difficult circumstances, the practical-minded Washington publicly accepted segregation and disfranchisement as immovable realities. He argued that industrial training and individual effort would gradually build black business skill and wealth. And he thought blacks would gain their civil rights in time. Washington's compromise approach became the principal political target of a very different kind of New Negro, one mainly based in northern cities and who refused to trade with racists on what he regarded as basic human rights. Led most prominently by the multitalented intellectual W. E. B. Du Bois, this group served as a harbinger of events to come—but much would have to change in black American life before this direction became apparent.

Among the many changes that would radicalize blacks in the early twentieth century, migration to the North, precipitated by World War I (1914–1918), was the most important. The war in Europe virtually cut off European immigration, forcing Northern industry to turn to black labor from the South at a time when southern blacks were eager to escape the unrelenting racial cruelty and poverty endemic to the cotton industry. Therefore, economic and social influences both "pushed" and "pulled" black migrants toward the North. In deciding to leave familiar surroundings for an inviting but virtually unknown "Promised Land," they transformed their own lives as they altered the course of African American history. Between 1915 and 1918, 500,000 blacks migrated to the North. A second wave of 700,000 followed during the 1920s. Together, these two large migrations urbanized about one-tenth of the black American population within fifteen years.

As the northern black population rose, so did expectations. But the North rarely met them. When blacks began to arrive in northern cities such as Chicago and New York, whites restricted them to segregated neighborhoods that quickly became overcrowded. Many working-class whites feared that black laborers would take their jobs, act as strikebreakers, or accept lower wages. Although blacks did this much less often than whites suspected, such fears sparked racial violence in industrial cities.[2] In 1917, rioting white workers in East St. Louis, Illinois, who claimed to be attacking "scabs" and "strikebreakers," left more than forty African Americans dead and six thousand homeless. In response to the increasingly dangerous racial atmosphere, the National Association for the Advancement of Colored People (NAACP) held a Silent March from Harlem to downtown Manhattan. This dramatic protest not only announced the powerful new black presence in urban America, but also protested the government's unwillingness to protect black citizens and, through the silence of its 10,000 participants, the government suppression of dissent through wartime measures such as the Espionage Act (1917). One silent protester carried a sign beseeching President Woodrow Wilson, who promised that the war would "make the world safe for democracy," to make America safe for democracy, too.[3] Clearly, urbanized blacks were beginning to view their situation in national and international terms.

African American soldiers in World War I served in a segregated military that did everything possible to restrict their activities to ditch digging and fence mending. Of the 325,000 black soldiers in the war, only 20 percent served in combat roles; among this 20 percent was

Harlem's 369th Regiment, whom the Germans called the Hell Fighters. For fighting 191 consecutive days in the trenches without a single man captured or an inch of ground lost to the enemy and for spearheading the Allied invasion of the Rhine, the regiment was awarded the Croix-de-Guerre for bravery by the French command, even as American commanders cast aspersions on the courage of black soldiers.[4] Upon its return to the United States in 1919, the 369th marched triumphantly and symbolically up Fifth Avenue in tight French formation (see Figure 1). When it finally reached the adoring crowds of Harlem, the soldiers broke ranks and rushed into the arms of friends and family as the regimental band, led by James Reese Europe, played "Here Comes My Daddy Now." At that bright moment of jubilation, it seemed that the New Negro had arrived in his rightful place of glory. Yet the moment would not last. W. E. B. Du Bois, now editor of *The Crisis*, the journal of the NAACP, described the predicament with singular eloquence in "Returning Soldiers" (see Document 1). Having

Figure 1. *The 369th Regiment Marching up Fifth Avenue, New York City, February 17, 1919.*
National Archives.

fought for the cause of democracy on the battlefields of Europe, black soldiers returned to fight for democracy at home.[5]

"Returning Soldiers" declared Du Bois's dogged resolve to continue the fight for equality, but it also tacitly admitted that his support for war had been too optimistic. Against a vocal minority of black leaders who questioned whether black Americans ought to fight for a country that had done nothing but betray them, Du Bois had urged blacks in 1918 to "close ranks" with whites and put their grievances aside.[6] He had hoped that such a gesture might soften white racism, but it did not, as the return of soldiers after World War I only intensified American race prejudice. Under the pressure of postwar economic readjustment and widespread fear of a new black militancy, a long and bloody series of race riots, collectively referred to as the Red Summer of 1919, broke out in Chicago, Washington, and twenty-four other cities. In the rabid violence of that year, seventy-six African Americans were lynched, including ten soldiers in uniform.[7] In response, the Jamaican writer Claude McKay published "If We Must Die" (see Document 6), a poem seething with the indignation and determination of the political underdog.

Contributing to the heightened racial tensions was a revived Ku Klux Klan, a racist paramilitary organization now dedicated to intimidating not only African Americans, but also immigrants. The Klan quickly gained members and extended its reach to northern states, where it gave voice to white working-class fears.[8] At the same time, the Communist Revolution in Russia (1917–1918) generated fears that outsiders would attempt to overthrow the American political and economic system. This "Red Scare" eventually was used to justify a series of government raids in the early 1920s, led by Attorney General A. Mitchell Palmer, against "communist sympathizers"—a broad label that included almost anyone who questioned sharply and publicly the laws and economic practices of the United States.

This included A. Philip Randolph and Chandler Owen, editors of the Socialist journal *The Messenger*, who had campaigned loudly against World War I, denouncing it as a "capitalist war" in which millions of workers sacrificed their lives only to enrich the owners of weapons factories, steel mills, and other war industries. Randolph and Owen also viewed the race problem in economic terms. Ruling-class whites promoted racism, they said, because it divided white workers from black workers. Randolph and Owen urged black socialism, collective ownership of factories, and working-class unity across racial lines. Their "The New Negro—What Is He?" (see Document 2) asserts this program as it roundly denounces the political ideas of an older generation of black leaders.

Although New Negroes such as Randolph, Owen, and Du Bois advocated what they saw as the interest of ordinary black people, they never came close to capturing the mass imagination. This honor went to the Jamaican Marcus Garvey. While the majority of black leaders advocated integration, Garvey secured a large following by promoting a vision of independent black economic and political power. Through his organization, the Universal Negro Improvement Association (UNIA), and its shipping fleet, the Black Star Line, he hoped to establish an independent state in Africa that would link black people all over the world economically, politically, and spiritually. The sheer size and energy of the Garvey movement—which exceeded 500,000 members in the early 1920s—alarmed leaders such as Du Bois and Randolph, and its antics embarrassed them. Built in part on the idea of making the dream of an African empire tangible to ordinary blacks, the UNIA held huge conventions (see Document 3) and large, garish parades on the streets of Harlem that put on display the "dukes" and "duchesses" that made up its leadership. Also, by the standards of many black leaders, Garvey's version of "black is beautiful" rhetoric, which urged blacks to rise up as a "mighty race," appeared dangerously chauvinistic and out of place in a racial atmosphere marked by such threats as the Ku Klux Klan and the Red Scare.

Initially, A. Philip Randolph's *Messenger* led the charge against Garvey with a vitriolic "Garvey Must Go" campaign that attempted to turn the tide of black American opinion against the Jamaican. Garvey added to the controversy surrounding himself when he met with Ku Klux Klan leaders in 1922. Although Garvey said he believed in facing the enemy, his explanations did little to help defuse the denouncements of him in black journals and newspapers. The NAACP and Randolph's group then worked together to have Garvey investigated by the federal government. Ultimately tried for mail fraud charges stemming from his sloppy conduct of stock sales for the Black Star Line, Garvey went to jail in 1925. In 1927, he was deported, never to return to the United States. His demise, which placed in bold relief the willingness of New Negro leadership to use the government against one of its own, corresponded with the decline of black political radicalism in the 1920s. This decline would in turn play a decisive role in the rise of the Harlem Renaissance, a cultural movement that preserved some elements of the earlier radicalism even as it made a less direct and less dangerous assault on racial injustice.

HARLEM REAL AND IMAGINED

Although debates about the New Negro had national and international significance, they occurred for the most part in a single neighborhood in upper Manhattan (see Figure 2). In 1920, Harlem stretched six blocks from Lexington Avenue on the east side to St. Nicholas Avenue on the west. From north to south it covered about twenty blocks, or approximately one mile, between 125th and 145th streets. In this area, which expanded fifteen blocks to the south and ten blocks to the north by 1930 and grew in population from about 92,000 in 1910 to 328,000 in 1930, one could find the main headquarters of many significant civil rights organizations, including the UNIA and the National Urban League.[9] Here were the homes and offices of many civil rights leaders of national importance, including W. E. B. Du Bois, James Weldon Johnson, and A. Philip Randolph. The major journals connected to important civil rights organizations, such as *Opportunity* (published by Urban League) and *Negro World* (published by the UNIA), and major newspapers such as the *New York Age* and the *Amsterdam News* had offices here. The Silent March originated in Harlem; Marcus Garvey's colorful parades always occurred here; and the victorious 369th Regiment called it home.

Yet Harlem represented much more than a political center in the decade after World War I. Because of its location in New York City, a great entry point for immigrants, Harlem became in the 1920s a primary destination for black people from all over the world. Immigrants from the West Indies and Africa mixed freely with migrants from the South and with black New Yorkers whose families had resided in the city since the colonial period. In Harlem, blacks with college degrees circulated among uneducated people, and the richest resided within easy walking distance of the poor. As New York was the major American center for theater and publishing, Harlem attracted writers and artists of all sorts.[10] It was a center of black intellectual and artistic activity and, as poems by Helene Johnson, Claude McKay, and Countée Cullen demonstrate (see Documents 5, 6, and 8), a constant site of return for the artistic imagination of the 1920s and 1930s.

In his study *Black Manhattan* (see Document 4), James Weldon Johnson, one of the older artists and theorists of the Harlem Renaissance,

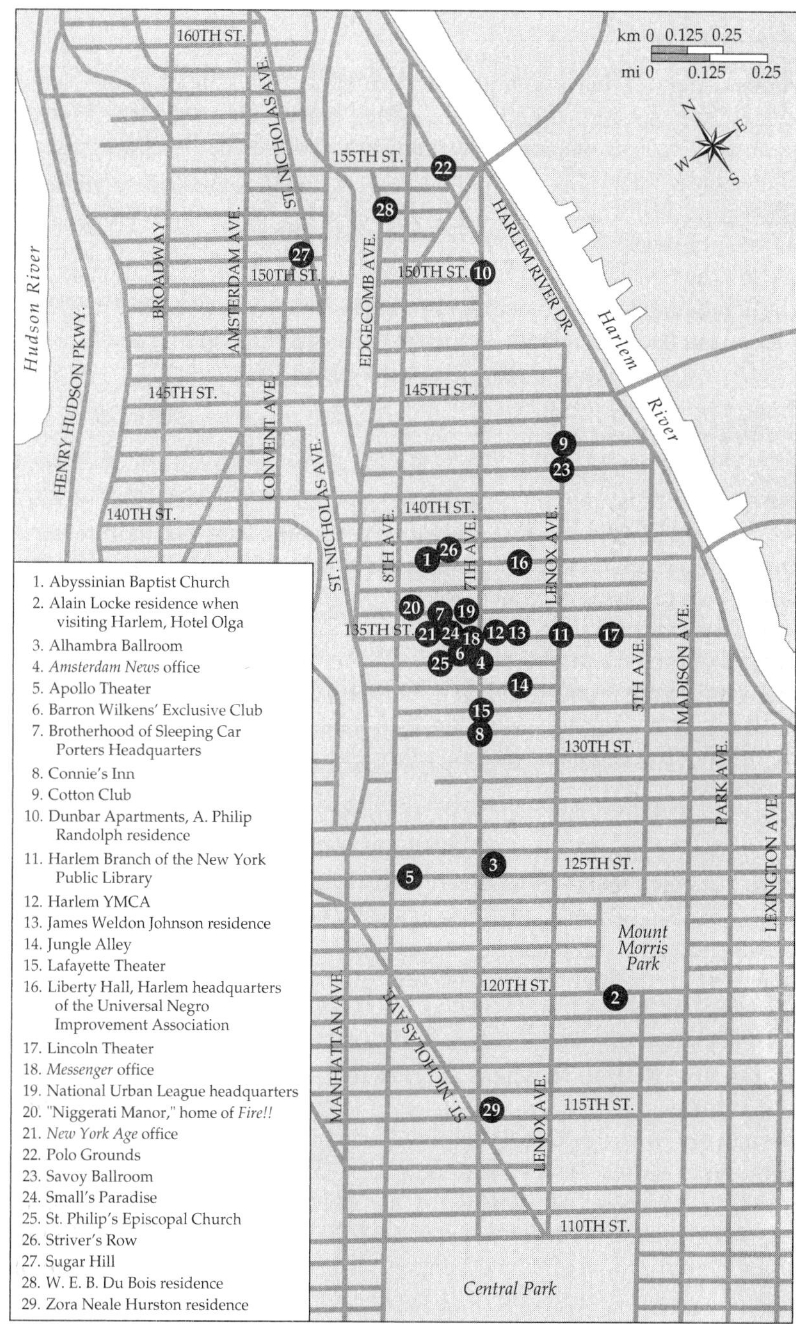

Figure 2. *Map of Important Harlem Renaissance Locations.*

claimed that Harlem's connection with New York City explained how its concrete realities—its broad streets, brownstones, diverse population, and varied employment opportunities—could produce imaginative dynamism. In "Harlem" (see Document 11), former Rhodes Scholar and Howard University philosophy professor Alain Locke similarly emphasizes Harlem's unique sociological features in casting it as the birthplace of a new black consciousness. These conceptions of Harlem as a place of rebirth and modernization competed with others that construed the "Mecca of the New Negro" in negative terms as an overcrowded ghetto, a site of class conflict, or a place of spiritual destruction. Walking down Seventh Avenue, where well-dressed Harlemites displayed their finery on Sunday afternoons, one might have agreed with Johnson and Locke, but after a brief encounter with overcrowded Fifth Avenue, where the desperate and the homeless of Harlem circulated among ramshackle tenements, one might well have come to the opposite opinion.[11] In the poems "The Harlem Dancer" and "Harlem Shadows" (see Document 6), Claude McKay reflects on this unsavory side of Harlem life by imagining the struggles of women caught in the trap of poverty.

By focusing on suffering prostitutes in these two poems, McKay not only offers an alternative to the most romantic outbursts of the optimistic "race capital" school, he also deflates attempts to view Harlem as a haven of sexual pleasure. During the 1920s, spurred in large part by a booming economy and the widespread desire to enjoy the good life after the war, Americans turned to the pleasures of party-going, alcohol consumption, and sexual play. Although Prohibition (1919–1933) outlawed the use of alcohol, underground bars, or "speakeasies," turned a heavy profit distributing illegal gin, beer, and whiskey, to the vast enrichment of organized crime. In this new environment of forbidden pleasure, Harlem became one of America's favorite nighttime playgrounds. Although some upstanding intellectuals such as W. E. B. Du Bois decried the nightly traffic of thrill seekers—and the criminal underworld of bootleggers, pimps, and prostitutes that they supported—Harlem's vigorous nightlife contributed to its romantic reputation in the 1920s, which in turn made it an almost irresistible subject for songwriters, dramatists, novelists, poets, and visual artists.

Driven by Prohibition and by a growing rebellion against repressive moral standards, many whites yearned to experience the rush of an outing in the regions north of 125th Street. There they could listen to some of the most innovative jazz and blues music in the world, watch some of the most energetic dancing, drink illegal gin and whiskey, and dance the night away in places like the Cotton Club and Connie's Inn, which served only whites, and Barron Wilkens' Exclusive Club, which catered to the upper class of both races. The more adventurous visitors to Harlem might hazard a trip to "Jungle Alley," a strip of nightclubs with names like Tillie's Chicken Shack and Pod's & Jerry's that catered predominantly to blacks.[12] Certainly, many whites who toured Harlem's nightclubs viewed blacks as exotic sexual creatures rather than as full human beings. Nevertheless, interracial nightlife also contained undeniably democratic potential. Poet Langston Hughes had something like this in mind in the poem "Harlem Nightclub," in which he celebrated interracial sexual attraction (see Document 9). Although much of Harlem tried mightily to define itself against, or outside of, the white world that surrounded it, such playful experimentation across conventional categories, in the face of American racism, remained throughout the 1920s one of the foundational strengths of this quintessentially racial, but profoundly mixed, crossroads of black creativity.

BEGINNINGS OF THE HARLEM RENAISSANCE

Events of the New Negro Era such as the black migration to the North, the Silent March, the return of the troops from World War I, and the recognition of Harlem as a "race capital" signaled key economic and political changes in black American life, but they involved cultural transformation as well. The shift from South to North, from rural to urban, and from regional to national political concerns made black Americans more politically assertive, more visible, and more aware of their visibility. Yet few white Americans thought of them this way. Negative black stereotypes emphasizing laziness, stupidity, uncontrolled sexual desire, aggression, and other distasteful characteristics abounded in film, literature, and theater. Minstrel shows, in which actors masked in "blackface" comically projected these stereotypes through humorous dances, songs, and speeches, etched such images in the minds of whites. Stereotypes like the Mammy, a loyal, asexual female domestic; the "tragic" mulatto, an emotionally conflicted mixed-blood; and the black rapist, a violent pursuer of white females, contributed to a veritable arsenal of negative black images that were used to justify racial exploitation.

Invented during the era of slavery, negative black stereotypes found new life during the World War I era in the work of many artists, including the filmmaker D. W. Griffiths, whose white supremacist movie *Birth of a Nation* (1915) celebrated the rise of the Ku Klux Klan. Playing to record audiences and praised by President Woodrow Wilson after a special viewing at the White House, this film prompted a nationwide boycott by the NAACP. As part of this protest, the Washington-based poet and short-story writer Angelina Weld Grimké produced *Rachel* (1916), the first play in the United States to feature an all-black cast. Its theme—the refusal of its main character to bear children for whites to punish and kill—suited the protest-oriented concerns of the New Negro. Its all-black cast signaled a resolve to make racial grievances the subject of serious theater by contesting the comic distortions that had dominated the black image to that point. In this way, *Rachel* prefigured themes that the Harlem Renaissance would develop more fully.

The next year, three one-act plays written by the white playwright Ridgeley Torrence and performed by all-black casts appeared at New York's Provincetown Playhouse, an experimental theater in Greenwich Village devoted to realistic presentation of contemporary themes. These theatrical presentations generated positive interest, and, two years later, *The Emperor Jones*, playwright Eugene O'Neill's story of the rise and fall of a black dictator on a Caribbean island, opened at the same playhouse before packed audiences. Notwithstanding its unfortunate tendency to depict blacks as primitives, this highly popular play further indicated that whites had begun to take a new and somewhat more hopeful look across the color line.

On Broadway, the musical *Shuffle Along*, opening in 1921, answered through energetic song and dance the postwar desire for cheerful moods exuberantly expressed. Written by the black comedy team Flournoy Miller and Aubrey Lyles, with music by black composers Hubie Blake and Noble Sissle, and featuring an all-black cast, this musical signaled an improving black image, and its extensive run on Broadway incited an explosion of black and black-inspired musicals and reviews throughout the 1920s.[13] Some, such as *Blackbirds* (1928), *Porgy* (1927), and *Showboat* (1927), appeared on Broadway, while many others played in such Harlem theaters as the Lafayette, the Lincoln, and the Alhambra.[14] Among its many achievements, *Shuffle Along* launched the careers of singer and actress Florence Mills, a much-loved performer whose death in 1927 gave rise to the largest public funeral in the history of Harlem, and singer Josephine Baker, who would later be a sensation on the stages of Paris (see Figure 3).

Figure 3. *Josephine Baker performing in the Review Nègre in Paris during the mid-1920s.*

Yale Collection of American Literature, Beinecke Rare Book and Manuscript Library.

While theatrical events signaled the rise of the Harlem Renaissance, literary events stood closer to its center. In the late 1910s and early 1920s, several outstanding writers heightened expectations for a rising generation of black poets and novelists of unprecedented size and talent. Of these, Claude McKay made the earliest mark with the publication in 1917 of "The Harlem Dancer" (see Document 6) in the cutting-edge literary journal *The Seven Arts.* Soon after, McKay became an editor of the Marxist journal *The Liberator,* in which he published much of his poetry, and a member of its Greenwich Village–based group of communist radicals. In 1922, before leaving the United States to attend the Third Communist International in the Soviet Union, the much-traveled McKay published some of his best verse in *Harlem Shadows* (see Document 6), his fourth and most important collection of poetry.

A year before McKay's landmark collection, eighteen-year-old Langston Hughes published his first poem, "The Negro Speaks of Rivers" (see Document 9), a lyric that demonstrates his ability to convey elevated meanings in plain language reminiscent of Walt Whitman and Carl Sandburg, poets who celebrated the ordinary events of American life. This poem reappeared in Hughes's much anticipated first collection, *The Weary Blues* (1926) (see Document 9), which he followed with *Fine Clothes to the Jew* (1927) (see Document 14), a collection featuring some of his most innovative poetry modeled on blues music and lower-class themes.

In 1923, two years after the appearance of "The Negro Speaks of Rivers," Jean Toomer, who spent most of his time in artistic circles in New York's Greenwich Village rather than in Harlem, startled critics with the moving and powerful prose poem *Cane* (see Document 7). Weaving the sounds and imagery of the rural South, *Cane* testifies to the enduring qualities of the black folk spirit. Like the poetry of McKay and Hughes, Toomer's *Cane* reflected a new level of formal sophistication and assertion in black writing. Departing from every known literary genre, it signified the willingness of black writers to reject all preestablished rules in fashioning modes of expression directly around their heritage and racial experience.

The year following the publication of *Cane,* "Shroud of Color," by twenty-one-year-old Countée Cullen, appeared in *The American Mercury,* the leading mainstream intellectual journal of the day. With his first collection of poems, *Color* (1925) (see Document 8), which he quickly followed by *Copper Sun* (1927) (see Document 8) and *Ballad for the Brown Girl* (1927), Cullen became the most celebrated black poet in America. Both his youth and his New York origin made his name synonymous with the expressive potential of a new generation.[15]

Also in 1924, Jessie Fauset published *There Is Confusion*, the first novel of the Harlem Renaissance. Although less celebrated than Cullen and many other male figures of the period, Fauset had a large impact on the direction of literary events not only as a prolific novelist but also as literary editor of *The Crisis*, for which she shepherded young literary talent. Yet the historical importance of *There Is Confusion*, a story of two racially mixed middle-class families, hinges less on its artistic excellence than on the role it played in bringing about further events. As a result of its publication, prominent sociologist Charles S. Johnson—editor of the Urban League journal *Opportunity* and a guiding force of the Harlem Renaissance—arranged a dinner in honor of Fauset at the fancy downtown Civic Club. The event, which took place on March 21, 1924, stands as the greatest symbolic moment of the Harlem Renaissance[16] (see Document 10). Perhaps more clearly than any other figure of the period, Johnson recognized that a combination of black talent, a thick network of white intellectuals and publishers, and the ever-increasing visibility of black Americans in popular culture could positively alter the black image in the national mind-set. With this aim in mind, he worked hard to turn the Civic Club dinner into a special occasion in which the most prominent writers and publishers could make contact with the new generation of black talent. He could not have been more successful.

Together, the various guests at the Civic Club dinner stood at the center of a network of journals and publishers that would promote the writers of the Harlem Renaissance in the upcoming years. They included powerful white publishers and editors such as Horace Liveright of the publishing house Boni and Liveright, editor and dean of American letters H. L. Mencken of the *The American Mercury*, editor and civil liberties activist Paul Kellogg of *The Survey Graphic*, and managing editor Freda Kirchwey of *The Nation*. Prominent white intellectuals such as novelist Sherwood Anderson, art critic Albert Barnes, and Columbia University professor of literature Carl Van Doren also attended.[17] Philosopher Alain Locke of Howard University served as master of ceremonies, while editor W. E. B. Du Bois of *The Crisis*; novelist, poet, and literary critic James Weldon Johnson; and poet Georgia Douglass Johnson represented the so-called older generation of black writers. Countée Cullen and Langston Hughes—both of whom read from their poetry—novelist Zora Neale Hurston, and poet Gwendolyn Bennett, who read the poem "To Usward" (see Document 10), written just for the occasion, represented a rising group of young writers. So did Walter White, a civil rights activist whose novel *Fire in the Flint* would soon be published. In his address, Carl Van Doren delighted the organizers of the event by testifying to the need for new life and color in American literature through the expression of the "gay and desperate moods" that black American writers could provide.[18]

Of the many important consequences of the Civic Club dinner, the most important was Kellogg's proposal to devote a full issue of *The Survey Graphic*, an influential social reform journal containing illustrated feature essays, to the cultural events centered in Harlem. Guest edited by Alain Locke, this popular and historic issue, which included articles on Harlem life, representative samples from the best young writers, and illustrations by the German artist Winold Reiss (see Document 11), led to the equally historic publication of *The New Negro* (1925) (see Document 12), again edited by Locke, with an expanded list of articles on black life, a wider representation of literary output, and illustrations by the African American artist Aaron Douglas. In both publications, Locke trenchantly stated his version of the New Negro concept, shifting the emphasis from politics to culture. Diverging sharply from the embattled ideas of the New Negro expressed by McKay, Randolph, and Garvey, Locke's pluralist New Negro promoted democracy through the development of an outlook at once internal to the group and radiating outward toward the rest of the world.

THEMES IN BLACK IDENTITY

Looked at one way, the chain of events from the New Negro movement to the publication of *The New Negro* marks a period of ever-increasing race consciousness. Yet the strong and necessary presence of white publishers and writers at the Civic Club dinner and the enthusiastic waves of white visitors to Harlem nightclubs demonstrate an important irony regarding race in the 1920s: Just when blacks had become most artistically and politically interested in asserting themselves in racially independent terms, they became most interesting to whites. Some scholars of the Harlem Renaissance consider this irony a compromising contradiction, while others have regarded it as an important indicator of the new place of black culture within the larger cultural matrix of the United States in the 1920s.

The Harlem Renaissance occurred at the nexus of a complex racial discussion that went in many directions. Still, it makes sense to see in it an overriding concern with the general question of identity, because the writers and thinkers of the Harlem Renaissance focused intensely on matters of heritage, black culture, black consciousness, and many other issues related to the general questions "Who am I?" "Who are we?" and "Where do we find ourselves?" During the 1920s, many of these writers and thinkers agreed that a new kind of black person had emerged, but hardly anyone could identify him or her exactly. Some writers looked to Africa, some to the American South, some to Pan-African and other global identities. Still others wondered how to balance ideas of racial unity with loyalties within the group, including class, gender, and nation. Ambiguities of every sort attended these reflections—between newness and tradition, sameness and otherness, invention and imitation.

In search of black identity, inspiration, and experience, several black writers of the period, such as McKay and Hughes, traveled constantly. Like their white contemporaries such as the poet Ezra Pound and the novelist Ernest Hemingway, they found Paris an especially attractive destination—but for very different reasons (see Documents 13 and 14). A magnet for intellectuals from various nations, including the French colonies of Africa and the Caribbean, Paris in the 1920s served as a center for Pan-African and anticolonial activism, which gained greater legitimacy after World War I. There, one could find poets such as Aimé Césaire of Martinique and Léopold Sédar Senghor of Senegal, major voices in the negritude movement, which attempted to convey the essence of black pride, beauty, and spirit. One could also find the novelist René Maran of Martinique and Gabon, author of the prize-winning anticolonialist novel *Batouala* (1922).[19] Like New York, Paris went wild over jazz and black entertainers in this period. American singer Josephine Baker flourished there, and African American jazz bands filled the nightclubs with their music. Thus, like Harlem, Paris provided an outpost of sorts for a wide array of displaced blacks from all over the world.

The same fundamental desire for discovery, connection, and identity that led McKay and Hughes to visit Europe in the 1920s also spurred them to visit Africa. They, and many other artists of the Harlem Renaissance who could not make such a visit, regarded Africa as a powerful symbol of origin, destiny, dignity, and hope. The idea of African beauty issued directly from the concepts of black beauty and pride that dominated the 1920s. It also flowed from the larger intellectual developments of the day. The unprecedented carnage of World War I prompted some thinkers to theorize a decline of the West and others to seek sources of truth and vitality among non-Western peoples formerly regarded as backward. The Spanish artist Pablo Picasso, for example, found inspiration in the abstract, expressive qualities of African painting and sculpture. Such recognition of African genius among Western intellectuals enhanced the symbolic value of Africa for Harlem Renaissance writers and thinkers, even as they gravitated toward it for their own varied reasons. Their ideas ranged from the thoughtful but conflicted confessions of Countée Cullen's "Heritage" (see Document 15), to the romantic affirmations of Gwendolyn Bennett's "Heritage" (see Document 16), to the bohemian primitivism of Richard Bruce Nugent's "Sahdji" (see Document 17).

The search for usable folk origins followed the same fundamental logic, and inspired some of the same ambivalent feelings, as the quest for African cultural connections. Again, the issue reduced to whether black cultural distinctiveness could provide a basis for pride and artistic creativity. In the midst of rapid urbanization, many blacks felt uncomfortable locating this basis in the South that they had gladly left behind. Yet, in the 1920s, 80 percent of African Americans remained in the South, and many of those who had migrated to the North maintained an avid interest in their place of origin, where most of their relatives and friends still lived. This sentiment comes out clearly in novelist Zora Neale Hurston's account of her return home to collect folklore in *Mules and Men* (1935) (see Document 18).

Hurston's autobiographical account also reflects the importance of a new school of cultural anthropology, centered at Columbia University and led by her teacher Franz Boas, which challenged biological conceptions of race.[20] In the hands of such popular theorists as Madison Grant, whose *Passing of the Great Race* (1915) urged so-called Nordic whites to prevent the "inferior" darker races from reproducing, such conceptions reinforced the widely held belief that granting civil rights would never erase gaps in moral, intellectual, and cultural capacity between the races. Boas argued, instead, that race was a cultural conception, providing a scientific basis for artist/researchers such as Hurston to see black folk culture as a product of invention and art rather than of instincts and proclivities. The poet Sterling Brown also advanced this idea in his poetry, employing the language and storytelling forms of folk culture to convey the tragedy, strength, violence, humor, and dignity of black southern life (see Document 19).

The creative exploration of folk origins during the Harlem Renaissance connected naturally with the wide interest in the blues and jazz, whose arrival as foundational American musical forms in the 1920s shaped the atmosphere within which the literature and visual art of the period developed. Although its precise origins remain obscure, the blues began in the South during the 1880s and 1890s, when oppressive laws and social practices began to make a mockery of African American freedom. An invention of the first generation of African Americans born outside of slavery, it captured in its emphasis on tragic turns of fate the devastating ironies of betrayal that characterized black life in this era. Yet the blues most characteristically focused on universal themes of sex and romance, which it used as a metaphor for almost everything else, rather than on politics.

Instead of the standard musical scale, the blues used a series of inflected or "blue" notes, as well as guttural slurs and wails, to achieve its unique musical effect. Often referred to as a healing music, it usually featured an individual singer who seemingly celebrated his or her troubled existence through artful song, thus giving testament to the possibility of spiritual enhancement and self-determination through suffering. The blues gained early popularity in 1914 when the black bandleader and composer W. C. Handy, who became known as "The Father of the Blues," published his "St. Louis Blues" as sheet music. Through the World War I years, black migration and technological innovation in the radio and recording industries created a new mass market for "race records," a category that included both jazz and the blues. In 1920, Mamie Smith recorded the first big blues hit with "Crazy Blues," which sold more than 750,000 copies. Throughout the 1920s, other artists such as Ma Rainey (see Document 20) and "The Empress of the Blues" Bessie Smith (see Document 21) would continue black women's domination of commercial blues. In the 1930s, male blues singers such as Robert Johnson and Huddie Ledbetter (Ledbelly) also rose to prominence.

Jazz became popular in the 1920s for many of the same reasons as the blues. Developed by black New Orleans bands during the first decade of the twentieth century, it combined marching band music, the blues, and ragtime—a piano-based style that altered, or "ragged," the rhythms of existing songs—into a distinctive form that came north with the black migration to Chicago and New York (see Document 22). Typically, jazz involved a band playing a strong but flexible alternating or syncopated rhythm that provided the backdrop for individual performances by its members. In contrast to performers of classical music, who rarely strayed from a composer's score, jazz musicians invented, or improvised, the song as they played it, thus involving listeners emotionally and intellectually. As dance music, jazz was incessantly promoted by radio stations for the post–World War I party culture, and rose to such prominence that the decade of the 1920s is sometimes called "The Jazz Age." Carried to Europe by black soldiers during World War I, it also made a sensation abroad. During the 1920s, the major figures of jazz included trumpeter Louis "Satchmo" Armstrong, who played mostly in Chicago; bandleader and pianist Duke Ellington, who performed for white audiences at downtown Manhattan's Hollywood Club; and bandleader Fletcher Henderson, who also played in downtown Manhattan, at the Roseland Ballroom. In Harlem, stride piano—where a player's left hand held a strong alternating beat while the right played an improvised melody—dominated the jazz scene under its masters James P. Johnson, Willie "The Lion" Smith, and Thomas Wright "Fats" Waller. Known for their flamboyance, these figures often held "cutting" competitions, or battles to decide the best player, at "rent" parties, where guests paid an entry fee to cover food, entertainment, and the host's rent.

During the 1920s, jazz and the blues had both black and white detractors as well as fans. Some critics found jazz and the blues aesthetically undisciplined and thought that their wild infectious rhythms threatened social order. Others loved them for the same reason. Some black detractors associated these musical forms with the rude simplicity of folk origins or with the dangers of nightlife and the criminal element, associations that made them even more attractive to rebellious artists such as Hughes, Hurston, and Brown. These artists understood keenly that the amazing popularity of jazz and the blues bespoke the power of artistic forms rooted in the black experience to transcend boundaries of class, race, and nation while maintaining the integrity of their origins.[21] For this reason, both Hughes and Brown modeled many of their poems on the spirit and form of this innovative music (see Documents 9, 14, and 19).

Among its many connections, the interest in jazz and the blues during the Harlem Renaissance indicated a much larger fascination with transgressive cultural energies, not only those that ran against Victorian prudery, but also those that tended to complicate simple ideas of black and white. In addition, the emphasis on race pride and racial origins during the Harlem Renaissance practically dictated a corresponding interest in racial intermixture. In many ways, the mere existence of people who were "neither white nor black, yet both" exposed the hypocrisy of the American "one-drop" rule (that only one drop of "black blood" made a person black) and the absurdity of racist theories that insisted on a natural white aversion to sexual contact with "lower" races.[22] These issues were explored in a literature of "passing" that demonstrated how easily black people who looked white could also fit in with white people socially and culturally. Yet, in order to "pass," these characters had to leave their loved ones behind, live in constant fear of discovery, and sometimes cooperate with racists. By highlighting the dilemmas of mixed blood, the literature of "passing" dramatized the larger psychological costs of American racism, which insisted on an absolute line of separation between the races that it could not maintain.

Passing and the experiences of interracial people already had long standing as major themes in black and American literature. *Clotel or the President's Daughter* (1855), by William Wells Brown; *Iola Leroy* (1892), by Frances Harper; *Pudd'nhead Wilson* (1894), by Mark Twain; and *Autobiography of an Ex-Colored Man* (1912), by James Weldon Johnson helped establish this tradition, but it took on a new significance after World War I when the context for representing mixed-race identity shifted radically. Passing thrived in anonymous urban environments where social and geographical mobility prevailed.[23] In contrast to small southern towns, where most people knew one another, the large cities of the North permitted black people free anonymous interaction with whites, who usually lived only a subway or trolley car ride away. Yet notions of race pride and group loyalty among blacks added tension and drama to the idea of "passing." For those who wanted to make the case for black solidarity, the choice to become white seemed unwise at best and an outright betrayal of the group at worst. Because it symbolized new possibilities and new tensions around race, passing received unprecedented attention in the literature of the Harlem Renaissance. Novelist Nella Larsen in *Quicksand* (1928) (see Document 25) and *Passing* (1929) (see Document 23); Jessie Fauset in *Plum Bun* (1929) (see Document 24), *The Chinaberry Tree* (1931), and *Comedy American Style* (1932); novelist and NAACP activist Walter White in *Flight* (1926); and satirist George S. Schuyler in *Black No More* (1931) each explored trenchantly different sides of this multifaceted theme.

Because it deals so centrally with issues of interracial sex (miscegenation) and reproduction, the theme of passing connects naturally to a wider concern with gender and with relations between and within the sexes. For this reason, Fauset and Larsen regarded the theme of passing as a crucial entryway into criticism of conventional gender roles and the limitations of black radicalism in the 1920s. Because of its association with submissiveness and other characteristics traditionally considered feminine, racial oppression has always carried with it the implication of deficient manhood. At its core, many blacks held, racism attacked black men more directly than it did black women. By taking away a man's right to an equal political voice, economic opportunity, and the means to defend his family, some argued, it assaulted the fundamental male prerogatives. Thus many New Negroes placed the defense of manhood at the very center of their racial values. Regarded this way, the race problem becomes the special province of the black man, who must reestablish his compromised masculinity through acts of self-assertion and courage. The black woman plays her best role in this narrative by making her endangered and embattled counterpart feel manly. She serves the race, and herself, by serving him. Any personal aspirations or righteous objections to gender inequality open her to charges of disloyalty to the group.

Although it could count many feminists, both male and female, within its ranks, the Harlem Renaissance provided unprecedented impetus to the quest for black manhood. Its dominant rhetoric grouped aggression, pride, anger, intellect, self-awareness, and self-expression together under the celebrated label "New Negro," even as it vilified the submissive, symbolically female characteristics of the old plantation Negro. The resulting equation of manhood and race created significant challenges for women artists, who had to find ways either to oppose or to accommodate the prevailing masculinist orientation of the era without appearing disloyal to the group. Yet, in the course of this difficult task, women artists of the Harlem Renaissance had to show care in avoiding black female stereotypes, such as the supersexual primitive—an aggressive and crass female pursuer of sexual pleasure—that tended to develop the image of the black woman partly along male lines. Nor did it help that racist standards regarded white women as models of feminine daintiness, beauty, and motherhood to the exclusion of black women, whose kinky hair, dark skin, and flat noses marked them as ugly in conventional eyes. Although many other important themes animate their works, the ability of Harlem Renaissance woman novelists such as Nella Larsen (see Documents 23 and 25), Jessie Fauset (see Document 24), and Zora Neale Hurston (see Documents 18 and 34); poets like Georgia Douglass Johnson (see Document 26) and Anne Spencer (see Document 27); and blues singers such as Ma Rainey (Document 20) and Bessie Smith (Document 21) to invent stories, attitudes, and modes of self-fashioning around this difficult predicament contributes to their lasting importance in the era and in the discourse on race and gender in general.[24]

CONTROVERSIES IN ART AND POLITICS

As the previous section demonstrates, the Harlem Renaissance encompassed many overlapping and opposing perspectives on race. Sometimes these tensions ran below the surface of broad claims of black unity. At others times they expressed themselves in the form of controversies that the artists and thinkers of the period did not so much resolve as bequeath to later generations. Several such disputes emerged immediately on the heels of Alain Locke's anthology *The New Negro*, centering mainly on the question of art and politics: Could black artistic production play a role in advancing the black freedom struggle? Were black artists obligated to protest against racism? Should they attempt "high" art, or should they gravitate toward the artistic forms of the folk? Who should they write for, black or white audiences? Disputes around such questions provide some of the most dramatic moments of the Harlem Renaissance and offer the best guidance in reflecting on its legacy.

In the summer of 1926, not long after the appearance of *The New Negro*, *The Nation* published a controversial essay by *Messenger* editor and satirist George S. Schuyler called "The Negro-Art Hokum," which challenged several bedrock claims of the Harlem Renaissance (see Document 28). Most centrally, it questioned the existence of a separate black culture and accused black artists of pandering to racist white patrons. Schuyler characterized the Harlem Renaissance as false and harmful advertising by misguided members of the black leadership class rather than as an independent movement expressing the black soul. Langston Hughes's rebuttal, prepared at the invitation of *The Nation*'s editor, was less a comprehensive engagement with Schuyler's position than an independent statement that proved to be one of the most important essays of the period. In "The Negro Artist and the Racial Mountain" (see Document 29), Hughes boldly states the program of the young black artist, whose rooting in the cultural expression of the black masses provides a basis for independent effort that must develop along its own lines in order to reach maturity.

Only a few months after the Schuyler-Hughes debate in *The Nation*, Carl Van Vechten's controversial bestseller *Nigger Heaven* (1926) made its appearance. Along with Charlotte Osgood Mason, a domineering heiress who offered both her money and her Westfield, New Jersey, home to Hurston, Hughes, and other black artists, Van Vechten made a reputation as a major white promoter and patron of the Harlem Renaissance. A literary adviser of Hughes, Larsen, Hurston, and others, he had also achieved a more dubious notoriety for the parties he gave for the black and white intelligentsia and for the legendary tours of Harlem that he offered white friends.[25] Yet such well-intended efforts did him little good among the majority of black critics when his book *Nigger Heaven* appeared and became an almost instant bestseller. Some members of the black elite, including Du Bois, who called *Nigger Heaven* a "blow in the face," immediately took offense at the title of the novel and at some of its sensationalistic renderings of Harlem's criminal and sexual underworld.[26] Nevertheless, the novel did have its defenders, among them Hughes and Wallace Thurman, editor of the journal *Fire!!*, who saw lower-class black life as an inspiration, not an embarrassment, and who wanted to get beyond what they regarded as narrow and old-fashioned conceptions of black progress.

As the *Nigger Heaven* controversy raged on, late in 1926 a group of young writers led by Thurman and Hughes published the first and only issue of a new journal intended to state in powerful terms their independence from the "civil rights by copyright" wing of the Harlem Renaissance, which, according to them, focused more on the political uses of art than it did on the quality of the art itself. The result of their efforts, which emptied their pockets of what little money they had, contained short stories from Thurman, Bennett, and Nugent; poetry from Hughes and Cullen; a short play by Hurston; and cover art by Douglas. As the title *Fire!!* indicates, the editors intended their new journal to reflect strikingly the crossroads of race, desire, pain, and cultural rebellion—a combination that stood no chance of attracting a stable audience in 1926. *Fire!!* (see Document 30) celebrated jazz, paganism, homosexuality, and bohemianism in a bold fashion calculated to annoy artistic and social traditionalists.[27] Notably, the emphasis on gay themes in *Fire!!* reflected an important aspect of the identity of the Harlem Renaissance, as several of its artists were gay or bisexual, including Thurman, Nugent, Cullen, Locke, McKay, Ma Rainey, and Bessie Smith. One reviewer called the journal "effeminate tommyrot" and claimed to have thrown his copy of *Fire!!* "into the fire."[28] Later, in *Infants of the Spring* (1932), his devastating satire of the Harlem Renaissance, Thurman derided both the high idealism of *Fire!!* and the pragmatic genteelism of its detractors.

From March to November 1926, as each of the above controversies and literary events proceeded in turn, *The Crisis* published a symposium called "The Negro in Art—How Shall He Be Portrayed," in which a remarkably wide range of American writers and publishers answered a series of somewhat slanted questions, most likely composed by Du Bois, concerning white control of the black image and the obligations of black writers. Most of the respondents, whether black or white, tended to resist the bias of the questionnaire by supporting the freedom of black artists to invent as they pleased. Yet some did agree that the existing literature veered from realistic depiction of black life in overemphasizing its tawdry and sensational aspects. In October 1926, near the end of this symposium, *The Crisis* published "Criteria of Negro Art" (see Document 31), Du Bois's address to the annual meeting of the NAACP. At the high point of his address, Du Bois claimed not to "care a damn" for art that excludes propaganda, thus striking a blow at the younger black artists who had so boldly declared their independence in *Fire!!* and elsewhere. In *Harlem* (1928), another short-lived, one-volume attempt by Thurman to launch an independent black literary journal, Locke fired back by denouncing all literary propaganda while emphasizing the need for a wide-ranging and mature black discourse that reached out in all directions (see Document 32).

THE HARLEM RENAISSANCE: VOGUE OR WATERSHED?

Befitting the contentious cultural politics of the Harlem Renaissance, the end of the era in the late 1930s gave rise to a lively debate over whether it had indeed come to an end. Again, the fundamental issue reduced to the relationship between art and politics. By the mid-1930s, several events had dramatically changed the conditions for producing black art. The Great Depression, a severe twelve-year economic crisis beginning in 1929, had devastating effects on everyone, but it hurt black Americans disproportionately. In the South, it brought on increased racial violence, evictions, rural poverty, and rampant hunger. In the North, industrial contraction brought massive unemployment to a population that had barely begun to establish itself in the region. Moreover, new government programs and agencies aimed at bringing relief, collectively referred to as the New Deal, actively discriminated against black Americans.

In Harlem, the repeal of Prohibition in 1933 brought hardship to the formerly lucrative nightclub scene, which depended heavily on the trade in illegal liquor. Virtually drained of economic resources and frustrated at the turn of political events, Harlem residents rioted in March 1935 after rumors of police brutality against a black boy accused of stealing from a white-owned store spread throughout the neighborhood. Taking white-owned stores as their main target, Harlemites broke 600 store windows and inflicted millions of dollars in property damage. Such violence in the heart of America's largest and most sophisticated black neighborhood signaled to many black thinkers that the dream of the Harlem Renaissance had come to an end. If the New Negro would rise to his potential in the Promised Land of the North, they thought, it would not occur through cultural means, nor would it happen by convincing whites that blacks could achieve high art.

Some black thinkers claimed that tough economic realities required a new kind of writing rooted in realistic depictions of social conditions affecting ordinary black people. Hughes's reference to the Harlem Renaissance as a "vogue," or passing fad, in his autobiography, *The Big Sea* (1940), indicated his sympathy for this view.[29] McKay expressed a similar sentiment, referring in 1934 to the Harlem Renaissance as "a mushroom growth that could send no roots down into the soil of negro life."[30] Younger writers of the 1930s, such as Richard Wright and Margaret Walker, now looked to Chicago rather than New York as an intellectual mecca.

In fact, black artistic production did decline in the early 1930s. Like most Americans in this period, black writers found mere survival a challenge, so they wrote less. In an effort to revive the artistic spirit of the Harlem Renaissance, the Boston-based novelist and short-story writer Dorothy West started the independent black literary journal *Challenge* in 1934. She kept it alive for three years, but low circulation and poor submissions brought the project to a close. West then joined Richard Wright to launch *New Challenge* in 1937, but this journal published only two issues, the second of which appeared to deal a death blow to the Harlem Renaissance, as it contained Wright's "Blueprint for Negro Writing" (see Document 33). Arguing that the previous generation of black writers was politically shallow, Wright described them as excessively caught up in the ornamental, the foolish, and the flighty.

Also in 1937, Hurston published *Their Eyes Were Watching God* (see Document 34), a novel focused on questions of gender and personal maturation using folklore, mythology, and humor in a rural setting. Wright, a proponent of urban realism and class analysis, excoriated Hurston's novel in a review as smacking of the minstrel stage and almost every other retrograde gesture of black literature that he opposed.[31] Nevertheless, in Hurston, at least, the Harlem Renaissance lived on. In his 1939 retrospective of black American literature published in 1938, "The Negro: 'New' or Newer" (see Document 35), Locke claimed that the developments of the previous decade had made possible the best trends of the 1930s, even the ones that critics such as Wright regarded as departures from the past. Quoting his own words from *The New Negro*, written thirteen years earlier, he challenged the irresponsible typecasting of the Harlem Renaissance as a period lacking in social perspective. Where critics such as Wright saw contrast, he saw development, continuity, and legacy.

In our own age, at least for now, it seems that Locke and Hurston get the last word. Locke keenly recognized the irony of the so-called new generation of the 1930s declaring a total break with their predecessors, for he had done much the same thing in the previous decade. By this measure, the claim to newness had become quite old. Locke also understood that the propensity to denounce the Harlem Renaissance as a vogue or to criticize it for lacking social conscience had originated with the movement itself, which made cultural expression central to the broader debate concerning black American freedom for all future generations. At its best, it gave rise to racially expressive forms of art and thought rooted in the experiences of slavery, colonialism, and segregation and yet intricately intertwined with the larger complexities of modern civilization. In this regard, it serves as an indispensable point of reference for our own age, in which racial identity has ramifications far beyond the simple opposition of black and white. We look back to the Harlem Renaissance, a moment in American racial history when a striking array of artists and thinkers boldly declared themselves new in myriad ways, to see ourselves reflected. By doing so, we preserve the hope that we, too, might one day become new.

NOTES

[1]For more on the history and use of the term *New Negro*, see Henry Louis Gates, "The Trope of a New Negro and the Reconstruction of the Image of the Black," *The New American Studies: Essays from Representations*, ed. Philip Fisher (Berkeley: University of California Press, 1991), 319–45; and Wilson J. Moses, "The Lost World of the Negro, 1895–1919: Black Literary and Intellectual Life before the 'Renaissance,'" *Black American Literature Forum*, 1–2 (Spring–Summer 1987), 61–84.

[2]Eric Arneson, "The Great American Protest," *Black Protest and the Great Migration* (Boston: Bedford/St. Martins, 2003), 7–18.

[3]Ibid., 13.

[4]William E. Alt and Betty L. Alt, *Black Soldiers, White Wars: Black Warriors from Antiquity to the Present* (Westport, Conn.: Praeger, 2002), 80–82.

[5]David Levering Lewis, *When Harlem Was in Vogue* (New York: Oxford University Press, 1989), 3–5.

[6]W. E. B. Du Bois, "Close Ranks," *The Crisis*, 16 (July 1918): 111.

[7]Arneson, "Great American Protest," 33.

[8]For more on the Ku Klux Klan, see David M. Chalmers, *Hooded Americanism: The First Century of the Ku Klux Klan, 1865–1965* (New York: Doubleday, 1965), and for more on the federal government's attempt to disrupt black radicalism after World War I, see Theodore Kornweibel Jr., *"Seeing Red": Federal Campaigns against Black Militancy, 1919–1925* (Bloomington: Indiana University Press, 1998).

[9]Cary D. Wintz, *Black Culture and the Harlem Renaissance* (College Station: Texas A&M University Press, 1996), 14.

[10]George Hutchinson, *The Harlem Renaissance in Black and White* (Cambridge, Mass.: Harvard University Press, 1995), 5–6.

[11]The most notable modern exponent of the "Harlem as ghetto" school is Gilbert Osofsky, *Harlem: The Making of a Ghetto: Negro New York, 1890–1930* (New York: Harper and Row, 1966), 105–49.

[12]Jervis Anderson, *This Was Harlem: A Cultural Portrait 1900–1950* (New York: Farrar, Straus and Giroux, 1981), 168–76.

[13]In his autobiography, Langston Hughes claims to have based his decision to attend Columbia University on his desire to see *Shuffle Along*. Langston Hughes, *The Big Sea* (1940; New York: Hill and Wang, 1993), 224.

[14]David Krasner, *A Beautiful Pageant: African American Theater, Drama, and Performance in the Harlem Renaissance, 1910–1927* (New York: Palgrave Macmillan, 2002).

[15]Gerald Early, ed., introduction to *My Soul's High Song: The Collected Writings of Countée Cullen, Voice of the Harlem Renaissance* (New York: Doubleday, 1991), 15–23.

[16]Lewis, *When Harlem Was in Vogue*, 89–95.

[17]Ibid.

[18]Carl Van Doren, "The Younger Generation of Negro Writers," *Opportunity*, 2 (May 1924): 144–45.

[19]For more on the international dimension of the Renaissance, see Brent Hayes Edwards, *The Practice of Diaspora: Literature, Translation, and the Rise of Black Internationalism* (Cambridge, Mass.: Harvard University Press, 2003).

[20]Hutchinson, *Harlem Renaissance in Black and White*, 62–77.

[21]Ann Douglas, *Terrible Honesty: Mongrel Manhattan in the 1920s* (New York: Farrar, Straus and Giroux, 1995), 387–433, and Anderson, *This Was Harlem*, 167–217.

[22]For a broad perspective on the whole question of interracial literature and passing in the Harlem Renaissance and beyond, see Werner Sollors, *Neither Black Nor White Yet Both: Thematic Explorations of Interracial Literature* (New York: Oxford University Press, 1997), 247–84.

[23]Ibid., 248–49.

[24]Cheryl A. Wall, *Women of the Harlem Renaissance* (Bloomington: Indiana University Press, 1995), 1–32. On the blues women, see Douglas, *Terrible Honesty*, 407–26.

[25]Lewis, *When Harlem Was in Vogue*, 182–85.

[26]W. E. B. Du Bois, "Review of *Nigger Heaven* by Carl Van Vechten," *The Crisis*, 33 (December 1926): 81–82.

[27]A. B. Christa Schwartz, *Gay Voices of the Harlem Renaissance* (Bloomington: Indiana University Press, 2003).

[28]Cited in Steven Watson, *The Harlem Renaissance: Hub of African-American Culture 1920–1930* (New York: Pantheon, 1995), 92. See also Hughes, *Big Sea*, 237.

[29]The chapter is called "When the Negro Was in Vogue." Hughes, *Big Sea*, 223–33.

[30]Claude McKay, "For a Negro Magazine," a 1934 circular reprinted in *Voices from*

the Harlem Renaissance, ed. Nathan Irvin Huggins (New York: Oxford University Press, 1976), 403.

[31]Wright's review appeared originally as "Between Laughter and Tears" in *The New Masses* on October 5, 1937. It is reprinted in *Zora Neale Hurston: Critical Perspectives Past and Present*, ed. Henry Louis Gates and K. Anthony Appiah (New York: Amistad, 1993), 16–17.

Major Harlem Renaissance Figures and Publications

Individuals

Gwendolyn Bennett (1902–1981) Poet, graphic designer, short-story writer, literary editor, author of the poems "To Usward" (1924) (see Document 10) and "Heritage" (1923) (see Document 16) and of the art news and criticism column "The Ebony Flute" in ***Opportunity**** magazine.

Sterling Brown (1901–1989) Poet best known for his compelling depictions of African American folk life and philosophy in the collection *Southern Road* (1932) (see Document 19).

Countée Cullen (1903–1946) One of the most popular poets of the Harlem Renaissance, famous for "Heritage" (see Document 15), "Yet Do I Marvel," and "From the Dark Tower," published in the collections *Color* (1925) and *Copper Sun* (1927) (Document 8).

Aaron Douglas (1898–1979) Painter and illustrator sometimes referred to as "the Dean of African American painters" for his groundbreaking style based on flat forms, hard edges, and repetitive geometric shapes. Illustrator of ***The New Negro*** (1925) (see Document 17) and ***Fire!!*** (1926) (see Document 30), and most famous as a painter for the four-part mural "Aspects of Negro Life" (1934) at the Harlem Branch of the New York Public Library.

W. E. B. Du Bois (1868–1963) Leading African American intellectual and civil rights activist, head editor and editorialist of ***The Crisis*** from 1910 to 1934, author of *The Souls of Black Folk* (1903), "Returning Soldiers" (see Document 1), "Criteria of Negro Art" (1926) (see Document 31), the novel *Dark Princess* (1928), and many other groundbreaking books in history, literature, and sociology.

*Names and journal titles in boldface within the descriptions also are referenced elsewhere in this list.

Lieutenant James Reese Europe (1881–1919) Early jazz innovator and leader of Harlem's 369th Regiment band during World War I.

Jessie Fauset (1882–1961) Author of *There Is Confusion* (1924), the first novel of the Harlem Renaissance, and *Plum Bun* (1929) (see Document 24), and literary editor of ***The Crisis*** from 1919 to 1926.

Marcus Garvey (1887–1940) Jamaican immigrant and black nationalist leader of the Universal Negro Improvement Association (UNIA), which drew more than 400,000 members in the United States and many more around the world (see Document 3). He went to federal prison in 1925 on mail fraud charges in connection with stock sales for the Black Star Line, a shipping fleet intended to promote trade and communication among blacks around the world.

Langston Hughes (1902–1967) Poet, short-story writer, and novelist renowned for his poetry based on the ordinary cadences and rhythms of African American life, including jazz and the blues. In addition to the poetry collections *The Weary Blues* (1926) (see Document 9) and *Fine Clothes to the Jew* (1927) (see Document 14), he published the literary manifesto "The Negro Artist and the Racial Mountain" (1926) (see Document 29), the novel *Not without Laughter* (1930), and the short-story collection *The Ways of White Folk* (1934).

Zora Neale Hurston (1891–1960) Short-story writer, playwright, and novelist. A student of anthropology under Franz Boaz at Columbia University, she published the folklore collection *Mules and Men* in 1935 (see Document 18) and a series of novels informed by her scientific investigations, including *Jonah's Gourd Vine* (1934) and her best-known work, *Their Eyes Were Watching God* (1937) (Document 34).

Charles S. Johnson (1893–1956) Leading black sociologist, editor of ***Opportunity***, and a great promoter of black art. In 1924, he organized the Civic Club dinner (see Document 10), a landmark meeting of black artists and white editors and publishers.

Georgia Douglass Johnson (1880–1966) Washington, D.C.–based playwright, musician, and poet, author of "The Heart of a Woman" (1918) (see Document 26), and best known for her three poetry collections *The Heart of a Woman* (1918), *Bronze: A Book of Verse* (1922), and *Autumn Love Cycle* (1928) and for her syndicated column "The Homely Philosophy," which appeared in twenty black newspapers.

Helene Johnson (1906–1995) Leading female poet, author of "Sonnet to a Negro in Harlem" (see Document 5) and many other poems published in ***Opportunity***, *Vanity Fair*, and ***Fire!!***

James Weldon Johnson (1871–1938) Journalist, songwriter, poet, novelist, cultural theorist, diplomat, first black secretary of the NAACP, and author of the black national anthem "Lift Every Voice and Sing." The multitalented Johnson's seminal works include a novel, *Autobiography of an Ex-Colored Man* (1912); an edited collection, *The Book of American Negro Poetry* (1922, expanded ed., 1931); and a social history of black New York, *Black Manhattan* (1930) (see Document 4).

Nella Larsen (1893–1964) Novelist, author of *Quicksand* (1928) (see Document 25) and *Passing* (1929) (see Document 23), two complexly woven works focusing on interracial themes and the experiences of women.

Alain Locke (1886–1954) Howard University professor, leading cultural theorist, and editor of two important publications, ***The Survey Graphic, Harlem Issue*** (1925) (see Document 11), and ***The New Negro*** (1925) (see Document 12).

Claude McKay (1889–1948) Jamaican immigrant, socialist poet, and novelist. Author of the poems "The Harlem Dancer" (1917) and "If We Must Die" (1919), collected in *Harlem Shadows* (1922) (see Document 6); the novel *Home to Harlem* (1928); the autobiography *A Long Way from Home* (1937) (see Document 13); and many other works.

Richard Bruce Nugent (1906–1987) Graphic artist and short-story writer known for his bohemianism. Contributor to ***The New Negro*** (1925) (see Document 17) and ***Fire!!*** (1926).

Chandler Owen (1889–1967) With **A. Philip Randolph**, co-author of "The New Negro—What Is He?" (1920) (see Document 2) and socialist co-editor of ***The Messenger***.

Ma Rainey (1886–1939) Popular blues artist, singer of "See See Rider" (1924) (see Document 20) and many other songs, and subject of the poem "Ma Rainey" (1930) by **Sterling Brown** (see Document 19).

A. Philip Randolph (1889–1979) Socialist labor leader, civil rights activist, and with **Chandler Owen**, co-author of "The New Negro—What Is He?" (1920) (see Document 2) and co-editor of ***The Messenger***.

Winold Reiss (1886–1953) German immigrant, graphic artist, painter, a teacher of the black artist **Aaron Douglas**, and illustrator of ***The Survey Graphic, Harlem Issue*** (1925) (see Document 11).

Joel A. Rogers (1880–1966) Jamaican immigrant, journalist, historian, author of *From Superman to Man* (1917), "Jazz at Home"

(1925) (see Document 22), the collection of biographical sketches *The World's Greatest Men of African Descent* (1931), and many other books aimed at destroying racist theories of the human past.

George S. Schuyler (1895–1977) Journalist, satirist, editor of ***The Messenger***, and author of the column "Views and Reviews" in the black newspaper *The Pittsburgh Courier*, the controversial article "The Negro-Art Hokum" (1926) (see Document 28), and *Black No More* (1931), the first full-length satire by a black American writer.

Bessie Smith (1895–1937) Popular blues artist, singer of "Young Woman's Blues" (1926) (see Document 21), "Downhearted Blues," and many other hit songs.

Anne Spencer (1882–1976) Poet and civil rights activist, author of "Lady, Lady" (1925) and "Letter to My Sister" (1928) (see Document 27).

Wallace Thurman (1902–1934) Novelist, short-story writer, editor of the journals ***Fire!!*** (1926) (see Document 30) and *Harlem* (1928), and author of "Cordelia the Crude" (1926) (see Document 30) and the novels *The Blacker the Berry* (1929) and *Infants of the Spring* (1932), which satirized the Harlem Renaissance.

Jean Toomer (1894–1967) Poet and author of the stylistically innovative book *Cane* (1923) (see Document 7).

Carl Van Vechten (1880–1964) Important white patron and promoter of black art, personal adviser to many black artists, and author of the best-selling and controversial novel *Nigger Heaven* (1926).

Dorothy West (1907–1998) Novelist and short-story writer, founder and editor of ***Challenge*** from 1934–1937, and co-founder, with **Richard Wright**, of the journal *New* ***Challenge*** (see Document 33).

Walter White (1893–1955) Civil rights leader and novelist, served as assistant secretary of the NAACP from 1918 until 1929 and as executive secretary from 1929 until 1955. White published two novels, *The Fire in the Flint* (1924) and *Flight* (1926), and a study of lynching, *Rope and Faggot: A Biography of Judge Lynch* (1929).

Richard Wright (1908–1960) Principal novelist of the African American literary tradition known for his hard-boiled realism. A communist from the early 1930s until 1944, Wright is the author of the literary manifesto "Blueprint for Negro Writing" (1937) (see Document 33), the short-story collection *Uncle Tom's Children* (1938), the novel *Native Son* (1940), and many other important novels and essays.

Publications

Challenge (1934–1937) Literary journal founded by **Dorothy West** to give young black writers a place to publish during the Great Depression. Its failure signaled a decline in black artistic production during the 1930s.

The Crisis (1910–) Journal of the NAACP, edited by **W. E. B. Du Bois** from 1910 to 1934.

Fire!! (1926) Literary journal edited by **Wallace Thurman**, illustrated by **Aaron Douglas**, and produced by a group of younger artists and contributors including **Langston Hughes**, **Zora Neale Hurston**, and **Richard Bruce Nugent**. The first attempt by black artists to produce a journal devoted exclusively to art, it protested attempts by publishers, editors, and civil rights leaders to control the thematic and stylistic range of black expression. Because of expense and its risky cutting-edge treatments of racial themes, only one issue was published.

The Messenger (1917–1928) Black socialist journal edited by **A. Philip Randolph** and **Chandler Owen**, and with **George S. Schuyler** as an editor and a principal contributor from 1923 to 1928.

New Challenge (1937) Literary journal founded by **Dorothy West** and **Richard Wright**, intended to succeed where the journal ***Challenge*** failed by providing an outlet for a new generation of black writers devoted to urban realism. The second and last issue featured Wright's "Blueprint for Negro Writing" (see Document 33), which declared explicitly his opposition to the Harlem Renaissance.

The New Negro (1925) Edited by **Alain Locke** and illustrated by **Aaron Douglas**, an important collection of essays, poetry, and short stories by almost every important black artist of the period. Locke's foreword to this volume remains one of the most important statements of the significance of cultural diversity for American democracy.

Opportunity (1923–) Journal of the National Urban League, edited by sociologist **Charles S. Johnson** from 1923 to 1928. Along with ***The Crisis***, one of the leading publishers and promoters of black art.

The Survey Graphic, Harlem Issue (1925) Special issue of *The Survey Graphic*, a liberal progressive journal, edited by activist Paul Kellogg and featuring illustrated articles focusing on ethnic minorities and the poor. This issue, edited by **Alain Locke** and illustrated by **Winold Reiss**, includes articles, poetry, and short stories by the major contributors to the Harlem Renaissance.

PART TWO

The Documents

1

Background and Beginnings

1

W. E. B. DU BOIS

Returning Soldiers

May 1919

At the time the United States entered World War I in 1917, W. E. B. Du Bois was black America's most important intellectual and civil rights leader. Born in Great Barrington, Massachusetts, he attended both historically black Fisk College and Harvard College, where in 1895 he became the first black American to earn a PhD. In 1903, he published his classic collection of essays, The Souls of Black Folk, *and in 1910 he became editor of* The Crisis, *the journal of the NAACP. In this editorial from* The Crisis, *Du Bois assesses the predicament of black soldiers returning from World War I. How does he equate the African American choice to fight "race arrogance" in Europe with fighting racism at home? Pay close attention to his use of language—his constant use of short sentences, italics, and repetition, especially of the pronoun "it" in reference to the United States—to make his most important points.*

We are returning from war! *The Crisis* and tens of thousands of black men were drafted into a great struggle. For bleeding France and what she means and has meant and will mean to us and humanity and against the threat of German race arrogance, we fought gladly and to the last drop of blood; for America and her highest ideals, we fought

W. E. B. Du Bois, "Returning Soldiers," *The Crisis*, 18 (May 1919): 13–14.

in far-off hope; for the dominant southern oligarchy entrenched in Washington, we fought in bitter resignation. For the America that represents and gloats in lynching, disfranchisement, caste, brutality and devilish insult—for this, in the hateful upturning and mixing of things, we were forced by vindictive fate to fight, also.

But today we return! We return from the slavery of uniform which the world's madness demanded us to don to the freedom of civil garb. We stand again to look America squarely in the face and call a spade a spade. We sing: This country of ours, despite all its better souls have done and dreamed, is yet a shameful land.

It *lynches*.

And lynching is barbarism of a degree of contemptible nastiness unparalleled in human history. Yet for fifty years we have lynched two Negroes a week, and we have kept this up right through the war.

It *disfranchises* its own citizens.

Disfranchisement is the deliberate theft and robbery of the only protection of poor against rich and black against white. The land that disfranchises its citizens and calls itself a democracy lies and knows it lies.

It encourages *ignorance*.

It has never really tried to educate the Negro. A dominant minority does not want Negroes educated. It wants servants, dogs, whores and monkeys. And when this land allows a reactionary group by its stolen political power to force as many black folk into these categories as it possibly can, it cries in contemptible hypocrisy: "They threaten us with degeneracy; they cannot be educated."

It *steals* from us.

It organizes industry to cheat us. It cheats us out of our land; it cheats us out of our labor. It confiscates our savings. It reduces our wages. It raises our rent. It steals our profit. It taxes us without representation. It keeps us consistently and universally poor, and then feeds us on charity and derides our poverty.

It *insults* us.

It has organized a nation-wide and latterly a world-wide propaganda of deliberate and continuous insult and defamation of black blood wherever found. It decrees that it shall not be possible in travel nor residence, work nor play, education nor instruction for a black man to exist without tacit or open acknowledgment of his inferiority to the dirtiest white dog. And it looks upon any attempt to question or even discuss this dogma as arrogance, unwarranted assumption and treason.

This is the country to which we Soldiers of Democracy return. This is the fatherland for which we fought! But it is *our* fatherland. It was right for us to fight. The faults of *our* country are *our* faults. Under similar circumstances, we would fight again. But by the God of Heaven, we are cowards and jackasses if now that that war is over, we do not marshal every ounce of our brain and brawn to fight a sterner, longer, more unbending battle against the forces of hell in our own land.

We *return.*

We *return from fighting.*

We *return fighting.*

Make way for Democracy! We saved it in France, and by the Great Jehovah, we will save it in the United States of America, or know the reason why.

2

A. PHILIP RANDOLPH AND CHANDLER OWEN

The New Negro—What Is He?

August 1920

The heated debate surrounding the meaning of the term "New Negro" in the years following World War I prompted the editors of the conservative black newspaper The New York Age *to ask readers for their opinions on the new radical spirit. Although many respondents, whose letters appeared in a "symposium" in the newspaper from January 24 to March 20, 1920, enthusiastically endorsed "protest" and "manhood," A. Philip Randolph and Chandler Owen, editors of socialist journal* The Messenger, *objected to the business-oriented* Age *claiming any association with black militancy. In this article from* The Messenger, *they explain their unique version of the New Negro concept. Randolph migrated to New York in 1912 from Jacksonville, Florida, to attend New York's City College. A native of North Carolina, Owen also migrated to New York, in 1913, to attend Columbia University. The pair met in 1916, joined the*

A. Philip Randolph and Chandler Owen, "The New Negro—What Is He?" *The Messenger,* 2 (August 1920): 73–74.

Socialist Party in the same year, and started The Messenger *in 1917. In the early days of their association, they argued against American participation in World War I and for the rights of workers, especially black workers. They were arrested in 1918 for violating the Espionage Act (1917), which made public statements against the war illegal, but were quickly freed when the judge refused to believe that two black men could write so eloquently. In 1925, Randolph organized the Brotherhood of Sleeping Car Porters union, which achieved a historic collective bargaining agreement with the Pullman Company in 1937.*

Our title was the subject of an editorial in the New York Age which formed the basis of an extensive symposium. Most of the replies, however, have been vague and nebulous. THE MESSENGER, therefore, undertakes to supply the New York Age and the general public with a definite and clear portrayal of the New Negro.

It is well nigh axiomatic that the most accurate test of what a man or institution or a movement is, is first, what its aims are; second, what its methods are, or how it expects to achieve its aims; and third, its general relations to current movements.

Now, what are the aims of the New Negro? The answer to this question will fall under three general heads, namely, political, economic, and social.

In politics, the New Negro, unlike the Old Negro, cannot be lulled into a false sense of security with political spoils and patronage. A job is not the price of his vote. He will not continue to accept political promissory notes from a political debtor, who has already had the power, but who has refused to satisfy his political obligations. The New Negro demands political equality. He recognizes the necessity of selective as well as elective representation. He realizes that so long as the Negro votes for the Republican or Democratic party, he will have only the right and privilege to elect but not to select his representatives. And he who selects the representatives controls the representative. The New Negro stands for universal suffrage.

A word about the economic aims of the New Negro. Here, as a worker, he demands the full product of his toil. His immediate aim is more wages, shorter hours and better working conditions. As a consumer, he seeks to buy in the market, commodities at the lowest possible price.

The social aims of the New Negro are decidedly different from those of the Old Negro. Here he stands for absolute and unequivocal "*social equality.*" He realizes that there cannot be any qualified equality. He insists that a society which is based upon justice can only be a society composed of *social equals.* He insists upon identity of social treatment. With respect to intermarriage, he maintains that it is the only logical, sound and correct aim for the Negro to entertain. He realizes that the acceptance of laws against intermarriage is tantamount to the acceptance of the stigma of inferiority. Besides, laws against intermarriage expose Negro women to sexual exploitation, and deprive their offspring, by white men, of the right to inherit the property of their father. Statistics show that there are nearly four million mulattoes in America as a result of miscegenation.[1]

So much then for the aims of the New Negro. A word now about his methods. It is with respect to methods that the essential difference between the New and Old Negro relates.

First, the methods by which the New Negro expects to realize his political aims are radical. He would repudiate and discard both of the old parties—Republican and Democratic. His knowledge of political science enables him to see that a political organization must have an economic foundation. A party whose money comes from working people, must and will represent working people. Now, everybody concedes that the Negro is essentially a worker. There are no big capitalists among them. There are a few petit bourgeoisie,[2] but the process of money concentration is destined to weed them out and drop them down into the ranks of the working class. In fact, the interests of all Negroes are tied up with the workers. Therefore, the Negro should support a working class political party. He is a fool or insane, who opposes his best interests by supporting his enemy. As workers, Negroes have nothing in common with their employers. The Negro wants high wages; the employer wants to pay low wages. The Negro wants to work short hours; the employer wants to work him long hours. Since this is true, it follows as a logical corollary that the Negro should not support the party of the employing class. Now, it is a question of fact that the Republican and Democratic Parties are parties of the employing or capitalist class.

On the economic field, the New Negro advocates that the Negro join the labor unions. Wherever white unions discriminate against the Negro worker, then the only sensible thing to do is to form independent unions to fight both the white capitalists for more wages and

[1]Sex between the races.
[2]The owners of small shops and businesses.

shorter hours, on the one hand, and white labor unions for justice, on the other. It is folly for the Negro to fight labor organization because some white unions ignorantly ignore or oppose him. It is about as logical and wise as to repudiate and condemn writing on the ground that it is used by some crooks for forgery. As a consumer, he would organize cooperative societies to reduce the high cost of living.

The social methods are: education and physical action in self defense. That education must constitute the basis of all action, is beyond the realm of question. And to fight back in self defense, should be accepted as a matter of course. No one who will not fight to protect his life is fit to live. Self defense is recognized as a legitimate weapon in all civilized countries. Yet the Old Crowd Negroes have counseled the doctrine of non-resistance.

As to current movements, the Negro would accept, praise and support that which his enemies reject, condemn and oppose. He is tolerant. He would restore free speech, a free press and freedom of assemblage. He would release Debs.[3] He would recognize the right of Russia to self determination. He is opposed to the Treaty and the League of Nations. Yet, he rejects Lodge's reservations.[4] He knows that neither will help the people. As to Negro leaders, his object is to destroy them all and build up new ones.

Finally, the New Negro arrived upon the scene at the time of all other forward, progressive groups and movements—after the great world war. He is the product of the same world wide forces that have brought into being the great liberal and radical movements that are now seizing the reins of political, economic and social power in all of the civilized countries of the world.

His presence is inevitable in these times of economic chaos, political upheaval and social distress. Yes, there is a New Negro. And it is he who will pilot the Negro through this terrible hour of storm and stress.

[3]Eugene V. Debs (1855–1926), labor leader, who ran as a socialist candidate for president five times between 1904 and 1920. During his last campaign in 1919, Debs went to jail under the Espionage Act (1917) for speaking out against U.S. participation in World War I.

[4]Henry Cabot Lodge (1850–1894), Republican senator from Massachusetts who opposed U.S. participation in the League of Nations after World War I and was instrumental in defeating ratification of the Versailles Treaty in the Senate (1919).

3

MARCUS GARVEY

Speech to the Second International Convention of Negroes

August 14, 1921

In this speech, delivered on August 14, 1921, during the Second International Convention of Negroes held at Liberty Hall, the Harlem headquarters of the Universal Negro Improvement Association, the popular Jamaican leader Marcus Garvey urges his followers to fight for a free Africa. At the first International Convention of Negroes, held in the previous year in New York's Madison Square Garden, 20,000 members of the UNIA representing twenty-five countries across Africa, the Caribbean, and North America had elected Garvey provisional president of Africa; declared red, black, and green the colors of the organizational flag; and adopted "The Declaration of Rights of the Negro Peoples of the World." The Second International Convention consolidated the success of the first. Held at the height of Garvey's power, it drew 6,000 delegates from all over the world every day for a month. Notice how Garvey justifies his demand of "Africa for the Africans" by employing the rhetoric of democracy and national self-determination used by President Woodrow Wilson to justify American involvement in World War I.

Four years ago, realizing the oppression and the hardships from which we suffered, we organized ourselves into an organization for the purpose of bettering our condition, and founding a government of our own. The four years of organization have brought good results, in that from an obscure, despised race we have grown into a mighty power, a mighty force whose influence is being felt throughout the length and breadth of the world. The Universal Negro Improvement Association existed but in name four years ago, today it is known as the greatest moving force among Negroes. We have accomplished this through

---

Marcus Garvey, "Speech Delivered at Liberty Hall, N.Y.C. during the Second International Convention of Negroes, August, 1921," *The Philosophy and Opinions of Marcus Garvey*, ed. Amy Jaques Garvey (New York: Universal Publishing House, 1923), 93–97.

unity of effort and unity of purpose, it is a fair demonstration of what we will be able to accomplish in the very near future, when the millions who are outside the pale of the Universal Negro Improvement Association will have linked themselves up with us.

By our success of the last four years we will be able to estimate the grander success of a free and redeemed Africa. In climbing the heights to where we are today, we have had to surmount difficulties, we have had to climb over obstacles, but the obstacles were stepping stones to the future greatness of this Cause we represent. Day by day we are writing a new history, recording new deeds of valor performed by this race of ours. It is true that the world has not yet valued us at our true worth but we are climbing up so fast and with such force that every day the world is changing its attitude towards us. Wheresoever you turn your eyes today you will find the moving influence of the Universal Negro Improvement Association among Negroes from all corners of the globe. We hear among Negroes the cry of "Africa for the Africans." This cry has become a positive, determined one. It is a cry that is raised simultaneously the world over because of the universal oppression that affects the Negro. You who are congregated here tonight as Delegates representing the hundreds of branches of the Universal Negro Improvement Association in different parts of the world will realize that we in New York are positive in this great desire of a free and redeemed Africa. We have established this Liberty Hall as the centre from which we send out the sparks of liberty to the four corners of the globe, and if you have caught the spark of your section, we want you to keep it a-burning for the great Cause we represent.

There is a mad rush among races everywhere towards national independence. Everywhere we hear the cry of liberty, of freedom, and a demand for democracy. In our corner of the world we are raising the cry for liberty, freedom and democracy. Men who have raised the cry for freedom and liberty in ages past have always made up their minds to die for the realization of the dream. We who are assembled in this Convention as Delegates representing the Negroes of the world give out the same spirit that the fathers of liberty in this country gave out over one hundred years ago. We give out a spirit that knows no compromise, a spirit that refuses to turn back, a spirit that says "Liberty or Death,"[1] and in prosecution of this great ideal—the ideal of a free and redeemed Africa, men may scorn, men may spurn us, and may say

[1]Here Garvey quotes Patrick Henry (1736–1799), a leader of the American Revolution.

that we are on the wrong side of life, but let me tell you that way in which you are travelling is just the way all peoples who are free have travelled in the past. If you want liberty you yourselves must strike the blow. If you must be free you must become so through your own effort, through your own initiative. Those who have discouraged you in the past are those who have enslaved you for centuries and it is not expected that they will admit that you have a right to strike out at this late hour for freedom, liberty and democracy.

At no time in the history of the world, for the last five hundred years, was there ever a serious attempt made to free Negroes. We have been camouflaged into believing that we were made free by Abraham Lincoln. That we were made free by Victoria of England, but up to now we are still slaves, we are industrial slaves, we are social slaves, we are political slaves, and the new Negro desires a freedom that has no boundary, no limit. We desire a freedom that will lift us to the common standard of all men, whether they be white men of Europe or yellow men of Asia, therefore, in our desire to lift ourselves to that standard we shall stop at nothing until there is a free and redeemed Africa. . . .

It falls to our lot to tear off the shackles that bind Mother Africa. Can you do it? You did it in the Revolutionary War. You did it in the Civil War; You did it at the Battles of the Marne and Verdun; You did it in Mesopotamia. You can do it marching up the battle heights of Africa. Let the world know that 400,000,000 Negroes are prepared to die or live as free men. Despise us as much as you care. Ignore us as much as you care. We are coming 400,000,000 strong.[2] We are coming with our woes behind us, with the memory of suffering behind us—woes and suffering of three hundred years—they shall be our inspiration. My bulwark of strength in the conflict for freedom in Africa, will be the three hundred years of persecution and hardship left behind in this Western Hemisphere. The more I remember the suffering of my fore-fathers, the more I remember the lynchings and burnings in the Southern States of America, the more I will fight on even though the battle seems doubtful. Tell me that I must turn back, and I laugh you to scorn. Go on! Go on! Climb ye the heights of liberty and cease not in well doing until you have planted the banner of the Red, the Black and the Green on the hilltops of Africa.

[2]The approximate size of the worldwide black population at that time.

4

JAMES WELDON JOHNSON

Black Manhattan

1930

A thinker of astonishing range, James Weldon Johnson (1871–1938) wrote poetry, songs, essays, and novels. A native of Jacksonville, Florida, he served as a journalist, a diplomat, and the first black secretary of the NAACP, from 1920 to 1930. He also co-authored with his brother John Rosamond Johnson the African American national anthem "Lift Every Voice and Sing." In this selection from his classic study Black Manhattan, *he recalls the transformation of Harlem from a white, middle-class neighborhood to a center of black urban life, focusing on the economic, social, and geographic features that made Harlem an intimate part of New York City. How, according to Johnson, did racial, ethnic, and other forms of mixture come together to make Harlem a hub for black art and identity in the 1920s?*

If you ride northward the length of Manhattan Island, going through Central Park and coming out on Seventh Avenue or Lenox Avenue at One Hundred and Tenth Street, you cannot escape being struck by the sudden change in the character of the people you see. In the middle and lower parts of the city you have, perhaps, noted Negro faces here and there; but when you emerge from the Park, you see them everywhere, and as you go up either of these two great arteries leading out from the city to the north, you see more and more Negroes, walking in the streets, looking from the windows, trading in the shops, eating in the restaurants, going in and coming out of the theaters, until, nearing One Hundred and Thirty-fifth Street, ninety per cent of the people you see, including the traffic officers, are Negroes. And it is not until you cross the Harlem River that the population whitens again, which it does as suddenly as it began to darken at One Hundred and Tenth Street. You have been having an outside glimpse of Harlem, the Negro metropolis.

James Weldon Johnson, *Black Manhattan* (New York: Alfred A. Knopf, 1930), 145–59.

In nearly every city in the country the Negro section is a nest or several nests situated somewhere on the borders; it is a section one must "go out to." In New York it is entirely different. Negro Harlem is situated in the heart of Manhattan and covers one of the most beautiful and healthful sites in the whole city. It is not a fringe, it is not a slum, nor is it a "quarter" consisting of dilapidated tenements. It is a section of new-law apartment houses and handsome dwellings, with streets as well paved, as well lighted, and as well kept as in any other part of the city. Three main highways lead into and out from upper Manhattan, and two of them run straight through Harlem. So Harlem is not a section that one "goes out to," but a section that one goes through.

Roughly drawn, the boundaries of Harlem are: One Hundred and Tenth Street on the south; on the east, Lenox Avenue to One Hundred and Twenty-sixth Street, then Lexington Avenue to the Harlem River, and the Harlem River on the east and north to a point where it passes the Polo Grounds,[1] just above One Hundred and Fifty-fifth Street; on the west, Eighth Avenue to One Hundred and Sixteenth Street, then St. Nicholas Avenue up to a juncture with the Harlem River at the Polo Grounds. To the east of the Lenox Avenue boundary there are a score of blocks of mixed colored and white population; and to the west of the Eighth Avenue boundary there is a solid Negro border, two blocks wide, from One Hundred and Sixteenth Street to One Hundred and Twenty-fifth Street. The heights north from One Hundred and Forty-fifth Street, known as Coogan's Bluff, are solidly black. Within this area of less than two square miles lie more than two hundred thousand Negroes, more to the square acre than in any other place on earth.

This city within a city, in these larger proportions, is actually a development of the last fifteen years. The trek to Harlem began when the West Fifty-third Street center had reached its utmost development; that is, early in the decade 1900–10. The move to West Fifty-third Street had been the result of the opportunity to get into better houses; and the move to Harlem was due to the same urge. In fact, Harlem offered the colored people the first chance in their entire history in New York to live in modern apartment houses. West Fifty-third Street was superior to anything they had ever enjoyed; and there they were, for the most part, making private dwellings serve the purpose of

[1]A stadium in upper Manhattan between 157th and 159th streets, longtime home of the New York Giants baseball team.

apartments, housing several families in each house. The move to Harlem, in the beginning and for a long time, was fathered and engineered by Philip A. Payton, a colored man in the real-estate business. But this was more than a matter of mere business with Mr. Payton: the matter of better and still better housing for colored people in New York became the dominating idea of his life, and he worked on it as long as he lived. When Negro New Yorkers evaluate their benefactors in their own race, they must find that not many have done more than Phil Payton; for much of what has made Harlem the intellectual and artistic capital of the Negro world is in good part due to this fundamental advantage: Harlem has provided New York Negroes with better, cleaner, more modern, more airy, more sunny houses than they ever lived in before. And this is due to the efforts made first by Mr. Payton.

Harlem had been overbuilt with new apartment houses. It was far uptown, and the only rapid transportation was the elevated running up Eighth Avenue—the Lenox Avenue Subway had not yet been built. This left the people on Lenox Avenue and to the east, with only the electric street-cars convenient. So landlords were finding it hard to fill their houses on that side of the section. Mr. Payton approached several of these landlords with the proposal to fill their empty houses with colored tenants and keep them filled. Economic necessity usually discounts race prejudice—or any other kind of prejudice—as much as ninety per cent, sometimes a hundred; so the landlords with empty houses whom Mr. Payton approached accepted his proposal, and one or two houses on One Hundred and Thirty-fourth Street were taken over and filled with colored tenants. Gradually other houses were filled. The white residents of the section showed very little concern about the movement until it began to spread to the west and across Lenox Avenue; then they took steps to check it. They organized, and formed plans to purchase through the Hudson Realty Company, a financial concern, all properties occupied by colored people and evict the tenants. Payton countered by forming the Afro-American Realty Company, a Negro corporation organized for the purpose of buying and leasing houses to be let to colored tenants. This counterstroke held the opposition in check for several years and enabled the Negroes to hold their own.

But the steady and increasing pressure of Negroes across the Lenox Avenue dead-line caused the opposition to break out anew; and this time the plans were more deeply laid and more difficult for the Negroes to defeat. These plans, formulated by several leading spirits, involved what was actually a conspiracy—the organization of whites to bring pressure on financial institutions to lend no money and renew no mortgages on properties occupied by colored people. These plans had considerable success and reached beyond the situation they were formed to deal with. They still furnish one of the hardest and most unjustifiable handicaps the Negro property-owner in Harlem has to contend with.

The Afro-American Realty Company, for lack of the large amount of capital essential, was now defunct; but several individual colored men carried on. Philip A. Payton and J. C. Thomas bought two five-story apartments, dispossessed the white tenants, and put in colored ones. John B. Nail bought a row of five apartments and did the same. St. Philip's Episcopal Church, one of the oldest and richest colored congregations in New York, bought a row of thirteen apartments on One Hundred and Thirty-fifth Street between Lenox and Seventh Avenues and rented them to colored tenants. The situation now resolved itself into an actual contest. But the Negro pressure continued constant. Colored people not only continued to move into apartments outside the zone east of Lenox Avenue, but began to purchase the fine private houses between Lenox and Seventh. Then, in the eyes of the whites who were antagonistic, the whole movement took on the aspect of an "invasion"—an invasion of both their economic and their social rights. They felt that Negroes as neighbors not only lowered the values of their property, but also lowered their social status. Seeing that they could not stop the movement, they began to flee. They took fright, they became panic-stricken, they ran amuck. Their conduct could be compared to that of a community in the Middle Ages fleeing before an epidemic of the black plague, except for the fact that here the reasons were not so sound. But these people did not stop to reason, they did not stop to ask why they did what they were doing, or what would happen if they didn't do it. The presence of a single colored family in a block, regardless of the fact that they might be well-bred people, with sufficient means to buy their new home, was a signal for precipitate flight. The stampeded whites actually deserted house after house and block after block. Then prices dropped; they dropped lower than the bottom, and such colored people as were able took advantage of these prices and bought. Some of the banks and lending companies that were compelled to take over deserted houses for the mortgages they held refused for a time to either sell or rent them to Negroes. Instead, they proposed themselves to bear the carrying charges and hold them vacant for what they evidently hoped would be a temporary period.

Prices continued to drop. And this was the property situation in Harlem at the outbreak of the World War in Europe.

With the outbreak of the war there came a sudden change. One of the first effects of the war was to draw thousands of aliens out of this country back to their native lands to join the colors. Naturally, there was also an almost total cessation of immigration. Moreover, the United States was almost immediately called upon to furnish munitions and supplies of all kinds to the warring countries. The result of these converging causes was an unprecedented shortage of labor and a demand that was imperative. From whence could the necessary supply be drawn? There was only one source, and that was the reservoir of black labor in the South. And it was at once drawn on to fill the existing vacuum in the great industries of the North. Every available method was used to get these black hands, the most effective being the sending of labor agents into the South, who dealt directly with the Negroes, arranged for their transportation, and shipped them north, often in single consignments running high up into the hundreds. I witnessed the sending north from a Southern city in one day a crowd estimated at twenty-five hundred. They were shipped on a train run in three sections, packed in day coaches, with all their baggage and other impedimenta. The exodus was on, and migrants came north in thousands, tens of thousands, hundreds of thousands—from the docks of Norfolk, Savannah, Jacksonville, Tampa, Mobile, New Orleans, and Galveston; from the cotton-fields of Mississippi, and the coal-mines and steel-mills of Alabama and Tennessee; from workshops and wash-tubs and brick-yards and kitchens they came, until the number, by conservative estimate, went well over the million and a half mark. For the Negroes of the South this was the happy blending of desire with opportunity.

It could not be otherwise in such a wholesale migration than that many who came were ignorant, inefficient, and worthless, and that there was also a proportion of downright criminals. But industry was in no position to be fastidious; it was glad to take what it could get. It was not until the return of more normal conditions that the process of elimination of the incapable and the unfit set in. Meanwhile, in these new fields, the Negro was acquiring all sorts of divergent reputations for capability. In some places he was rated A 1 and in others N. G.,[2] and in varying degrees between these two extremes. The explanation,

[2]"Great" and "No Good."

of course, is that different places had secured different kinds of Negroes. On the whole, New York was more fortunate in the migrants she got than were some of the large cities. Most of the industries in the manufacturing cities of the Middle West—except the steel mills, which drew largely on the skilled and semi-skilled labor from the mills of Alabama and Tennessee—received migrants from the cotton-raising regions of the lower Mississippi Valley, from the rural, even the backwoods, districts, Negroes who were unused to city life or anything bearing a resemblance to modern industry. On the other hand, New York drew most of her migrants from cities and towns of the Atlantic seaboard states, Negroes who were far better prepared to adapt themselves to life and industry in a great city. Nor did all of New York's Negro migrants come from the South. The opportunity for Negro labor exerted a pull that reached down to the Negroes of the West Indies, and many of them came, most of them directly to New York. Those from the British West Indies average high in intelligence and efficiency. There is practically no illiteracy among them, and many have a sound English common school education. They are characteristically sober-minded and have something of a genius for business, differing almost totally, in these respects, from the average rural Negro of the South. Those from British possessions constitute the great majority of the West Indians in New York; but there is also a large number who are Spanish-speaking and a considerable, though smaller, number who are French-speaking. The total West Indian population of Harlem is approximately fifty thousand.

With thousands of Negroes pouring into Harlem month by month, two things happened: first, a sheer physical pressure for room was set up that was irresistible; second, old residents and new-comers got work as fast as they could take it, at wages never dreamed of, so there was now plenty of money for renting and buying. And the Negro in Harlem did, contrary to all the burlesque notions about what Negroes do when they get hold of money, take advantage of the low prices of property and begin to buy. Buying property became a contagious fever. It became a part of the gospel preached in the churches. It seems that generations of the experience of an extremely precarious foothold on the land of Manhattan Island flared up into a conscious determination never to let that condition return. So they turned the money from their new-found prosperity into property. All classes bought. It was not an unknown thing for a colored washerwoman to walk into a real-estate office and lay down several thousand dollars on a house. There was Mrs. Mary Dean, known as "Pig Foot Mary" because of her high reputation in the business of preparing and selling that particular delicacy, so popular in Harlem. She paid $42,000 for a five-story apartment house at the corner of Seventh Avenue and One Hundred and Thirty-seventh Street, which was sold later to a colored undertaker for $72,000. The Equitable Life Assurance Company held vacant for quite a while a block of 106 model private houses, designed by Stanford White, which the company had been obliged to take over following the hegira of the whites from Harlem. When they were put on the market, they were promptly bought by Negroes at an aggregate price of about two million dollars. John E. Nail, a colored real-estate dealer of Harlem who is a member of the Real Estate Board of New York and an appraisal authority, states that Negroes own and control Harlem real property worth, at a conservative estimate, between fifty and sixty million dollars. Relatively, these figures are amazing. Twenty years ago barely a half-dozen colored individuals owned land on Manhattan. Down to fifteen years ago the amount that Negroes had acquired in Harlem was by comparison negligible. Today a very large part of the property in Harlem occupied by Negroes is owned by Negroes.

It should be noted that Harlem was taken over without violence. In some of the large Northern cities where the same sort of expansion of the Negro population was going on, there was not only strong antagonism on the part of whites, but physical expression of it. In Chicago, Cleveland, and other cities houses bought and moved into by Negroes were bombed. In Chicago a church bought by a colored congregation was badly damaged by bombs. In other cities several formerly white churches which had been taken over by colored congregations were bombed. In Detroit, mobs undertook to evict Negroes from houses bought by them in white neighborhoods. The mob drove vans up to one house just purchased and moved into by a colored physician, ordered him out, loaded all his goods into the vans, and carted them back to his old residence. These arrogated functions of the mob reached a climax in the celebrated Sweet case. A mob gathered in the evening round a house in a white neighborhood which Dr. O. H. Sweet, a colored physician, had bought and moved into the day before. When the situation reached a critical point, shots fired from within the house killed one person in the crowd and seriously wounded another. Dr. Sweet, his wife, and eight others, relatives and friends, who were in the house at the time, were indicted and tried for murder in the first degree. They were defended in two long trials by the National Association for the Advancement of Colored People, through Clarence Darrow and Arthur Garfield Hays, assisted by several local attorneys, and were acquitted.[3] This was the tragic end of eviction by mob in Detroit.

Although there was bitter feeling in Harlem during the fifteen years of struggle the Negro went through in getting a foothold on the land, there was never any demonstration of violence that could be called serious. Not since the riot of 1900 has New York witnessed, except for minor incidents, any interracial disturbances. Not even in the memorable summer of 1919—that summer when the stoutest-hearted Negroes felt terror and dismay; when the race got the worst backwash of the war, and the Ku Klux Klan was in the ascendant; when almost simultaneously there were riots in Chicago and in Longview, Texas; in Omaha and in Phillips County, Arkansas; and hundreds of Negroes, chased through the streets or hunted down through the swamps, were beaten and killed; when in the national capital an anti-Negro mob held sway for three days, in which time six persons were killed and scores severely beaten—not even during this period of massacre did New York, with more than a hundred thousand Negroes grouped together in Harlem, lose its equanimity.

It is apparent that race friction, as it affects Harlem as a community, has grown less and less each year for the past ten years; and the signs are that there will not be a recrudescence. The signs are confirmed by certain basic conditions. Although Harlem is a Negro community, the newest comers do not long remain merely "Harlem Negroes"; astonishingly soon they become New Yorkers. One reason for this is that, by comparison with Chicago, Detroit, Pittsburgh, or Cleveland, there is no gang labor among Negroes in New York. The longshoremen are an exception, but the Negro longshoremen are highly unionized and stand on an equal footing with their white fellow-workers. Employment of Negroes in New York is diversified; they are employed more as individuals than as non-integral parts of a gang. This gives them the opportunity for more intimate contacts with the life and spirit of the city as a whole. A thousand Negroes from Mississippi brought up and put to work in a Pittsburgh plant will for a long time remain a thousand Negroes from Mississippi. Under the conditions that prevail in

[3]Clarence Darrow (1857–1938), American lawyer famous for defending the downtrodden and for representing high school biology teacher John Scopes (1925), whom the state of Tennessee had charged with illegally teaching the theory of evolution. Arthur Garfield Hays (1881–1954), a lawyer and free speech advocate known for his participation in high-profile civil liberties cases, including the Scopes Trial.

New York, they would all, inside of six months, be pretty good New Yorkers. One of the chief factors in the Chicago race riot in 1919 was the fact that at the time more than twelve thousand Negroes were employed at the stockyards. Moreover, there is the psychology of New York, the natural psychology of a truly cosmopolitan city, in which there is always the tendency to minimize rather than magnify distinctions of this sort, in which such distinctions tend to die out, unless kept alive by some intentional agency. New York, more than any other American city, maintains a matter-of-fact, a taken-for-granted attitude towards her Negro citizens. Less there than anywhere else in the country are Negroes regarded as occupying a position of wardship; more nearly do they stand upon the footing of common and equal citizenship. It may be that one of the causes of New York's attitude lies in the fact that the Negro there has achieved a large degree of political independence; that he has broken away from a political creed based merely upon traditional and sentimental grounds. Yet, on the other hand, this itself may be a result of New York's attitude.

At any rate, there is no longer any apparent feeling against the occupancy of Harlem by Negroes. Within the past five years the colony has expanded to the south, the north, and the west. It has gone down Seventh Avenue from One Hundred and Twenty-seventh Street to Central Park at One Hundred and Tenth Street. It has climbed upwards between Eighth Avenue and the Harlem River from One Hundred and Forty-fifth Street to One Hundred and Fifty-fifth. It has spread to the west and occupies the heights of Coogan's Bluff, overlooking Colonial Park. And to the east and west of this solid Negro area, there is a fringe where the population is mixed, white and colored. This expansion of the past five years has taken place without any physical opposition, or even any considerable outbreak of antagonistic public sentiment.

The question inevitably arises: Will the Negroes of Harlem be able to hold it? Will they not be driven still farther northward? Residents of Manhattan, regardless of race, have been driven out when they lay in the path of business and greatly increased land values. Harlem lies in the direction that path must take; so there is little probability that Negroes will always hold it as a residential section. But this is to be considered: the Negro's situation in Harlem is without precedent in all his history in New York; never before has he been so securely anchored, never before has he owned the land, never before has he had so well established a community life. It is probable that land through the heart of Harlem will some day so increase in value that

Negroes may not be able to hold it—although it is quite as probable that there will be some Negroes able to take full advantage of the increased values—and will be forced to make a move. But the next move, when it comes, will be unlike the others. It will not be a move made solely at the behest of someone else; it will be more in the nature of a bargain. Nor will it be a move in which the Negro will carry with him only his household goods and utensils; he will move at a financial profit to himself. But at the present time such a move is nowhere in sight.

5

HELENE JOHNSON

Sonnet to a Negro in Harlem

1927

Originally from Boston and a cousin of the short-story writer and editor Dorothy West, Helene Johnson attended Boston University and moved to New York City in 1926. There, while in her twenties, she published her best work in Opportunity, Vanity Fair, *and* Fire!! *"Sonnet to a Negro in Harlem" appeared in Countée Cullen's anthology* Caroling Dusk *(1927). In this poem, Harlem appears as a proud and disdainful character that sings barbaric songs as others work. Why does Johnson celebrate such a figure? (For an explanation of the sonnet form, see the headnote to Document 6.)*

You are disdainful and magnificent—
Your perfect body and your pompous gait,
Your dark eyes flashing solemnly with hate,
Small wonder that you are incompetent
To imitate those whom you so despise—
Your shoulders towering high above the throng,

Helene Johnson, "Sonnet to a Negro in Harlem," *Caroling Dusk*, ed. Countée Cullen (New York: Harper & Brothers, 1927), 217.

Your head thrown back in rich, barbaric song,
Palm trees and mangoes stretched before your eyes
Let others toil and sweat for labor's sake
And wring from grasping hands their meed of gold.
Why urge ahead your supercilious feet?
Scorn will efface each footprint that you make.
I love your laughter arrogant and bold.
You are too splendid for this city street!

6

CLAUDE MCKAY

Harlem Shadows and *The Liberator*

1922

Claude McKay immigrated to the United States from his native Jamaica in 1912 having already published two books of poetry, Songs of Jamaica *(1912) and* Constab Ballads *(1912). He enrolled in Booker T. Washington's Tuskegee Institute, where he first encountered the cruelty of American racism that became an enduring subject of his poetry. Moving to New York City in 1914, he associated with radical circles in Greenwich Village and became an editor of Max Eastman's Marxist journal* The Liberator *in 1917, one of several avant-garde journals in which McKay published most of the poetry that later appeared in his collection* Harlem Shadows *(1922). "The Harlem Dancer" (1917), which McKay published under the name Eli Edwards to avoid government repression of radicals, uses the image of an unhappy prostitute to represent the*

Claude McKay, *Harlem Shadows: The Poems of Claude McKay* (New York: Harcourt, Brace, 1922), 6, 22, 42, 53; "The Harlem Dancer," first published under the pseudonym Eli Edwards in *The Seven Arts*, 2 (October 1917): 2; "Harlem Shadows," first published in *Pearsons Magazine*, 34 (September 1918): 276; "If We Must Die," first published in *The Liberator*, 2 (July 1919): 21; "America," first published in *The Liberator*, 4 (August 1921): 9; "The White House," *The Liberator*, 5 (May 1922): 9.

tough but vital underside of Harlem life. Like most of his later verse, it employs the sonnet, a fourteen-line poem with a fixed rhyme scheme, to achieve its effect. Typically, the first twelve lines of a sonnet set out a thought or problem that the last two lines, or the couplet, reflect on by providing an opposing or complicating insight. Notice how the last two lines of "The Harlem Dancer" amplify its meaning. "Harlem Shadows" (1918), the poem that would eventually lead off his famous collection of the same title, repeats many of the themes of "The Harlem Dancer." Here McKay calls attention to the unromantic underside of Harlem life by evoking the image of a spiritually lost prostitute—symbolic of a debauched and fallen race—wandering, poor and halfhearted, through the streets in search of business. In "If We Must Die" (1919), McKay uses the sonnet form to express unforgettably the fighting spirit of the New Negro immediately following World War I. Two more sonnets, "America" (1921) and "The White House" (1922), extend the embattled attitude of "If We Must Die" to more specific thematic territory. What do these poems say about how McKay views the United States?

The Harlem Dancer

Applauding youths laughed with young prostitutes
And watched her perfect, half-clothed body sway;
Her voice was like the sound of blended flutes
Blown by black players upon a picnic day.
She sang and danced on gracefully and calm,
The light gauze hanging loose about her form;
To me she seemed a proudly-swaying palm
Grown lovelier for passing through a storm.
Upon her swarthy neck black shiny curls
Luxuriant fell; and tossing coins in praise,
The wine-flushed, bold-eyed boys, and even the girls,
Devoured her shape with eager, passionate gaze;
But looking at her falsely-smiling face,
I knew her self was not in that strange place.

Harlem Shadows

I hear the halting footsteps of a lass
In Negro Harlem when the night lets fall
Its veil. I see the shapes of girls who pass
To bend and barter at desire's call.
Ah, little dark girls who in slippered feet
Go prowling through the night from street to street!

Through the long night until the silver break
Of day the little gray feet know no rest;
Through the lone night until the last snow-flake
Has dropped from heaven upon the earth's white breast,
The dusky, half-clad girls of tired feet
Are trudging, thinly shod, from street to street.

Ah, stern harsh world, that in the wretched way
Of poverty, dishonor and disgrace,
Has pushed the timid little feet of clay,
The sacred brown feet of my fallen race!
Ah, heart of me, the weary, weary feet
In Harlem wandering from street to street.

If We Must Die

If we must die—let it not be like hogs
Hunted and penned in an inglorious spot,
While round us bark the mad and hungry dogs,
Making their mock at our accursed lot.
If we must die—oh, let us nobly die,
So that our precious blood may not be shed
In vain; then even the monsters we defy
Shall be constrained to honor us though dead!

Oh, kinsmen! We must meet the common foe;
Though far outnumbered, let us still be brave,
And for their thousand blows deal one death-blow!
What though before us lies the open grave?
Like men we'll face the murderous, cowardly pack,
Pressed to the wall, dying, but—fighting back!

America

Although she feeds me bread of bitterness,
And sinks into my throat her tiger's tooth,
Stealing my breath of life, I will confess
I love this cultured hell that tests my youth!
Her vigor flows like tides into my blood,
Giving me strength erect against her hate.
Her bigness sweeps my being like a flood.
Yet as a rebel fronts a king in state,
I stand within her walls with not a shred
Of terror, malice, not a word of jeer.
Darkly I gaze into the days ahead,
And see her might and granite wonders there,
Beneath the touch of Time's unerring hand,
Like priceless treasures sinking in the sand.

The White House

Your door is shut against my tightened face,
And I am sharp as steel with discontent;
But I possess the courage and the grace
To bear my anger proudly and unbent.
The pavement slabs burn loose beneath my feet,
A chafing savage, down the decent street,
And passion reads my vitals as I pass,
Where boldly shines your shuttered door of glass.
Oh I must search for wisdom every hour,
Deep in my wrathful bosom sore and raw,
And find in it the superhuman power
To hold me to the letter of your law!
Oh I must keep my heart inviolate
Against the potent poison of your hate.

7

JEAN TOOMER

Cane

1923

Although Jean Toomer declined the political radicalism and anger of figures such as Claude McKay, he published in the same journals and, like McKay, gravitated toward Greenwich Village literary and intellectual circles. A native of Washington, D.C., he first came to New York City in 1917. After returning briefly to Washington, he took a teaching job in Spartanburg, Georgia, in 1921. There he observed for the first time southern black life in a rural setting and received the inspiration and theme for his moving prose-poem Cane, *which advances a three-part circular movement from the decaying industrial South, to the spiritually dead urban North, to an evocation of the sources of nature, primitive truth, and interracial unity still alive in the black southern soul. The only major work by Toomer,* Cane *rewards close attention. Take note of repeated images (pines, the mound, smoke), sounds (the wind, the whispering of the pines, and the* s *sound of reaping), and rhythms (the steady beat within and between the lines of both poems, reflecting the rhythms of work and rural black American work songs) that shape and connect the stories of the beautiful black woman Karintha, the exiled white woman Becky, and the intervening poems "Reapers" and "November Cotton Flower."*

Karintha

Her skin is like dusk on the eastern horizon,
O cant you see it, O cant you see it,
Her skin is like dusk on the eastern horizon
. . . When the sun goes down.

Men had always wanted her, this Karintha, even as a child, Karintha carrying beauty, perfect as dusk when the sun goes down. Old men

---

Jean Toomer, *Cane* (New York: Boni and Liveright, 1923), 1–7.

rode her hobby-horse upon their knees. Young men danced with her at frolics when they should have been dancing with their grown-up girls. God grant us youth, secretly prayed the old men. The young fellows counted the time to pass before she would be old enough to mate with them. This interest of the male, who wishes to ripen a growing thing too soon, could mean no good to her.

Karintha, at twelve, was a wild flash that told the other folks just what it was to live. At sunset, when there was no wind, and the pine-smoke from over by the sawmill hugged the earth, and you couldn't see more than a few feet in front, her sudden darting past you was a bit of vivid color, like a black bird that flashes in light. With the other children one could hear, some distance off, their feet flopping in the two-inch dust. Karintha's running was a whir. It had the sound of the red dust that sometimes makes a spiral in the road. At dusk, during the hush just after the sawmill had closed down, and before any of the women had started their supper-getting-ready songs, her voice, high-pitched, shrill, would put one's ears to itching. But no one ever thought to make her stop because of it. She stoned the cows, and beat her dog, and fought the other children. . . Even the preacher, who caught her at mischief, told himself that she was as innocently lovely as a November cotton flower. Already, rumors were out about her. Homes in Georgia are most often built on the two-room plan. In one, you cook and eat, in the other you sleep, and there love goes on. Karintha had seen or heard, perhaps she had felt her parents loving. One could but imitate one's parents, for to follow them was the way of God. She played "home" with a small boy who was not afraid to do her bidding. That started the whole thing. Old men could no longer ride her hobby-horse upon their knees. But young counted faster.

Her skin is like dusk,
O cant you see it,
Her skin is like dusk,
When the sun goes down.

Karintha is a woman. She who carries beauty, perfect as dusk when the sun goes down. She has been married many times. Old men remind her that a few years back they rode her hobby-horse upon their knees. Karintha smiles, and indulges them when she is in the mood for it. She has contempt for them. Karintha is a woman. Young men run stills to make her money. Young men go to the big cities and run on the road. Young men go away to college. They all want to bring her money. These are the young men who thought that all they had to do was to count time. But Karintha is a woman, and she has had a child. A child fell out of her womb onto a bed of pine-needles in the forest. Pine-needles are smooth and sweet. They are elastic to the feet of rabbits. . . A sawmill was nearby. Its pyramidal sawdust pile smouldered. It is a year before one completely burns. Meanwhile, the smoke curls up and hangs in odd wraiths about the trees, curls up, and spreads itself out over the valley. . . Weeks after Karintha returned home the smoke was so heavy you tasted it in water. Some one made a song:

Smoke is on the hills. Rise up.
Smoke is on the hills, O rise
And take my soul to Jesus.

Karintha is a woman. Men do not know that the soul of her was a growing thing ripened too soon. They will bring their money; they will die not having found it out. . . Karintha at twenty, carrying beauty, perfect as dusk when the sun goes down. Karintha. . .

Her skin is like dusk on the eastern horizon,
O cant you see it, O cant you see it,
Her skin is like dusk on the eastern horizon
. . . When the sun goes down.

Goes down. . .

Reapers

Black reapers with the sound of steel on stones
Are sharpening scythes. I see them place the hone
In their hip-pockets as a thing that's done,
And start their silent swinging, one by one.
Black horses drive a mower through the weeds,
And there, a field rat, startled, squealing bleeds,
His belly close to ground. I see the blade,
Blood-stained, continue cutting weeds and shade.

November Cotton Flower

Boll-weevil's coming, and the winter's cold,
Made cotton-stalks look rusty, seasons old,
And cotton, scarce as any southern snow,

Was vanishing; the branch, so pinched and slow,
Failed in its function as the autumn rake;
Drouth fighting soil had caused the soil to take
All water from the streams; dead birds were found
In wells a hundred feet below the ground—
Such was the season when the flower bloomed.
Old folks were startled, and it soon assumed
Significance. Superstition saw
Something it had never seen before:
Brown eyes that loved without a trace of fear,
Beauty so sudden for that time of year.

Becky

Becky was the white woman who had two Negro sons. She's dead; they've gone away. The pines whisper to Jesus. The Bible flaps its leaves with an aimless rustle on her mound.

Becky had one Negro son. Who gave it to her? Damn buck nigger, said the white folks' mouths. She wouldnt tell. Common, God-forsaken, insane white shameless wench, said the white folks' mouths. Her eyes were sunken, her neck stringy, her breasts fallen, till then. Taking their words, they filled her, like a bubble rising—then she broke. Mouth setting in a twist that held her eyes, harsh, vacant, staring... Who gave it to her? Low-down nigger with no self-respect, said the black folks' mouths. She wouldnt tell. Poor Catholic poor-white crazy woman, said the black folks' mouths. White folks and black folks built her cabin, fed her and her growing baby, prayed secretly to God who'd put His cross upon her and cast her out.

When the first was born, the white folks said they'd have no more to do with her. And black folks, they too joined hands to cast her out... The pines whispered to Jesus... The railroad boss said not to say he said it, but she could live, if she wanted to, on the narrow strip of land between the railroad and the road. John Stone, who owned the lumber and the bricks, would have shot the man who told he gave the stuff to Lonnie Deacon, who stole out there at night and built the cabin. A single room held down to earth... O fly away to Jesus... by a leaning chimney...

Six trains each day rumbled past and shook the ground under her cabin. Fords, and horse- and mule-drawn buggies went back and forth along the road. No one ever saw her. Trainmen, and passengers who'd heard about her, threw out papers and food. Threw out little crumpled slips of paper scribbled with prayers, as they passed her eye-shaped piece of sandy ground. Ground islandized between the road and railroad track. Pushed up where a blue-sheen God with listless eyes could look at it. Folks from the town took turns, unknown, of course, to each other, in bringing corn and meat and sweet potatoes. Even sometimes snuff. . . O thank y Jesus. . . Old David Georgia, grinding cane and boiling syrup, never went her way without some sugar sap. No one ever saw her. The boy grew up and ran around. When he was five years old as folks reckoned it, Hugh Jourdon saw him carrying a baby. "Becky has another son," was what the whole town knew. But nothing was said, for the part of man that says things to the likes of that had told itself that if there was a Becky, that Becky now was dead.

The two boys grew. Sullen and cunning. . . O pines, whisper to Jesus; tell Him to come and press sweet Jesus-lips against their lips and eyes. . . It seemed as though with those two big fellows there, there could be no room for Becky. The part that prayed wondered if perhaps she'd really died, and they had buried her. No one dared ask. They'd beat and cut a man who meant nothing at all in mentioning that they lived along the road. White or colored? No one knew, and least of all themselves. They drifted around from job to job. We, who had cast out their mother because of them, could we take them in? They answered black and white folks by shooting up two men and leaving town. "Godam the white folks; godam the niggers," they shouted as they left town. Becky? Smoke curled up from her chimney; she must be there. Trains passing shook the ground. The ground shook the leaning chimney. Nobody noticed it. A creepy feeling came over all who saw that thin wraith of smoke and felt the trembling of the ground. Folks began to take her food again. They quit it soon because they had a fear. Becky if dead might be a hant, and if alive— it took some nerve even to mention it. . . O pines, whisper to Jesus. . .

It was Sunday. Our congregation had been visiting at Pulverton, and were coming home. There was no wind. The autumn sun, the bell from Ebenezer Church, listless and heavy. Even the pines were stale, sticky, like the smell of food that makes you sick. Before we turned the bend of the road that would show us the Becky cabin, the horses stopped stock-still, pushed back their ears, and nervously whinnied. We urged, then whipped them on. Quarter of a mile away thin smoke curled up from the leaning chimney. . . O pines, whisper to Jesus. . . Goose-flesh came on my skin though there still was neither chill nor wind. Eyes left their sockets for the cab. Ears burned and throbbed.

Uncanny eclipse! fear closed my mind. We were just about to pass... Pines shout to Jesus!... the ground trembled as a ghost train rumbled by. The chimney fell into the cabin. Its thud was like a hollow report, ages having passed since it went off. Barlo and I were pulled out of our seats. Dragged to the door that had swung open. Through the dust we saw the bricks in a mound upon the floor. Becky, if she was there, lay under them. I thought I heard a groan. Barlo, mumbling something, threw his Bible on the pile. (No one has ever touched it.) Somehow we got away. My buggy was still on the road. The last thing that I remember was whipping old Dan like fury; I remember nothing after that—that is, until I reached town and folks crowded round to get the true word of it.

Becky was the white woman who had two Negro sons. She's dead; they've gone away. The pines whisper to Jesus. The Bible flaps its leaves with an aimless rustle on her mound.

8

COUNTÉE CULLEN

Color and *Copper Sun*

1925 and 1927

The adopted son of a Harlem minister, Countée Cullen published Color *(1925) during his senior year at New York University and* Copper Sun *(1927) almost directly after. These poems represent some of the best from these two collections. In contrast to Claude McKay, who gravitated to indignation, and Jean Toomer, who rejected traditional verse forms and traditional poets in his quest for a genuine black voice, Cullen wrote polished "white" verse—ballads, quatrains, and sonnets in the manner of English poets John Keats and Lord Byron. In "To John Keats, Poet. At*

Countée Cullen, *Color* (New York: Harper & Brothers, 1925), 3, 13, 102–4. Countée Cullen, *Copper Sun* (New York: Harper & Brothers, 1927), 3. "To John Keats, Poet. At Spring Time," first published in *Vanity Fair*, 24 (June 1925): 62. "Yet Do I Marvel," first published in *Century Magazine*, 109 (November 1924): 122. "From the Dark Tower," first published in the *New York Herald Tribune*, January 16, 1924. "Harlem Wine," first published in *The Survey Graphic*, 6 (March 1925): 674.

Spring Time" (1925), Cullen uses Keats's assertion of the importance of beauty and ambiguity to invoke his own effort to disentangle the ambiguities of race and oppression without explicitly mentioning race. His dominant contemplative mood, tinged with melancholy, reappears in two of his most famous poems, "Yet Do I Marvel" (1924) and "From the Dark Tower" (1924), in which he addresses the race problem directly. In "Harlem Wine" (1925), Cullen calls forth the image of wine—symbolic of blood sacrifice, heritage, intoxication, and many other associations—flowing relentlessly down the streets of Harlem. What makes this wine so powerful? Why must it flow on?

To John Keats, Poet. At Spring Time

For Carl Van Vechten

I cannot hold my peace, John Keats;
There never was a spring like this;
It is an echo, that repeats
My last year's song and next year's bliss.
I know, in spite of all men say
Of Beauty, you have felt her most.
Yea, even in your grave her way
Is laid. Poor, troubled, lyric ghost,
Spring never was so fair and dear
As Beauty makes her seem this year.

I cannot hold my peace, John Keats,
I am as helpless in the toil
Of Spring as any lamb that bleats
To feel the solid earth recoil
Beneath his puny legs. Spring beats
Her tocsin call to those who love her,
And lo! the dogwood petals cover

And while my head is earthward bowed
To read new life sprung from your shroud,
Folks seeing me must think it strange
That merely spring should so derange
My mind. They do not know that you,
John Keats, keep revel with me, too.

Yet Do I Marvel

I doubt not God is good, well-meaning, kind,
And did He stoop to quibble could tell why
The little buried mole continues blind,
Why flesh that mirrors Him must some day die,
Make plain the reason tortured Tantalus[1]
Is baited by the fickle fruit, declare
If merely brute caprice dooms Sisyphus[2]
To struggle up a never-ending stair.
Inscrutable His ways are, and immune
To catechism by a mind too strewn
With petty cares to slightly understand
What awful brain compels His awful hand.
Yet do I marvel at this curious thing:
To make a poet black, and bid him sing!

[1]Tantalus, a king in Greek mythology condemned by the gods to stand in water that receded when he tried to drink it and below a tree with fruit that receded when he reached for it.

[2]Sisyphus, a cruel king in Greek mythology condemned by the gods forever to roll a huge stone up a hill in Hades only to have it roll down again upon nearing the top.

From the Dark Tower

To Charles S. Johnson

We shall not always plant while others reap
The golden increment of bursting fruit,
Not always countenance, abject and mute,
That lesser men should hold their brothers cheap;
Not everlastingly while others sleep
Shall we beguile their limbs with mellow flute,
Not always bend to some more subtle brute;
We were not made eternally to weep.

The night whose sable breast relieves the stark,
White stars is no less lovely being dark,
And there are buds that cannot bloom at all
In light, but crumple, piteous, and fall;
So in the dark we hide the heart that bleeds,
And wait, and tend our agonizing seeds.

Harlem Wine

This is not water running here,
   These thick rebellious streams
That hurtle flesh and bone past fear
   Down alleyways of dreams.

This is a wine that must flow on
   Not caring how nor where,
So it has ways to flow upon
   Where song is in the air.

So it can woo an artful flute
   With loose, elastic lips,
Its measurement of joy compute
   With blithe, ecstatic hips.

9

LANGSTON HUGHES

The Weary Blues

1926

Born in Joplin, Missouri, and raised in many locations from Lawrence, Kansas, to Mexico City, Langston Hughes first came to New York in 1921 to attend Columbia University, where he lasted only a year pursuing an engineering degree at the behest of his father. Turning away from engineering and from his father's support, Hughes decided, after the publication of his poem "The Negro Speaks of Rivers" in the NAACP jour-

Langston Hughes, *The Weary Blues* (New York: Alfred A. Knopf, 1926), 23–24, 32, 43, 51, 109. "The Negro Speaks of Rivers" first published in *The Crisis*, 22 (June 1921): 36. "The Weary Blues," first published in *Opportunity*, 3 (May 1925): 143. "Dream Variation," first published in *Current Opinion*, 77 (September 1924): 361. "Epilogue: I, Too, Sing America," first published as "I, Too" in *The Survey Graphic*, 6 (March 1925): 664.

nal, The Crisis, *to attempt a writing career. Like Jean Toomer, Hughes found his greatest inspiration in the voices and artistic creations of ordinary black Americans, whose experiences he regarded as intimately his own. In "The Negro Speaks of Rivers" (1921), he conveys the emotional and spiritual depth of ordinary blacks in part by representing the collective black voice, which transcends time and space, as that of a single individual relating the events of his life directly to another. Similarly, "The Weary Blues" (1925) celebrates the creativity and insight of black folk music by using its rhythms as a basis for poetry. More abstractly, "Dream Variation" (1924) extols blackness itself as a source of comfort and joyful integration with the universe, while "Harlem Nightclub" memorializes the breaking of interracial sexual taboos under the intoxicating influence of jazz. In "Epilogue: I, Too, Sing America," the last poem of* The Weary Blues, *Hughes speaks directly to the nineteenth-century American poet Walt Whitman, whose poem "Song of Myself" declares, "I hear America singing, their varied carols I hear." Evoking this thought, Hughes reminds his audience that black Americans have a special place in the cultural creation of the nation.*

The Negro Speaks of Rivers

To W. E. B. Du Bois

I've known rivers:
I've known rivers ancient as the world and older than the flow of human blood in human veins.

My soul has grown deep like the rivers.

I bathed in the Euphrates when dawns were young.
I built my hut near the Congo and it lulled me to sleep.
I looked upon the Nile and raised the pyramids above it.
I heard the singing of the Mississippi when Abe Lincoln went down to New Orleans, and I've seen its muddy bosom turn all golden in the sunset.

I've known rivers:
Ancient, dusky rivers.

My soul has grown deep like the rivers.

The Weary Blues

Droning a drowsy syncopated tune,
Rocking back and forth to a mellow croon,
  I heard a Negro play.
Down on Lenox Avenue the other night
By the pale dull pallor of an old gas light
  He did a lazy sway. . . .
  He did a lazy sway. . . .
To the tune o' those Weary Blues.
With his ebony hands on each ivory key
He made that poor piano moan with melody.
  O Blues!
Swaying to and fro on his rickety stool
He played that sad raggy tune like a musical fool.
  Sweet Blues!
Coming from a black man's soul.
  O Blues!
In a deep song voice with a melancholy tone
I heard that Negro sing, that old piano moan—
  "Ain't got nobody in all this world,
  Ain't got nobody but ma self.
  I's gwine to quit ma frownin
  And put ma troubles on the shelf."
Thump, thump, thump, went his foot on the floor.
He played a few chords then he sang some more—
  "I got the Weary Blues
  And I can't be satisfied.
  Got the Weary Blues
  And can't be satisfied—
  I ain't happy no mo'
  And I wish that I had died."
And far into the night he crooned that tune.
The stars went out and so did the moon.
The singer stopped playing and went to bed
While the Weary Blues echoed through his head.
He slept like a rock or a man that's dead.

Dream Variation

To fling my arms wide
In some place of the sun,
To whirl and to dance
Till the white day is done.
Then rest at cool evening
Beneath a tall tree
While night comes on gently,
   Dark like me,—
That is my dream!

To fling my arms wide
In the face of the sun,
Dance! whirl! whirl!
Till the quick day is done.
Rest at pale evening. . . .
A tall, slim tree. . . .
Night coming tenderly
   Black like me.

Harlem Nightclub

Sleek black boys in a cabaret.
Jazz-band, jazz-band,—
Play, plAY, PLAY!
Tomorrow. . . . who knows?
Dance today!

White girls' eyes
Call gay black boys.
Black boys' lips
Grin jungle joys.

Dark brown girls
In blond men's arms.
Jazz-band, jazz-band,—
Sing Eve's charms!

White ones, brown ones,
What do you know
About tomorrow
Where all paths go?

Jazz-boys, jazz-boys,—
Play, plAY, PLAY!
Tomorrow. . . . is darkness.
Joy today!

Epilogue: I, Too, Sing America

I, too, sing America.

I am the darker brother.
They send me to eat in the kitchen
When company comes,
But I laugh,
And eat well,
And grow strong.

Tomorrow,
I'll sit at the table
When company comes.
Nobody'll dare
Say to me,
"Eat in the kitchen,"
Then.

Besides,
They'll see how beautiful I am
And be ashamed,—

I, too, am America.

10

OPPORTUNITY

The Debut of the Younger School of Negro Writers

Including GWENDOLYN BENNETT, *To Usward*

May 1924

Two months after the Civic Club dinner in March 1924, where important white intellectuals, publishers, and editors gathered to recognize the important cultural events occurring in Harlem, the Urban League journal Opportunity *published an account of the event and its participants. Although Charles S. Johnson, editor of* Opportunity, *planned the event supposedly to honor Jessie Fauset, the literary editor of* The Crisis *for* There Is Confusion *(1924), the first novel of the Harlem Renaissance, he used the occasion deftly to launch his own journal into the lead over* The Crisis *in the promotion of black art in the 1920s.*

The article includes black writer and critic Gwendolyn Bennett's poem "To Usward," written especially for the occasion. Originally from Giddings, Texas, Bennett wrote poems, short stories, and "The Ebony Flute," a lively column on art and literature in Opportunity, *in which she published much of her work. Bennett also published in other important journals of the day, including* The American Mercury, The Crisis, *and* Fire!!

Interest among the literati of New York in the emerging group of younger Negro writers found an expression in a recent meeting of the Writers' Guild, an informal group whose membership includes Countee Cullen, Eric Walrond,[1] Langston Hughes, Jessie Fauset, Gwendolyn Bennett, Harold Jackman, Regina Anderson[2] and a few others. The

[1]Eric Walrond (1898–1966), originally from British Guiana, author of the short-story collection *Tropic Death* (1926).

[2]Regina Anderson (1901–1993), African American playwright, librarian at the Harlem Branch of the New York Public Library, and one of the organizers of the Civic Club dinner.

"The Debut of the Younger School of Negro Writers," *Opportunity*, 2 (May 1924): 143–44.

occasion was a "coming out party," at the Civic Club, on March 21—a date selected around the appearance of the novel "There Is Confusion" by Jessie Fauset. The responses to the invitations sent out were immediate and enthusiastic and the few regrets that came in were genuine.

Although there was no formal, prearranged program, the occasion provoked a surprising spontaneity of expression both from the members of the writers' group and from the distinguished visitors present.

A brief interpretation of the object of the Guild was given by Charles S. Johnson, Editor of *Opportunity*, who introduced Alain Locke, virtual dean of the movement, who had been selected to act as Master of Ceremonies and to interpret the new currents manifest in the literature of this younger school. Alain Locke has been one of the most resolute stimulators of this group, and although he has been writing longer than most of them, he is distinctly a part of the movement. One excerpt reflects the tenor of his remarks. He said: "They sense within their group—meaning the Negro group—a spiritual wealth which if they can properly expound will be ample for a new judgment and re-appraisal of the race."

Horace Liveright, publisher, told about the difficulties, even yet, of marketing books of admitted merit. The value of a book cannot be gauged by the sales. He regarded Jean Toomer's "Cane" as one of the most interesting that he had handled, and yet, less than 500 copies had been sold. In his exhortations to the younger group he warned against the danger of reflecting in one's writing the "inferiority complex" which is so insistently and frequently apparent in an overbalanced emphasis on "impossibly good" fiction types. He felt that to do the best writing it was necessary to give a rounded picture which included bad types as well as good ones since both of these go to make up life.

Dr. W. E. B. Du Bois made his first public appearance and address since his return to this country from Africa. He was introduced by the chairman with soft seriousness as a representative of the "older school." Dr. Du Bois explained that the Negro writers of a few years back were of necessity pioneers, and much of their style was forced upon them by the barriers against publication of literature about Negroes of any sort.

James Weldon Johnson was introduced as an anthologist of Negro verse and one who had given invaluable encouragement to the work of this younger group.

Carl Van Doren, Editor of the *Century*, spoke on the future of imaginative writing among Negroes. . . .

Another young Negro writer, Walter F. White, whose novel "Fire in Flint" has been accepted for publication, also spoke and made reference to the passing of the stereotypes of the Negroes of fiction.

Professor Montgomery Gregory of Howard University, who came from Washington for the meeting, talked about the possibilities of Negroes in drama and told of the work of several talented Negro writers in this field, some of whose plays were just coming into recognition.

Another visitor from Philadelphia, Dr. Albert C. Barnes, art connoisseur and foremost authority in America on primitive Negro art, sketched the growing interest in this art which had had such tremendous influence on the entire modern art movement.

Miss Jessie Fauset was given a place of distinction on the program. She paid her respects to those friends who had contributed to her accomplishments, acknowledging a particular debt to her "best friend and severest critic," Dr. Du Bois.

The original poems read by Countee Cullen were received with a tremendous ovation. Miss Gwendolyn Bennett's poem, dedicated to the occasion, is reproduced. It is called

GWENDOLYN BENNETT

To Usward

Let us be still
As ginger jars are still
Upon a Chinese shelf,
And let us be contained
By entities of Self. . . .

Not still with lethargy and sloth,
But quiet with the pushing of our growth:
Not self-contained with smug identity,
But conscious of the strength in entity.

If any have a song to sing that's different from the rest,
Oh, let him sing before the urgency of Youth's behest!

And some of us have songs to sing
Of jungle heat and fires;
And some of us are solemn grown
With pitiful desires;

And there are those who feel the pull
Of seas beneath the skies;
And some there be who want to croon
Of Negro lullabies.
We claim no part with racial dearth,
We want to sing the songs of birth!

And so we stand like ginger jars,
Like ginger jars bound round
With dust and age;
Like jars of ginger we are sealed
By nature's heritage.
But let us break the seal of years
With pungent thrusts of song,
For there is joy in long dried tears,
For whetted passions of a throng!

11

ALAIN LOCKE, Editor

The Survey Graphic, Harlem Issue

Cover Art by Winold Reiss

March 1925

An important social reform journal of the 1920s, The Survey Graphic *brought the lives and struggles of lower-class people to the attention of middle- and upper-class readers through feature articles by progressive social thinkers and activists, accompanied by striking drawings and photographs. This special issue of the journal, published in March 1925, directly resulted from the Civic Club dinner, where editor Paul Kellogg of the* Survey Graphic *pledged his magazine to the promotion of the cultural movement centered in Harlem. The leading cultural theorist of the Harlem Renaissance, Alain Locke served as its editor and contributed "Harlem," the essay that follows. Locke played a crucial role in advancing the careers of Countée Cullen, Claude McKay, Aaron Douglas, Zora*

Alain Locke, ed., *The Survey Graphic*, 6 (March 1925): cover art by Winold Reiss, and "Harlem" by Alain Locke, 629–30.

Special Collections, University of Virginia Library.

Neale Hurston, and many others. Originally from Philadelphia, Locke attended Harvard College and Oxford University, where he was the first black American Rhodes Scholar, before becoming a professor of philosophy at Howard University in Washington, D.C. In "Harlem," Locke expounds on the spiritual import of Harlem as a "race capital" and as an example of democratic progress. The German immigrant Winold

Reiss, a teacher of the black artist Aaron Douglas and a pioneer in the depiction of blacks as individuals rather than as stereotypes, illustrated the issue with several drawings, including the cover depicting the talented tenor and New Negro icon Roland Hayes (1887–1977), who gave concerts both in Europe and in the United States.

ALAIN LOCKE

Harlem

If we were to offer a symbol of what Harlem has come to mean in the short span of twenty years it would be another statue of liberty on the landward side of New York. It stands for a folk-movement which in human significance can be compared only with the pushing back of the western frontier in the first half of the last century, or the waves of immigration which have swept in from overseas in the last half. Numerically far smaller than either of these movements, the volume of migration is such none the less that Harlem has become the greatest Negro community the world has known—without counterpart in the South or in Africa. But beyond this, Harlem represents the Negro's latest thrust towards Democracy.

The special significance that today stamps it as the sign and center of the renaissance of a people lies, however, layers deep under the Harlem that many know but few have begun to understand. Physically Harlem is little more than a note of sharper color in the kaleidoscope of New York. The metropolis pays little heed to the shifting crystallizations of its own heterogeneous millions. Never having experienced permanence, it has watched, without emotion or even curiosity, Irish, Jew, Italian, Negro, a score of other races drift in and out of the same colorless tenements.

So Harlem has come into being and grasped its destiny with little heed from New York. And to the herded thousands who shoot beneath it twice a day on the subway, or the comparatively few whose daily travel takes them within sight of its fringes or down its main arteries, it is a black belt and nothing more. The pattern of delicatessen store and cigar shop and restaurant and undertaker's shop which repeats itself a thousand times on each of New York's long avenues is unbroken through Harlem. Its apartments, churches and storefronts antedated the Negroes and, for all New York knows, may outlast them there. For most of New York, Harlem is merely a rough rectangle of common-place city blocks, lying between and to east and west of Lenox and Seventh Avenues, stretching nearly a mile north and south—and unaccountably full of Negroes.

Another Harlem is savored by the few—a Harlem of racy music and racier dancing, of cabarets famous or notorious according to their kind, of amusement in which abandon and sophistication are cheek by jowl—a Harlem which draws the connoisseur in diversion as well as the undiscriminating sightseer. This Harlem is the fertile source of the "shufflin'" and "rollin'" and "runnin' wild" revues that establish themselves season after season in "downtown" theaters. It is part of the exotic fringe of the metropolis.

Beneath this lies again the Harlem of the newspapers—a Harlem of monster parades and political flummery, a Harlem swept by revolutionary oratory or draped about the mysterious figures of Negro "millionaires," a Harlem preoccupied with naive adjustments to a white world—a Harlem, in short, grotesque with the distortions of journalism.

Yet in final analysis, Harlem is neither slum, ghetto, resort or colony, though it is in part all of them. It is—or promises at least to be—a race capital. Europe seething in a dozen centers with emergent nationalities, Palestine full of a renascent Judaism—these are no more alive with the spirit of a racial awakening than Harlem; culturally and spiritually it focuses a people. Negro life is not only founding new centers, but finding a new soul. The tide of Negro migration, northward and city-ward, is not to be fully explained as a blind flood started by the demands of war industry coupled with the shutting off of foreign migration, or by the pressure of poor crops coupled with increased social terrorism in certain sections of the South and Southwest. Neither labor demand, the bollweevil[1] nor the Ku Klux Klan is a basic factor, however contributory any or all of them may have been. The wash and rush of this human tide on the beach line of the northern city centers is to be explained primarily in terms of a new vision of opportunity, of social and economic freedom, of a spirit to seize, even in the face of an extortionate and heavy toll, a chance for the improvement of conditions. With each successive wave of it, the movement of the Negro migrant becomes more and more like that of the European waves at their crests, a mass movement toward the larger and the

[1]The bollweevil is a grayish beetle that destroys cotton buds. The bollweevil epidemic that began in 1916 brought great hardship to black sharecroppers, some of whom migrated to the North.

more democratic chance—in the Negro's case a deliberate flight not only from countryside to city, but from mediaeval America to modern.

The secret lies close to what distinguishes Harlem from the ghettos with which it is sometimes compared. The ghetto picture is that of a slowly dissolving mass, bound by ties of custom and culture and association, in the midst of a freer and more varied society. From the racial standpoint, our Harlems are themselves crucibles. Here in Manhattan is not merely the largest Negro community in the world, but the first concentration in history of so many diverse elements of Negro life. It has attracted the African, the West Indian, the Negro American; has brought together the Negro of the North and the Negro of the South; the man from the city and the man from the town and village; the peasant, the student, the business man, the professional man, artist, poet, musician, adventurer and worker, preacher and criminal, exploiter and social outcast. Each group has come with its own separate motives and for its own special ends, but their greatest experience has been the finding of one another. Proscription and prejudice have thrown these dissimilar elements into a common area of contact and interaction. Within this area, race sympathy and unity have determined a further fusing of sentiment and experience. So what began in terms of segregation becomes more and more, as its elements mix and react, the laboratory of great race-welding. Hitherto, it must be admitted that American Negroes have been race more in name than in fact, or to be exact, more in sentiment than in experience. The chief bond between them has been that of a common condition rather than a common consciousness; a problem in common rather than a life in common. In Harlem, Negro life is seizing upon its first chances for group expression and self-determination. That is why our comparison is taken with those nascent centers of folk-expression and self-determination which are playing a creative part in the world today. Without pretense to their political significance, Harlem has the same role to play for the New Negro as Dublin has had for the New Ireland or Prague for the New Czechoslovakia.

It is true the formidable centers of our race life, educational, industrial, financial, are not in Harlem, yet here, nevertheless, are the forces that make a group known and felt in the world. The reformers, the fighting advocates, the inner spokesmen, the poets, artists and social prophets are here, and pouring in toward them are the fluid ambitious youth and pressing in upon them the migrant masses. The professional observers, and the enveloping communities as well, are conscious of the physics of this stir and movement, of the cruder and more obvious facts of a ferment and a migration. But they are as yet largely unaware of the psychology of it, of the galvanizing shocks and reactions, which mark the social awakening and internal reorganization which are making a race out of its own disunited elements.

A railroad ticket and a suitcase, like a Baghdad carpet, transport the Negro peasant from the cotton-field and farm to the heart of the most complex urban civilization. Here, in the mass, he must and does survive a jump of two generations in social economy and of a century and more in civilization. Meanwhile the Negro poet, student, artist, thinker, by the very move that normally would take him off at a tangent from the masses, finds himself in their midst, in a situation concentrating the racial side of his experience and heightening his race-consciousness. These moving, half-awakened newcomers provide an exceptional seed-bed for the germinating contacts of the enlightened minority. And that is why statistics are out of joint with fact in Harlem, and will be for a generation or so.

Harlem, I grant you, isn't typical—but it is significant, it is prophetic. No sane observer, however sympathetic to the new trend, would contend that the great masses are articulate as yet, but they stir, they move, they are more than physically restless. The challenge of the new intellectuals among them is clear enough—the "race radicals" and realists who have broken with the old epoch of philanthropic guidance, sentimental appeal and protest. But are we after all only reading into the stirrings of a sleeping giant the dreams of an agitator? The answer is in the migrating peasant. It is the "man farthest down" who is most active in getting up. One of the most characteristic symptoms of this is the professional man himself migrating to recapture his constituency after a vain effort to maintain in some Southern corner what for years back seemed an established living and clientele. The clergyman following his errant flock, the physician or lawyer trailing his clients, supply the true clues. In a real sense it is the rank and file who are leading, and the leaders who are following. A transformed and transforming psychology permeates the masses.

When the racial leaders of twenty years ago spoke of developing race-pride and stimulating race-consciousness, and of the desirability of race solidarity, they could not in any accurate degree have anticipated the abrupt feeling that has surged up and now pervades the awakened centers. Some of the recognized Negro leaders and a powerful section of white opinion identified with "race work" of the older order have indeed attempted to discount this feeling as a "passing phase," an attack of "race nerves," so to speak, an "aftermath of the war," and the like. It has not abated, however, if we are to gage by the present tone and temper of the Negro press, or by the shift in popular support from the officially recognized and orthodox spokesmen to those of the independent, popular, and often radical type who are unmistakable symptoms of a new order. It is a social disservice to blunt the fact that the Negro of the Northern centers has reached a stage where tutelage, even of the most interested and well-intentioned sort, must give place to new relationships, where positive self-direction must be reckoned with in ever increasing measure.

As a service to this new understanding, the contributors to this Harlem number have been asked, not merely to describe Harlem as a city of migrants and as a race center, but to voice these new aspirations of a people, to read the clear message of the new conditions, and to discuss some of the new relationships and contacts they involve. First, we shall look at Harlem, with its kindred centers in the Northern and Mid-Western cities, as the way mark of a momentous folk movement; then as the center of a gripping struggle for an industrial and urban foothold. But more significant than either of these, we shall also view it as the stage of the pageant of contemporary Negro life. In the drama of its new and progressive aspects, we may be witnessing the resurgence of a race; with our eyes focussed on the Harlem scene we may dramatically glimpse the New Negro. A. L.

12

ALAIN LOCKE

Foreword to *The New Negro*

1925

In the foreword to The New Negro, *a volume that he also edited, Alain Locke explains the overall aim of this historic volume, which grew directly out of the Harlem issue of* The Survey Graphic, *published in March 1925. Following his statement in "Harlem" (see Document 11),*

Alain Locke, foreword, *The New Negro*, ed. Alain Locke (New York: Albert and Charles Boni, 1925), xxv–xxvii.

Locke insists that the Harlem Renaissance be seen as integral to wider national and international movements for self-determination, freedom, and expression. National movements such as those in Ireland and Palestine gained legitimacy and interest in the United States due to President Woodrow Wilson's pledge to promote the self-determination of all peoples, and thus his attempt to justify American participation in World War I as a way of extending democracy abroad. Playing on this logic without fully embracing it—and well aware of the irony involved in announcing a democratic movement in the very country that assigned itself the right to bring democracy to foreigners—Locke casts the Harlem Renaissance as a peaceful expression of the universal urge for justice everywhere.

This volume aims to document the New Negro culturally and socially,—to register the transformations of the inner and outer life of the Negro in America that have so significantly taken place in the last few years. There is ample evidence of a New Negro in the latest phases of social change and progress, but still more in the internal world of the Negro mind and spirit. Here in the very heart of the folk-spirit are the essential forces, and folk interpretation is truly vital and representative only in terms of these. Of all the voluminous literature on the Negro, so much is mere external view and commentary that we may warrantably say that nine-tenths of it is *about* the Negro rather than of him, so that it is the Negro problem rather than the Negro that is known, and mooted in the general mind. We turn therefore in the other direction to the elements of truest social portraiture, and discover in the artistic self-expression of the Negro to-day a new figure on the national canvas and a new force in the foreground of affairs. Whoever wishes to see the Negro in his essential traits, in the full perspective of his achievement and possibilities, must seek the enlightenment of that self-portraiture which the present developments of Negro culture are offering. In these pages, without ignoring either the fact that there are important interactions between the national and the race life, or that the attitude of America toward the Negro is as important a factor as the attitude of the Negro toward America, we have nevertheless concentrated upon self-expression and the forces and motives of self-determination. So far as he is culturally articulate, we shall let the Negro speak for himself.

Yet the New Negro must be seen in the perspective of a New World, and especially of a New America. Europe seething in a dozen centers with emergent nationalities, Palestine full of a renascent

Judaism—these are no more alive with the progressive forces of our era than the quickened centers of the lives of black folk. America seeking a new spiritual expansion and artistic maturity, trying to found an American literature, a national art, and national music implies a Negro-American culture seeking the same satisfactions and objectives. Separate as it may be in color and substance, the culture of the Negro is of a pattern integral with the times and with its cultural setting. The achievements of the present generation have eventually made this apparent. Liberal minds to-day cannot be asked to peer with sympathetic curiosity into the darkened Ghetto of a segregated race life. That was yesterday. Nor must they expect to find a mind and soul bizarre and alien as the mind of a savage or even as naive and refreshing as the mind of the peasant or the child. That too was yesterday, and the day before. Now that there is cultural adolescence and the approach to maturity,—there has come a development that makes these phases of Negro life only an interesting and significant segment of the general American scene.

Until recently, except for occasional discoveries of isolated talent here and there, the main stream of this development has run in the special channels of "race literature" and "race journalism." Particularly as a literary movement, it has gradually gathered momentum in the effort and output of such progressive race periodicals as the *Crisis* under the editorship of Dr. Du Bois and more lately, through the quickening encouragement of Charles Johnson, in the brilliant pages of *Opportunity*, a Journal of Negro Life. But more and more the creative talents of the race have been taken up into the general journalistic, literary and artistic agencies, as the wide range of the acknowledgments of the material here collected will in itself be sufficient to demonstrate. Recently in a project of *The Survey Graphic*, whose Harlem Number of March, 1925, has been taken by kind permission as the nucleus of this book, the whole movement was presented as it is epitomized in the progressive Negro community of the American metropolis. Enlarging this stage we are now presenting the New Negro in a national and even international scope. Although there are few centers that can be pointed out approximating Harlem's significance, the full significance of that event is a racial awakening on a national and perhaps even a world scale.

That is why our comparison is taken with those nascent movements of folk-expression and self-determination which are playing a creative part in the world to-day. The galvanizing shocks and reactions of the last few years are making by subtle processes of internal reorganization a race out of its own disunited and apathetic elements. A race experience penetrated in this way invariably flowers. As in India, in China, in Egypt, Ireland, Russia, Bohemia, Palestine and Mexico, we are witnessing the resurgence of a people: it has aptly been said,—"For all who read the signs aright, such a dramatic flowering of a new race-spirit is taking place close at home—among American Negroes."

Negro life is not only establishing new contacts and founding new centers, it is finding a new soul. There is a fresh spiritual and cultural focusing. We have, as the heralding sign, an unusual outburst of creative expression. There is a renewed race-spirit that consciously and proudly sets itself apart. Justifiably then, we speak of the offerings of this book embodying these ripening forces as culled from the first fruits of the Negro Renaissance.

2

Themes in Black Identity

13

CLAUDE McKAY

A Long Way from Home

1937

Although Claude McKay focused heavily on Harlem in his poetry and fiction, he spent the greater part of the 1920s in the Soviet Union, Europe, and North Africa. In this selection from his autobiography, appropriately titled A Long Way from Home, *he reflects on various aspects of the scene in Paris just after the publication of his controversial book* Home to Harlem *(1928) in the United States. Written in Paris,* Home to Harlem *became one of the best-selling novels of the Harlem Renaissance, but it offended some critics because of its frank depiction of black prostitutes, pimps, and other underworld figures. Two years earlier, the best-selling novel of the Harlem Renaissance,* Nigger Heaven *(1926), by Carl Van Vechten, an important white patron of black art, drew accusations of lewdness and racial exploitation, for the same reasons, from* Crisis *editor W. E. B. Du Bois and other members of the African American elite. Rather than deny the association of Van Vechten's novel with his own, McKay criticizes its critics on the way to relating the decidedly unsensational details of his meeting in Paris with Van Vechten. McKay also reveals his disagreement with Alain Locke, another frequent visitor to Europe, for changing the politically charged title of his poem "The White House" (see Document 6) to "White Houses" without his permission.*

Claude McKay, *A Long Way from Home* (New York: L. Furman, 1937), 306–23.

I finished my native holiday in Marrakesh. In Casablanca I found a huge pile of mail awaiting me. The handsomest thing was a fat envelope from a New York bank containing a gold-lettered pocket book. The pocket book enclosed my first grand from the sale of *Home to Harlem*.

There were stacks of clippings with criticisms of my novel; praise from the white press, harsh censure from the colored press. And a lot of letters from new admirers and old friends and associates and loves. One letter in particular took my attention. It was from James Weldon Johnson, inviting me to return to America to participate in the Negro renaissance movement. He promised to do his part to facilitate my return if there were any difficulty. And he did.

The Johnson letter set me thinking hard about returning to Harlem. All the reports stressed the great changes that had occurred there since my exile, pictured a Harlem spreading west and south, with splendid new blocks of houses opened up for the colored people. The reports described the bohemian interest in and patronage of Harlem, the many successful colored shows on Broadway, the florescence of Negro literature and art, with many promising aspirants receiving scholarships from foundations and patronage from individuals. Newspapers and magazines brought me exciting impressions of a more glamorous Harlem. Even in Casablanca a Moor of half-German parentage exhibited an article featuring Harlem in an important German newspaper, and he was eager for more information.

But the resentment of the Negro intelligentsia against *Home to Harlem* was so general, bitter and violent that I was hesitant about returning to the great Black Belt.[1] I had learned very little about the ways of the Harlem élite during the years I lived there. When I left the railroad and the companionship of the common blacks, my intellectual contacts were limited mainly to white radicals and bohemians. I was well aware that if I returned to Harlem I wouldn't be going back to the *milieu* of railroad men, from whom I had drifted far out of touch. Nor could I go back among radical whites and try to rekindle the flames of an old enthusiasm. I knew that if I did return I would have to find a new orientation among the Negro intelligentsia.

[1]The actual Black Belt was a crescent-shaped region from Texas to Virginia where 75 percent of the black American population resided in the 1930s. "Black" also refers to the fertile soil of this region, which facilitated the growing of cotton. Here McKay uses the term ironically to refer to Harlem.

One friend in Harlem had written that Negroes were traveling abroad *en masse* that spring and summer and that the élite would be camping in Paris. I thought that it might be less unpleasant to meet the advance guard of the Negro intelligentsia in Paris. And so, laying aside my experiment in wearing bags, bournous[2] and tarboosh,[3] I started out. . . .

After the strong dazzling colors of Morocco, Paris that spring appeared something like the melody of larks chanting over a gray field. It was over three years since I had seen the Metropolis. At that time it had a political and financial trouble hanging heavy round its neck. Now it was better, with its head up and a lot of money in every hand. I saw many copies of my book, *Banjo*,[4] decorating a shop window in the Avenue de l'Opéra and I was disappointed in myself that I could not work up to feeling a thrill such as I imagine an author should feel.

I took a fling at the cabarets in Montparnasse and Montmartre, and I was very happy to meet again a French West Indian girl whom I knew as a *bonne* in Nice when I was a valet. We ate some good dinners together and saw the excellent French productions of *Rose Marie* and *Show Boat* and danced a little at the Bal Negre and at Bricktop's Harlem hang-out in Montmartre. . . .

I had spruced myself up a bit to meet the colored élite. Observing that the Madrileños were well-tailored, I had a couple of suits made in Madrid, and chose a hat there. In Paris I added shoes and shirts and ties and gloves to my wardrobe.

The cream of Harlem was in Paris. There was the full cast of *Blackbirds* (with Adelaide Hall starring in the place of Florence Mills), just as fascinating a group off the stage as they were extraordinary on the stage. The *Porgy* actors had come over from London. There was an army of school teachers and nurses. There were Negro Communists going to and returning from Russia. There were Negro students from London and Scotland and Berlin and the French universities. There were presidents and professors of the best Negro colleges. And there were painters and writers and poets, of whom the most outstanding was Countee Cullen.

[2]Also spelled *burnoose*: a hooded cloak worn especially by Arabs and Berbers.

[3]A brimless, usually red felt, cap with a silk tassel, worn by Middle Eastern Muslim men.

[4]*Banjo: A Story Without a Plot* (New York: Harper & Brothers, 1929), McKay's second novel, a story of black beach boys in Marseilles, France.

I met Professor Alain Locke. He had published *The Anthology of the New Negro* in 1925 and he was the animator of the movement as well as the originator of the phrase "Negro renaissance." Commenting upon my appearance, Dr. Locke said, "Why, you are wearing the same kind of gloves as I am!" "Yes," I said, "but my hand is heavier than yours." Dr. Locke was extremely nice and invited me to dinner with President Hope of Atlanta University.[5] The dinner was at one of the most expensive restaurants in the *grands boulevards*. President Hope, who was even more Nordic-looking than Walter White, was very affable and said I did not look like the boxer-type drawings of me which were reproduced with the reviews of *Home to Harlem*. President Hope hoped that I would visit his university when I returned to America.

There had been an interesting metamorphosis in Dr. Locke. When we met for the first time in Berlin in 1923, he took me for a promenade in the Tiergarten. And walking down the row, with the statues of the Prussian kings supported by the famous philosophers and poets and composers on either side, he remarked to me that he thought those statues the finest ideal and expression of the plastic arts in the world. The remark was amusing, for it was just a short while before that I had walked through the same row with George Grosz,[6] who had described the statues as "the sugar-candy art of Germany." When I showed Dr. Locke George Grosz's book of drawings, *Ecce Homo*, he recoiled from their brutal realism. (Dr. Locke is a Philadelphia blue-black blood, a Rhodes scholar and graduate of Oxford University, and I have heard him described as the most refined Negro in America.)

So it was interesting now to discover that Dr. Locke had become the leading Negro authority on African Negro sculpture. I felt that there was so much more affinity between the art of George Grosz and African sculpture than between the Tiergarten insipid idealization of Nordic kings and artists and the transcending realism of the African artists.

Yet I must admit that although Dr. Locke seemed a perfect symbol of the Aframerican rococo[7] in his personality as much as in his prose

[5]John Hope (1868–1936), the first black American president of two historically black educational institutions, Morehouse College from 1903 to 1929 and Atlanta University from 1929 to 1936.

[6]George Grosz (1893–1959), German impressionist painter and illustrator known for his satirical cartoons of German politicians.

[7]James Weldon Johnson coined the term *Aframerican* to emphasize the common condition of blacks in North America, South America, and the Caribbean. *Rococo*: An artistic style that emerged in eighteenth-century France that emphasized, among many features, the carefree aristocratic life and lighthearted romance. In attributing these qualities to the "Aframerican" Locke, McKay pokes fun at his aristocratic pretense.

style, he was doing his utmost to appreciate the new Negro that he had uncovered. He had brought the best examples of their work together in a pioneer book. But from the indication of his appreciations it was evident that he could not lead a Negro renaissance. His introductory remarks were all so weakly winding round and round and getting nowhere. Probably this results from a kink in Dr. Locke's artistic outlook, perhaps due to its effete European academic quality.

When he published his *Anthology of the New Negro*, he put in a number of my poems, including one which was originally entitled "The White House." My title was symbolic, not meaning specifically the private homes of white people, but more the vast modern edifice of American Industry from which Negroes were effectively barred as a group. I cannot convey here my amazement and chagrin when Dr. Locke arbitrarily changed the title of my poem to "White Houses" and printed it in his anthology, without consulting me. I protested against the act, calling Dr. Locke's attention to the fact that my poem had been published under the original title of "The White House" in *The Liberator*. He replied that he had changed the title for political reasons, as it might be implied that the title meant the White House in Washington, and that that could be made an issue against my returning to America.

I wrote him saying that the idea that my poem had reference to the official residence of the President of the United States was ridiculous; and that, whether I was permitted to return to America or not, I did not want the title changed, and would prefer the omission of the poem. For his title "White Houses" was misleading. It changed the whole symbolic intent and meaning of the poem, making it appear as if the burning ambition of the black malcontent was to enter white houses in general. I said that there were many white folks' houses I would not choose to enter, and that, as a fanatical advocate of personal freedom, I hoped that all human beings would always have the right to decide whom they wanted to have enter their houses.

But Dr. Locke high-handedly used his substitute title of "White Houses" in all the editions of his anthology. I couldn't imagine such a man as the leader of a renaissance, when his artistic outlook was so reactionary.

The Negroid élite was not so formidable to meet after all. The financial success of my novel had helped soften hard feelings in some quarters. A lovely lady from Harlem expressed the views of many. Said she: "Why all this nigger-row if a colored writer can exploit his own people and make money and a name? White writers have been exploiting us long enough without any credit to our race. It is silly for the Negro critics to holler to God about *Home to Harlem* as if the social life of the characters is anything like that of the respectable class of Negroes. The people in *Home to Harlem* are our low-down Negroes and we respectable Negroes ought to be proud that we are not like them and be grateful to you for giving us a real picture of Negroes whose lives we know little about on the inside." I felt completely vindicated.

My agent in Paris gave a big party for the cast of *Blackbirds*, to which the lovely lady and other members of the black élite were invited. Adelaide Hall was the animating spirit of the *Blackbirds*. They gave some exhibition numbers, and we all turned loose and had a grand gay time together, dancing and drinking champagne. The French guests (there were some chic ones) said it was the best party of the season. And in tipsy accents some of the Harlem élite admonished me against writing a *Home-to-Harlem* book about *them*.

Thus I won over most of the Negro intelligentsia in Paris, excepting the leading journalist and traveler who remained intransigent.[8] Besides Negro news, the journalist specialized in digging up obscure and Amazing Facts for the edification of the colored people. In these "Facts" Beethoven is proved to be a Negro because he was dark and gloomy; also the Jewish people are proved to have been originally a Negro people! . . .

The Negro journalist argued violently against me. He insisted that I had exploited Negroes to please the white reading public. He said that the white public would not read good Negro books because of race prejudice; that he himself had written a "good" book which had not sold. I said that Negro writers, instead of indulging in whining and self-pity, should aim at reaching the reading public in general or creating a special Negro public; that Negroes had plenty of money to spend on books if books were sold to them. . . .

Nigger Heaven, the Harlem novel of Carl Van Vechten, also was much discussed. I met some of Mr. Van Vechten's Negro friends, who were not seeing him any more because of his book. I felt flattered that they did not mind seeing me! Yet most of them agreed that *Nigger Heaven* was broadly based upon the fact of contemporary high life in Harlem. Some of them said that Harlemites should thank their stars that *Nigger Heaven* had soft-pedaled some of the actually wilder

[8]Here McKay refers to the Jamaican American journalist and author Joel A. Rogers (see Document 22).

Harlem scenes. While the conventional Negro moralists gave the book a hostile reception because of its hectic bohemianism, the leaders of the Negro intelligentsia showed a marked liking for it. In comparing it with *Home to Harlem*, James Weldon Johnson said that I had shown a contempt for the Negro bourgeoisie. But I could not be contemptuous of a Negro bourgeoisie which simply does not exist as a class or a group in America. Because I made the protagonist of my novel a lusty black worker, it does not follow that I am unsympathetic to a refined or wealthy Negro.

My attitude toward *Nigger Heaven* was quite different from that of its Negro friends and foes. I was more interested in the implications of the book. It puzzled me a little that the author, who is generally regarded as a discoverer and sponsor of promising young Negro writers, gave Lascar, the ruthless Negro prostitute, the victory over Byron, the young Negro writer, whom he left, when the novel ends, in the hands of the police, destined perhaps for the death house in Sing Sing.

Carl Van Vechten also was in Paris in the summer of 1929. I had been warned by a white non-admirer of Mr. Van Vechten that I would not like him because he patronized Negroes in a subtle way, to which the Harlem élite were blind because they were just learning sophistication! I thought it would be a new experience to meet a white who was subtly patronizing to a black; the majority of them were so naïvely crude about it. But I found Mr. Van Vechten not a bit patronizing, and quite all right. It was neither his fault nor mine if my reaction was negative.

One of Mr. Van Vechten's Harlem sheiks introduced us after midnight at the Café de la Paix. Mr. Van Vechten was a heavy drinker at that time, but I was not drinking liquor. I had recently suffered from a cerebral trouble and a specialist had warned me against drinking, even wine. And when a French doctor forbids wine, one ought to heed. When we met at that late hour at the celebrated rendezvous of the world's cosmopolites, Mr. Van Vechten was full and funny. He said, "What will you take?" I took a soft drink and I could feel that Mr. Van Vechten was shocked.

I am afraid that as a soft drinker I bored him. The white author and the black author of books about Harlem could not find much of anything to make conversation. The market trucks were rolling by loaded with vegetables for Les Halles, and suddenly Mr. Van Vechten, pointing to a truck-load of huge carrots, exclaimed, "How I would like to have all of them!" Perhaps carrots were more interesting than conversation. But I did not feel in any way carroty. I don't know whether my looks betrayed any disapproval. Really I hadn't the slightest objection to Mr. Van Vechten's enthusiasm for the truck driver's raw carrots, though I prefer carrots *en casserole avec poulet cocotte.*[9] But he excused himself to go to the men's room and never came back. So, after waiting a considerable time, I paid the bill with some *Home to Harlem* money and walked in the company of the early dawn (which is delicious in Paris) back to the Rue Jean-Jacques Rousseau.

Mr. Van Vechten's sheik friend was very upset. He was a precious, hesitating sheik and very nervous about that introduction, wondering if it would take. I said that all was okay. But upon returning to New York he sent me a message from Mr. Van Vechten. The message said that Mr. Van Vechten was sorry for not returning, but he was so high that, after leaving us, he discovered himself running along the avenue after a truck load of carrots.

Among the Negro intelligentsia in Paris there was an interesting group of story-tellers, poets and painters. Some had received grants from foundations to continue work abroad; some were being helped by private individuals; and all were more or less identified with the Negro renaissance. It was illuminating to exchange ideas with them. I was an older man and not regarded as a member of the renaissance, but more as a forerunner. Indeed, some of them had aired their resentment of my intrusion from abroad into the renaissance set-up. They had thought that I had committed literary suicide because I went to Russia.

For my part I was deeply stirred by the idea of a real Negro renaissance. The Arabian cultural renaissance and the great European renaissance had provided some of my most fascinating reading. The Russian literary renaissance and also the Irish had absorbed my interest. My idea of a renaissance was one of talented persons of an ethnic or national group working individually or collectively in a common purpose and creating things that would be typical of their group.

I was surprised when I discovered that many of the talented Negroes regarded their renaissance more as an uplift organization and a vehicle to accelerate the pace and progress of smart Negro society. It was interesting to note how sharply at variance their artistic outlook was from that of the modernistic white groups that took a significant interest in Negro literature and art. The Negroes were

[9]The opposite of Van Vechten's preference: well-cooked carrots with smothered, slow-cooked chicken.

under the delusion that when a lady from Park Avenue or from Fifth Avenue, or a titled European, became interested in Negro art and invited Negro artists to her home that was a token of Negroes breaking into upper-class white society. I don't think that it ever occurred to them that perhaps such white individuals were searching for a social and artistic significance in Negro art which they could not find in their own society, and that the radical nature and subject of their interest operated against the possibility of their introducing Negroes further than their own particular homes in coveted white society.

Also, among the Negro artists there was much of that Uncle Tom[10] attitude which works like Satan against the idea of a coherent and purposeful Negro group. Each one wanted to be the first Negro, the one Negro, and the only Negro *for the whites* instead of for their group. Because an unusual number of them were receiving grants to do creative work, they actually and naïvely believed that Negro artists as a group would always be treated differently from white artists and be protected by powerful white patrons.

Some of them even expressed the opinion that Negro art would solve the centuries-old social problem of the Negro. That idea was vaguely hinted by Dr. Locke in his introduction to *The New Negro* (see Document 12). Dr. Locke's essay is a remarkable chocolate *soufflé* of art and politics, with not an ingredient of information inside.

They were nearly all Harlem-conscious, in a curious synthetic way, it seemed to me—not because they were aware of Harlem's intrinsic values as a unique and popular Negro quarter, but apparently because white folks had discovered black magic there. I understood more clearly why there had been so much genteel-Negro hostility to my *Home to Harlem* and to Langston Hughes's primitive Negro poems.

I wondered after all whether it would be better for me to return to the new *milieu* of Harlem. Much as all my sympathy was with the Negro group and the idea of a Negro renaissance, I doubted if going back to Harlem would be an advantage. I had done my best Harlem stuff when I was abroad, seeing it from a long perspective. I thought it might be better to leave Harlem to the artists who were on the spot, to give them their chance to produce something better than *Home to Harlem*. I thought that I might as well go back to Africa.

[10]A deeply Christian character in Harriet Beecher Stowe's *Uncle Tom's Cabin* (1852) and a popular synonym for black submissiveness.

14

LANGSTON HUGHES

Fine Clothes to the Jew

1927

Like Claude McKay, Langston Hughes traveled constantly during and after the period of the Harlem Renaissance. In 1923, a little more than a year after he dropped out of Columbia University, and badly in need of work, Hughes became a messboy on a freighter traveling between New York and the West African coast. At the close of this journey six months later, Hughes signed up for another job as a seaman on a ship headed for Rotterdam, Holland. After traveling three times across the Atlantic, he collected his twenty-five dollars in wages and headed for Paris, where he worked in a variety of restaurant and nightclub jobs before returning to the United States in 1925. In "Jazz Band in a Parisian Cabaret" (1925), a poem from his second collection, Fine Clothes to the Jew *(1927), in which he published some of his most ambitious poetry based on jazz, the blues, and African American religious music, Hughes conveys some of the feeling of Paris nightlife and celebrates the power of jazz to overcome distinctions of class, culture, and nation. "Song for a Dark Girl" (1922) takes Hughes's use of African American music in a much darker direction. Here Hughes mimics the call and response pattern of rural African American religious songs, in which a singer calls out and other singers answer or vocally support what the first singer has sung by calling back, usually with a refrain. The subject is the all-too-common practice of racial lynching—or execution, usually hanging by the neck without due process of law—but instead of focusing on a male victim, Hughes chooses a dark girl to highlight the tragedy and injustice of this practice, which punished black people just for being black. How does the choice and phrasing of words (for example, "Break the heart of me," instead of "Break my heart" or "My heart is broken") amplify the effect of this poem? What place does the idea of a "white Lord Jesus" play in its reflection on injustice?*

Langston Hughes, *Fine Clothes to the Jew* (New York: Alfred A. Knopf, 1927), 74, 75. "Jazz Band in a Parisian Cabaret" first published in *The Crisis*, 31 (December 1925): 67. "Song for a Dark Girl" first published in *The Crisis*, 25 (October 1922): 267.

Jazz Band in a Parisian Cabaret

Play that thing,
Jazz band!
Play it for the lords and ladies,
For the dukes and counts,
For the whores and gigolos,
For the American millionaires,
And the school teachers
Out for a spree.
Play it,
Jazz band!
You know that tune
That laughs and cries at the same time.
You know it.
    May I?
    Mais oui.
    Mein Gott!
    Parece una rumba.
Play it, jazz band!
You've got seven languages to speak in
And then some,
Even if you do come from Georgia.
    Can I go home wid yuh, sweetie?
    Sure.

Song for a Dark Girl

Way Down South in Dixie
    (Break the heart of me)
They hung my black young lover
    To a cross roads tree.

Way Down South in Dixie
    (Bruised body high in air)
I asked the white Lord Jesus
    What was the use of prayer.

Way Down South in Dixie
    (Break the heart of me)
Love is a naked shadow
    On a gnarled and naked tree.

15

COUNTÉE CULLEN

Heritage

1925

In "Heritage," Cullen reflects ambivalently on Africa, whose spiritual drumbeat reverberates powerfully in his soul (as in the driving beat of the poem) and animates his art. Yet Africa has no concrete cultural meaning to him, and he guards against its legacy, evident in the uncivilized passions of his soul. The dedication of this poem to his handsome longtime boyfriend, Harlem schoolteacher Harold Jackman (1900–1960), may indicate that Cullen's forbidden passions, and his ambivalence, derive from something other than his heritage.

For Harold Jackman

What is Africa to me:
Copper sun or scarlet sea,
Jungle star or jungle track,
Strong bronzed men, or regal black
Women from whose loins I sprang
When the birds of Eden sang?
One three centuries removed
From the scenes his fathers loved,
Spice grove, cinnamon tree,
What is Africa to me?

So I lie, who all day long
Want no sound except the song
Sung by wild barbaric birds
Goading massive jungle herds,
Juggernauts[1] of flesh that pass

[1]Unstoppable force.

Countée Cullen, "Heritage," in *Color* (New York: Harper & Brothers, 1925), 36–41.

Trampling tall defiant grass
Where young forest lovers lie,
Plighting troth beneath the sky.
So I lie, who always hear,
Though I cram against my ear
Both my thumbs, and keep them there
Great drums throbbing through the air.
So I lie, whose fount of pride,
Dear distress, and joy allied,
Is my somber flesh and skin,
With the dark blood dammed within
Like great pulsing tides of wine
That, I fear, must burst the fine
Channels of the chafing net
Where they surge and foam and fret.

Africa? A book one thumbs
Listlessly, till slumber comes.
Unremembered are her bats
Circling through the night, her cats
Crouching in the river reeds,
Stalking gentle flesh that feeds
By the river brink; no more
Does the bugle-throated roar
Cry that monarch claws have leapt
From the scabbards where they slept.
Silver snakes that once a year
Doff the lovely coats you wear,
Seek no covert in your fear
Lest a mortal eye should see;
What's your nakedness to me?
Here no leprous[2] flowers rear
Fierce corollas[3] in the air;

Here no bodies sleek and wet,
Dripping mingled rain and sweat,
Tread the savage measures of

[2]Scaly, like dry skin.
[3]The petals of a flower considered as a unit.

Jungle boys and girls in love.
What is last year's snow to me,
Last year's anything? The tree
Budding yearly must forget
How its past arose or set—
Bough and blossom, flower, fruit,
Even what shy bird with mute
Wonder at her travail there,
Meekly labored in its hair.
One three centuries removed
From the scenes his fathers loved,
Spicy grove, cinnamon tree,
What is Africa to me?

So I lie, who find no peace
Night or day, no slight release
From the unremittant beat
Made by cruel padded feet
Walking through my body's street.
Up and down they go, and back,
Treading out a jungle track.
So I lie, who never quite
Safely sleep from the rain at night—
I can never rest at all
When the rain begins to fall;
Like a soul gone mad with pain
I must match its weird refrain;
Ever must I twist and squirm,
Writhing like a baited worm,
While its primal measures drip
Through my body, crying, "Strip!
Doff this new exuberance.
Come and dance the Lover's Dance!"
In an old remembered way
Rain works on me night and day.

Quaint, outlandish heathen gods
Black men fashion out of rods,
Clay, and brittle bits of stone,
In a likeness like their own,
My conversion came high-priced;

I belong to Jesus Christ,
Preacher of humility;
Heathen gods are naught to me.

Father, Son, and Holy Ghost,
So I make an idle boast;
Jesus of the twice-turned cheek,
Lamb of God, although I speak
With my mouth thus, in my heart
Do I play a double part.
Ever at Thy glowing altar
Must my heart grow sick and falter,
Wishing He I served were black,
Thinking then it would not lack
Precedent of pain to guide it,
Let who would or might deride it;
Surely then this flesh would know
Yours had borne a kindred woe.
Lord, I fashion dark gods, too,
Daring even to give You
Dark despairing features where,
Crowned with a dark rebellious hair,
Patience wavers just so much as
Mortal grief compels, while touches
Quick and hot, of anger, rise
To smitten cheek and weary eyes.
Lord, forgive me if my need
Sometimes shapes a human creed.

All day long and all night through,
One thing only must I do:
Quench my pride and cool my blood,
Lest I perish in the flood.
Lest a hidden ember set
Timber that I thought was wet
Burning like the dryest flax,
Melting like the merest wax,
Lest the grave restore its dead.
Not yet has my heart or head
In the least way realized
They and I are civilized.

16

GWENDOLYN BENNETT

Heritage

1923

In this poem, Gwendolyn Bennett employs Africa as a metaphor for the true soul of her people, unburdened by oppression. In contrast to Countée Cullen's ambivalent portrayal of African heritage as a dangerous creative urge, Bennett casts it as a beautiful and sustaining desire for vitality and freedom. This poem progresses from day to night. It also moves from the image of a palm tree reaching upward toward white clouds to that of a (white) lotus plant reaching downward to the Nile, just before the culminating stanza. How would you explain this movement? Do you see any other patterns in the poem?

I want to see the slim palm-trees,
Pulling at the clouds
With little pointed fingers. . . .

I want to see lithe Negro girls,
Etched dark against the sky
While sunset lingers.

I want to hear the silent sands,
Singing to the moon
Before the Sphinx-still face. . . .

I want to hear the chanting
Around a heathen fire
Of a strange black race.

I want to breathe the Lotus flow'r,
Sighing to the stars
With tendrils drinking at the Nile. . . .

Gwendolyn Bennett, "Heritage," *Opportunity,* 1 (December 1923): 371.

I want to feel the surging
Of my sad people's soul
Hidden by a minstrel-smile.

17

RICHARD BRUCE NUGENT

Sahdji

Illustration by Aaron Douglas

1925

Richard Bruce Nugent's legacy may depend more on his flamboyant personality and enthusiastic embrace of bohemianism than on his writings or drawings. Originally from Washington, D.C., he first came to New York City in 1919 at the age of thirteen, where he held many jobs including errand boy, bellhop in an all-women's hotel, and elevator operator. The most outwardly decadent member of the circle that produced Fire!! *(1926) (see Document 30), he is known for the explicitly sexual and homosexual orientation of his artistic message, evident especially in his much anthologized story "Smoke, Lillies, and Jade" (1926). In "Sahdji," Nugent tells a strange and in some ways tragic story of primitive East African love between a fifty-nine-year-old chief and his eighteen-year-old wife, a story laced with father envy, veiled homosexual desire, murder, and suicide. Peppered with ellipses intended to resist conventional marks of punctuation, "Sahdji" strives for a flow of consciousness in which the unique breaks and rhythms fit the specific experiences that it relates. The story was illustrated by Aaron Douglas, the foremost visual artist of the Harlem Renaissance. Influenced by the emphasis on design in African art, Douglas uses two-dimensional figures and geometric juxtapositions to suggest dramatic movement. A black and white silhouette evokes the emotional qualities and broad thematic content of the black experience. This scene depicts Sahdji's final, tragic dance at the funeral of her fallen lover Konombju.*

Richard Bruce Nugent, "Sahdji," in *The New Negro*, ed. Alain Locke (New York: Albert and Charles Boni, 1925), 113, illustration by Aaron Douglas, 112.

That one now . . . . that's a sketch of a little African girl . . . delightfully black . . . I made it while I was passing through East Africa . . . her name was Sahdji . . . wife of Konombju . . . chieftain . . . of only a small tribe . . . Warpuri was the area of his sovereign domain . . . but to get back to Sahdji . . . with her beautiful dark body . . . rosy black . . . graceful as the tongues of flame she loved to dance around . . . and pretty . . . small features . . . . large liquid eyes . . . over-full sensuous lips . . . she knew how to dance too . . . better than any. . . . .

Sahdji was proud . . . she was the favorite wife . . . as such she had privileges . . . she did love Konombju . . .

Mrabo . . . son of Konombju, loved Sahdji . . . his father . . fifty-nine . . . . too old for her . . . fifty-nine and eighteen . . . he could wait . . . he loved his father . . . but . . . . maybe death . . . his father was getting old. . . . .

Numbo idolized Mrabo . . . Numbo was a young buck . . . . would do anything to make Mrabo happy. . . .

one day Sahdji felt restless . . . why . . . it was not unusual for Konombju to lead the hunt . . . even at his age . . . Sahdji jangled her bracelets . . . it was so still and warm . . . she'd wait at the door. . . . standing there . . . shifting . . . a blurred silhouette against the brown of the hut . . . she waited . . . waited. . .

maybe . . .

she saw the long steaming stream of natives in the distance . . . she looked for Konombju . . what was that burden they carried . . . why were they so solemn . . . where was Konombju. . . .

the column reached her door . . . placed their burden at her feet . . . Konombju . . . . . an arrow in his back . . . just accident . . . *Goare go shuioa go elui ruri*—(when men die they depart for ever)—they hadn't seen him fall . . hunting, one watches the hunt . . . a stray arrow . . . Konombju at her feet. . .

preparations for the funeral feast . . . the seven wives of Konombju went to the new chief's hut . . . Mrabo . . . one . . two . . three . . he counted . . . no Sahdji . . . six . . seven . . no Sahdji. . .

The funeral procession filed past the door . . . and Mrabo . . . Mrabo went to . . the drums beat their boom . . boom . . . deep pulsing heart-quivering boom . . . and the reeds added their weird dirge . . . the procession moved on . . . on to Konombju's hut . . . boom . . b-o-o-m. . . . .

there from the doorway stepped Sahdji . . . painted in the funeral red . . . the flames from the ground are already catching the branches . . . slowly to the funeral drums she swayed . . . danced . . . leading Konombju to his grave . . . her grave . . . their grave. . .

From *The New Negro*. Edited by Alain Locke. New York: Albert and Charles Boni, 1925.

they laid the body in the funeral hut . . . *Goa shoa motho go sale motho*— (when a man dies a man remains) —Sahdji danced slowly . . . sadly . . . looked at Mrabo and smiled . . . slowly triumphantly . . . and to the wails of the wives . . . boom-boom of the drums . . . gave herself again to Konombju . . . the grass-strewn couch of Konombju. . . .

Mrabo stood unflinching . . . but Numbo, silly Numbo had made an old . . old man of Mrabo.

18

ZORA NEALE HURSTON

Mules and Men

1935

Today Zora Neale Hurston receives the recognition that eluded her when she lived. Widely regarded as one of the very best writers and most notable personalities of the Harlem Renaissance, she also pioneered in the collection of folklore, which in turn inspired her art. A native of the all-black town Eatonville, Florida, Hurston first came to New York City in 1925 from Howard University, where one of the important leaders of the Harlem Renaissance, Professor Alain Locke (see Documents 11 and 12), had encouraged her to pursue a writing career. She enrolled in Columbia University as a transfer student on a scholarship and studied anthropology with Franz Boas, an important founder of the field under whose tutelage she conducted field research. In this passage from her folklore collection Mules and Men, *she describes the strangely alienating experience of returning as a researcher to her hometown to collect stories that she had heard as a little girl.*

I was glad when somebody told me, "You may go and collect Negro folklore."[1]

In a way it would not be a new experience for me. When I pitched headforemost into the world I landed in the crib of negroism. From the earliest rocking of my cradle, I had known about the capers Brer

[1]A play on Psalms 122:1, "I was glad when they said unto me, Let us go into the house of the Lord."

Zora Neale Hurston, introduction to *Mules and Men* (Philadelphia: J.B. Lippincott Co., 1935), 17–29.

Rabbit is apt to cut and what the Squinch Owl says from the house top.[2] But it was fitting me like a tight chemise. I couldn't see it for wearing it. It was only when I was off in college, away from my native surroundings, that I could see myself like somebody else and stand off and look at my garment. Then I had to have the spy-glass of Anthropology to look through at that.

Dr. Boas asked me where I wanted to work and I said, "Florida," and gave, as my big reason, that "Florida is a place that draws people—white people from all over the world, and Negroes from every Southern state surely and some from the North and West." So I knew that it was possible for me to get a cross section of the Negro South in the one state. And then I realized that I was new myself, so it looked sensible for me to choose familiar ground.

First place I aimed to stop to collect material was Eatonville, Florida.

And now, I'm going to tell you why I decided to go to my native village first. I didn't go back there so that the home folks could make admiration over me because I had been up North to college and come back with a diploma and a Chevrolet. I knew they were not going to pay either one of these items too much mind. I was just Lucy Hurston's daughter, Zora, and even if I had—to use one of our down-home expressions—had a Kaiser baby,[3] and that's something that hasn't been done in this County yet, I'd still be just Zora to the neighbors. If I had exalted myself to impress the town, somebody would have sent me word in a match-box that I had been up North there and had rubbed the hair off of my head against some college wall, and then come back there with a lot of form and fashion and outside show to the world. But they'd stand flat-footed and tell me that they didn't have me, neither my sham-polish, to study 'bout. And that would have been that.

I hurried back to Eatonville because I knew that the town was full of material and that I could get it without hurt, harm or danger. As early as I could remember it was the habit of the men folks particularly to gather on the store porch of evenings and swap stories. Even the women folks would stop and break a breath with them at times. As a child when I was sent down to Joe Clarke's store, I'd drag out my leaving as long as possible in order to hear more.

[2]Two figures from African American folklore, the first known for his tricks and the second for wisdom.

[3]To become an important person by having the child of the German emperor.

Folk-lore is not as easy to collect as it sounds. The best source is where there are the least outside influences and these people, being usually under-privileged, are the shyest. They are most reluctant at times to reveal that which the soul lives by. And the Negro, in spite of his open-faced laughter, his seeming acquiescence, is particularly evasive. You see we are a polite people and we do not say to our questioner, "Get out of here!" We smile and tell him or her something that satisfies the white person because, knowing so little about us, he doesn't know what he is missing. The Indian resists curiosity by a stony silence. The Negro offers a feather-bed resistance. That is, we let the probe enter, but it never comes out. It gets smothered under a lot of laughter and pleasantries.

The theory behind our tactics: "The white man is always trying to know into somebody else's business. All right, I'll set something outside the door of my mind for him to play with and handle. He can read my writing but he sho' can't read my mind. I'll put this play toy in his hand, and he will seize it and go away. Then I'll say my say and sing my song."

I knew that even *I* was going to have some hindrance among strangers. But here in Eatonville I knew everybody was going to help me. So below Palatka I began to feel eager to be there and I kicked the little Chevrolet right along.

I thought about the tales I had heard as a child. How even the Bible was made over to suit our vivid imagination. How the devil always outsmarted God and how that over-noble hero Jack or John—not *John Henry,* who occupies the same place in Negro folk-lore that Casey Jones does in white lore and if anything is more recent—outsmarted the devil. Brer Fox, Brer Deer, Brer 'Gator, Brer Dawg, Brer Rabbit, Ole Massa and his wife were walking the earth like natural men way back in the days when God himself was on the ground and men could talk with him. Way back there before God weighed up the dirt to make the mountains. When I was rounding Lily Lake I was remembering how God had made the world and the elements and people. He made souls for people, but he didn't give them out because he said:

> "Folks ain't ready for souls yet. De clay ain't dry. It's de strongest thing Ah ever made. Don't aim to waste none thru loose cracks. And then men got to grow strong enough to stand it. De way things is now, if Ah give it out it would tear them shackly bodies to pieces. Bimeby, Ah give it out."
>
> So folks went round thousands of years without no souls. All de time de soul-piece, it was setting 'round covered up wid God's loose

> raiment. Every now and then de wind would blow and hist up de cover and then de elements would be full of lightning and de winds would talk. So people told one 'nother that God was talking in de mountains.
>
> De white man passed by it way off and he looked but he wouldn't go close enough to touch. De Indian and de Negro, they tipped by cautious too, and all of 'em seen de light of diamonds when de winds shook de cover, and de wind dat passed over it sung songs. De Jew come past and heard de song from de soul-piece then he kept on passin' and all of a sudden he grabbed up de soul-piece and hid it under his clothes, and run off down de road. It burnt him and tore him and throwed him down and lifted him up and toted him across de mountain and he tried to break loose but he couldn't do it. He kept on hollerin' for help but de rest of 'em run hid 'way from him. Way after while they come out of holes and corners and picked up little chips and pieces that fell back on de ground. So God mixed it up wid feelings and give it out to 'em. 'Way after while when He ketch dat Jew, He's goin' to 'vide things up more ekal'.

So I rounded Park Lake and came speeding down the straight stretch into Eatonville, the city of five lakes, three croquet courts, three hundred brown skins, three hundred good swimmers, plenty guavas, two schools, and no jail-house.

Before I enter the township, I wish to make acknowledgments to Mrs. R. Osgood Mason of New York City.[4] She backed my falling in a hearty way, in a spiritual way, and in addition, financed the whole expedition in the manner of the Great Soul that she is. The world's most gallant woman.

As I crossed the Maitland-Eatonville township line I could see a group on the store porch. I was delighted. The town had not changed. Same love of talk and song. So I drove on down there before I stopped. Yes, there was George Thomas, Calvin Daniels, Jack and Charlie Jones, Gene Brazzle, B. Moseley and "Seaboard." Deep in a game of Florida-flip. All of those who were not actually playing were giving advice—"bet straightening" they call it.

"Hello, boys," I hailed them as I went into neutral.

[4]Charlotte Osgood Mason (1854–1946), one of the important white patrons of the Harlem Renaissance. She offered money and her Westfield, New Jersey, home to Hurston, Langston Hughes, and Alain Locke. A domineering woman, she insisted that her beneficiaries call her "Godmother." Here Hurston shows that she did not mind salving Mason's ego by paying her obsequious homage.

They looked up from the game and for a moment it looked as if they had forgotten me. Then B. Moseley said, "Well, if it ain't Zora Hurston!" Then everybody crowded around the car to help greet me.

"You gointer stay awhile, Zora?"

"Yep. Several months."

"Where you gointer stay, Zora?"

"With Mett and Ellis, I reckon."

"Mett" was Mrs. Armetta Jones, an intimate friend of mine since childhood and Ellis was her husband. Their house stands under the huge camphor tree on the front street.

"Hello, heart-string," Mayor Hiram Lester yelled as he hurried up the street. "We heard all about you up North. You back home for good, I hope."

"Nope, Ah come to collect some old stories and tales and Ah know y'all know a plenty of 'em and that's why Ah headed straight for home."

"What you mean, Zora, them big old lies we tell when we're jus' sittin' around here on the store porch doin' nothin'?" asked B. Moseley.

"Yeah, those same ones about Ole Massa, and colored folks in heaven, and—oh, y'all know the kind I mean."

"Aw shucks," exclaimed George Thomas doubtfully. "Zora, don't you come here and tell de biggest lie first thing. Who you reckon want to read all them old-time tales about Brer Rabbit and Brer Bear?"

"Plenty of people, George. They are a lot more valuable than you might think. We want to set them down before it's too late."

"Too late for what?"

"Before everybody forgets all of 'em."

"No danger of that. That's all some people is good for—set 'round and lie and murder groceries."

"Ah know one right now," Calvin Daniels announced cheerfully. "It's a tale 'bout John and de frog."

"Wait till she get out her car, Calvin. Let her get settled at 'Met's' and cook a pan of ginger bread then we'll all go down and tell lies and eat ginger bread. Dat's de way to do. She's tired now from all dat drivin'."

"All right, boys," I agreed. "But Ah'll be rested by night. Be lookin' for everybody."

So I unloaded the car and crowded it into Ellis' garage and got settled. Armetta made me lie down and rest while she cooked a big pan of ginger bread for the company we expected.

Calvin Daniels and James Moseley were the first to show up.

"Calvin, Ah sure am glad that you got here. Ah'm crazy to hear about John and dat frog," I said.

"That's why Ah come so early so Ah could tell it to you and go. Ah got to go over to Wood Bridge a little later on."

"Ah'm glad you remembered me first, Calvin."

"Ah always like to be good as my word, and Ah just heard about a toe-party over to Wood Bridge tonight and Ah decided to make it."

"A toe-party! What on earth is that?"

"Come go with me and James and you'll see!"

"But, everybody will be here lookin' for me. They'll think Ah'm crazy—tellin' them to come and then gettin' out and goin' to Wood Bridge myself. But Ah certainly would like to go to that toe-party."

"Aw, come on. They kin come back another night. You gointer like this party."

"Well, you tell me the story first, and by that time, Ah'll know what to do."

"Ah, come on, Zora," James urged. "Git de car out. Calvin kin tell you dat one while we're on de way. Come on, let's go to de toe-party."

"No, let 'im tell me this one first, then, if Ah go he can tell me some more on de way over."

James motioned to his friend. "Hurry up and tell it, Calvin, so we kin go before somebody else come."

"Aw, most of 'em ain't comin' nohow. They all 'bout goin' to Wood Bridge, too. Lemme tell you 'bout John and dis frog:

> It was night and Ole Massa sent John,[5] his favorite slave, down to the spring to get him a cool drink of water. He called John to him.
>
> "John!"
>
> "What you want, Massa?"
>
> "John, I'm thirsty. Ah wants a cool drink of water, and Ah wants you to go down to de spring and dip me up a nice cool pitcher of water."
>
> John didn't like to be sent nowhere at night, but he always tried to do everything Ole Massa told him to do, so he said, "Yessuh, Massa, Ah'll go git you some!"
>
> Ole Massa said: "Hurry up, John. Ah'm mighty thirsty."
>
> John took de pitcher and went on down to de spring. There was a great big ole bull frog settin' right on de edge of de spring, and

[5]Hurston defines John as "the great human culture hero of black folklore" (*Mules and Men*, 305). He defeats his enemies through trickery even when caught in seemingly hopeless situations.

when John dipped up de water de noise skeered de frog and he hollered and jumped over in de spring.

John dropped de water pitcher and tore out for de big house, hollerin' "Massa! Massa! A big ole booger[6] done got after me!"

Ole Massa told him, "Why, John, there's no such thing as a booger."

"Oh, yes it is, Massa. He down at dat Spring."

"Don't tell me, John. Youse just excited. Furthermore, you go git me dat water Ah sent you after."

"No, indeed, Massa, you and nobody else can't send me back there so dat booger kin git me."

Ole Massa begin to figger dat John musta seen somethin' sho nuff because John never had disobeyed him before, so he ast: "John, you say you seen a booger. What did it look like?"

John tole him, "Massa, he had two great big eyes lak balls of fire, and when he was standin' up he was sittin' down and when he moved, he moved by jerks, and he had most no tail."

Long before Calvin had ended his story James had lost his air of impatience.

"Now, Ah'll tell one," he said. "That is, if you so desire."

"Sure, Ah want to hear you tell 'em till daybreak if you will," I said eagerly.

"But where's the ginger bread?" James stopped to ask.

"It's out in the kitchen," I said. "Ah'm waiting for de others to come."

"Aw, naw, give us ours now. Them others may not get here before forty o'clock and Ah'll be done et nine and be in Wood Bridge. Anyhow Ah want a corner piece and some of them others will beat me to it."

So I served them with ginger bread and buttermilk.

"You sure going to Wood Bridge with us after Ah git thru tellin' this one?" James asked.

"Yeah, if the others don't show up by then," I conceded.

So James told the story about the man who went to Heaven from Johnstown.

You know, when it lightnings, de angels is peepin' in de lookin' glass; when it thunders, they's rollin' out de rain barrels; and when it rains, somebody done dropped a barrel or two and bust it.

One time, you know, there was going to be big doin's in Glory and all de angels had brand new clothes to wear and so they was all

[6]A bogey man [Hurston's note].

peepin' in the lookin' glasses, and therefore it got to lightning all over de sky. God tole some of de angels to roll in all de full rain barrels and they was in such a hurry that it was thunderin' from the east to the west and the zig-zag lightning went to join the mutterin' thunder and, next thing you know, some of them angels got careless and dropped a whole heap of them rain barrels, and didn't it rain!

In one place they call Johnstown they had a great flood. And so many folks got drownded that it looked jus' like Judgment day.

So some of de folks that got drownded in that flood went one place and some went another. You know, everything that happen, they got to be a nigger in it—and so one of de brothers in black went up to Heben from de flood.

When he got to the gate, Ole Peter let 'im in and made 'im welcome. De colored man was named John, so John ast Peter, says, "Is it dry in dere?"

Ole Peter tole 'im, "Why, yes it's dry in here. How come you ast that?"

"Well, you know Ah jus' come out of one flood, and Ah don't want to run into no mo'. Ooh, man! You ain't *seen* no water. You just oughter seen dat flood we had at Johnstown."[7]

Peter says, "Yeah, we know all about it. Jus' go wid Gabriel and let him give you some new clothes."

So John went on off wid Gabriel and come back all dressed up in brand new clothes and all de time he was changin' his clothes he was tellin' Ole Gabriel all about dat flood, jus' like he didn't know already."

So when he come back from changin' his clothes, they give him a brand new gold harp and handed him to a gold bench and made him welcome. They was so tired of hearing about dat flood they was glad to see him wid his harp 'cause they figgered he'd get to playin' and forget all about it. So Peter tole him, "Now you jus' make yo'self at home and play all de music you please."

John went and took a seat on de bench and commenced to tune up his harp. By dat time, two angels come walkin' by where John was settin' so he throwed down his harp and tackled 'em.

"Say," he hollered, "Y'all want to hear 'bout de big flood Ah was in down on earth? Lawd, Lawd! It sho rained, and talkin' 'bout water!"

Dem two angels hurried on off from 'im jus' as quick as they could. He started to tellin' another one and he took to flyin'. Gab'ull went over to 'im and tried to get 'im to take it easy, but John kept

[7]Johnstown, Pennsylvania, was the site of a large flood in 1899 that killed 2,100 people.

right on stoppin' every angel dat he could find to tell 'im about dat flood of water.

Way after while he went over to Ole Peter and said: "Thought you said everybody would be nice and polite?"

Peter said, "Yeah, Ah said it. Ain't everybody treatin' you right?"

John said, "Naw. Ah jus' walked up to a man as nice and friendly as Ah could be and started to tell 'im 'bout all dat water Ah left back there in Johnstown and instead of him turnin' me a friendly answer he said, 'Shucks! You ain't seen no water!' and walked off and left me standin' by myself."

"Was he a *ole* man wid a crooked walkin' stick?" Peter ast John.

"Yeah."

"Did he have whiskers down to here?" Peter measured down to his waist.

"He sho did," John tol' 'im.

"Aw shucks," Peter tol' 'im. "Dat was Ole Nora.[8] You can't tell *him* nothin' 'bout no flood."

[8]Noah [Hurston's note].

19

STERLING BROWN

Southern Road

1932

Originally from Washington, D.C., Sterling Brown joined Jean Toomer, Langston Hughes, and Zora Neale Hurston in finding his deepest inspiration in the experiences and voices of ordinary black Americans. A graduate of Washington's all-black Dunbar High School, he attended Williams College and Harvard University before becoming a professor at a series of historically black colleges, including Lincoln University in

Sterling Brown, *Southern Road* (New York: Harcourt, Brace, 1932), 5–7, 46–47, 51–53, 62–64. "Odyssey of Big Boy" first published in *Caroling Dusk*, ed. Countée Cullen (New York: Harper & Brothers, 1927), 130–33. "Ma Rainey" first published in *Folk Say: A Regional Miscellany*, ed. B. A. Botkin (Norman: University of Oklahoma Press, 1930), 2: 276–78. "Strong Men" first published in *The Book of American Negro Poetry*, 2nd ed., ed. James Weldon Johnson (New York: Harcourt, Brace, 1931), 258–60.

Missouri and Fisk University in Tennessee. Thus, like a number of Harlem Renaissance figures, he spent almost none of his time in Harlem. In Southern Road *(1932), Brown reinvented the idea of dialect poetry by giving it unprecedented comic and tragic range, thus remaking a form that once represented stereotype and degradation into a mode of affirmation. "Odyssey of Big Boy" (1932) and "Southern Road" (1931) provide two examples of his ability—unmatched by any other Harlem Renaissance writer—to distill poetic meaning from the ordinary events and voices of southern black folk. "Ma Rainey" (1930) pays tribute to the blues singer who drew crowds from all around by singing about hard luck and loneliness. Like many of the best blues artists, Ma Rainey brought people together by transforming their pain into hope and collective ritual through art. "Strong Men" (1931) shows how, in spite of his praise for Ma Rainey, Brown still followed the trend of the period in characterizing black strength in masculine terms.*

Odyssey of Big Boy

Lemme be wid Casey Jones,[1]
  Lemme be wid Stagolee,[2]
Lemme be wid such like men
  When Death takes hol' on me,
    When Death takes hol' on me. . . .

Done skinned as a boy in Kentucky hills,
  Druv steel dere as a man,
Done stripped tobacco in Virginia fiel's
  Alongst de River Dan,
    Alongst de River Dan;

Done mined de coal in West Virginia,
  Liked dat job jes' fine,
Till a load o' slate curved roun' my head,
  Won't work in no mo' mine,
    Won't work in no mo' mine;

[1]Casey Jones (1864–1900), American locomotive engineer and folk hero.
[2]Stacker Lee, African American folklore figure, a celebrated gambler, drinker, and "badman."

Done shocked de corn in Marylan',
  In Georgia done cut cane,
Done planted rice in South Caline,
  But won't do dat again,
    Do dat no mo' again.

Been roustabout in Memphis,
  Dockhand in Baltimore,
Done smashed up freight on Norfolk wharves,
  A fust class stevedore,
    A fust class stevedore. . . .

Done slung hash yonder in de North
  On de ole Fall River Line,
Done busted suds[3] in li'l New York,
  Which ain't no work o' mine—
    Lawd, ain't no work o' mine.

Done worked and loafed on such like jobs,
  Seen what dey is to see,
Done had my time wid a pint on my hip
  An' a sweet gal on my knee,
    Sweet mommer on my knee:

Had stovepipe blond in Macon,
  Yaller gal in Marylan',
In Richmond had a choklit brown,
  Called me huh monkey man—
    Huh big fool monkey man.

Had two fair browns in Arkansaw
  And three in Tennessee,
Had Creole gal in New Orleans,
  Sho Gawd did two time me—
    Lawd two time, fo' time me—

But best gal what I evah had
  Done put it over dem,
A gal in Southwest Washington
  At Four'n half and M—[4]
    Four'n half and M. . . .

[3]Washed dishes.
[4]On M Street between 4th and 5th streets.

Done took my livin' as it came,
  Done grabbed my joy, done risked my life;
Train done caught me on de trestle,[5]
  Man done caught me wid his wife,
    His doggone purty wife. . . .

I done had my women,
  I done had my fun;
Cain't do much complainin'
  When my jag[6] is done,
    Lawd, Lawd, my jag is done.

An' all dat Big Boy axes
  When time comes fo' to go,
Lemme be wid John Henry,[7] steel drivin' man,
  Lemme be wid old Jazzbo,
    Lemme be wid ole Jazzbo. . . .

Southern Road

Swing dat hammer—hunh—
Steady, bo';
Swing dat hammer—hunh—
Steady, bo';
Ain't no rush, bebby,
Long ways to go.

Burner[8] tore his—hunh—
Black heart away;
Burner tore his—hunh—
Black heart away;
Got me life, bebby,
An' a day.

Gal's on Fifth Street[9]—hunh—
Son done gone;

[5]Bridge.
[6]Spree.
[7]John Henry, African American folklore hero who died after outworking a steel driving machine.
[8]A gun.
[9]His daughter is a prostitute.

Gal's on Fifth Street—hunh—
Son done gone,
Wife's in de ward,[10] bebby,
Babe's not bo'n.

My ole man died—hunh—
Cussin' me;
My ole man died—hunh—
Cussin' me;
Ole lady rocks, bebby,
Huh misery.

Doubleshackled—hunh—
Guard behin';
Doubleshackled—hunh—
Guard behin';
Ball an' chain, bebby,
On my min'.

White man tells me—hunh—
Damn yo' soul;
White man tells me—hunh—
Damn yo' soul;
Got no need, bebby,
To be tole.

Chain gang nevah—hunh—
Let me go;
Chain gang nevah—hunh—
Let me go;
Po' los' boy, bebby,
Evahmo'. . . .

Ma Rainey

1

When Ma Rainey
Comes to town,
Folks from anyplace
Miles aroun',

[10] Hospital.

From Cape Girardeau,
Poplar Bluff,
Flocks in to hear
Ma do her stuff;
Comes flivverin'[11] in,
Or ridin' mules,
Or packed in trains,
Picknickin' fools. . . .
That's what it's like,
Fo' miles on down,
To New Orleans delta
An' Mobile town,
When Ma hits
Anywheres aroun'.

2

Dey comes to hear Ma Rainey from de little river settlements,
From blackbottom[12] cornrows and from lumber camps;
Dey stumble in de hall, jes' a-laughin' an' a-cacklin',
Cheerin' lak roarin' water, lak wind in river swamps.

An' some jokers keeps deir laughs a-goin' in de crowded aisles,
An' some folks sits dere waitin' wid deir aches an' miseries,
Till Ma comes out before dem, a-smilin' gold-toofed smiles
An' Long Boy ripples minors on de black an' yellow keys.[13]

3

O Ma Rainey,
Sing yo' song;
Now you's back
Whah you belong,
Git way inside us,
Keep us strong. . . .
O Ma Rainey,
Li'l an' low;
Sing us 'bout de hard luck

[11] Riding in a cheap car.
[12] Fertile land.
[13] Plays a song on the piano in the minor keys.

Roun' our do';
Sing us 'bout de lonesome road
We mus' go. . . .

4

I talked to a fellow, an' the fellow say,
"She jes' catch hold of us, somekindaway.
She sang Backwater Blues one day:
'It rained fo' days an' de skies was dark as night,
Trouble taken place in de lowlands at night.

'Thundered an' lightened an' the storm begin to roll
Thousan's of people ain't got no place to go.

'Den I went an' stood upon some high ol' lonesome hill,
An' looked down on the place where I used to live.'

An' den de folks, dey natchally bowed dey heads an' cried,
Bowed dey heavy heads, shet dey moufs up tight an' cried,
An' Ma lef' de stage, an' followed some de folks outside."

Dere wasn't much more de fellow say:
She jes' gits hold of us dataway.

Strong Men

The strong men keep coming on.
—Sandburg.[14]

They dragged you from homeland,
They chained you in coffles,[15]
They huddled you spoon-fashion in filthy hatches,
They sold you to give a few gentlemen ease.

They broke you in like oxen,
They scourged you,
They branded you,
They made your women breeders,
They swelled your numbers with bastards. . . .
They taught you the religion they disgraced.

[14]The epigraph is from the poem "Upstream" in the collection *Slabs of the Sunburnt West* (1922) by the American poet Carl Sandburg (1878–1967).
[15]Slaves chained together.

You sang:
  Keep a-inchin' along
  Lak a po' inch worm. . . .

You sang:
  Bye and bye
  I'm gonna lay down dis heaby load. . . .

You sang:
  Walk togedder, chillen,
  Dontcha git weary. . . .
    The strong men keep a-comin' on
    The strong men git stronger.

They point with pride to the roads you built for them,
They ride in comfort over the rails you laid for them.
They put hammers in your hands
And said—Drive so much before sundown.

You sang:
  Ain't no hammah
  In dis lan',
  Strikes lak mine, bebby,
  Strikes lak mine.

They cooped you in their kitchens,
They penned you in their factories,
They gave you the jobs that they were too good for,
They tried to guarantee happiness to themselves
By shunting dirt and misery to you.

You sang:
  Me an' muh baby gonna shine, shine
  Me an' muh baby gonna shine.
    The strong men keep a-comin' on
    The strong men git stronger. . . .

They bought off some of your leaders
You stumbled, as blind men will . . .
They coaxed you, unwontedly soft-voiced. . . .
You followed a way.
Then laughed as usual.

They heard the laugh and wondered;
Uncomfortable;

Unadmitting a deeper terror. . . .
The strong men keep a-comin' on
Gittin' stronger. . . .

What, from the slums
Where they have hemmed you,
What, from the tiny huts
They could not keep from you—
What reaches them
Making them ill at ease, fearful?
Today they shout prohibition at you
"Thou shalt not this"
"Thou shalt not that"
"Reserved for whites only"
You laugh.

One thing they cannot prohibit—
The strong men . . . coming on
The strong men gittin' stronger.
Strong men. . . .
Stronger. . . .

20

MA RAINEY

See See Rider

1924

Gertrude Pridgett, who later became "Ma" Rainey, was born in Columbus, Georgia, in a black show-business family. In 1902, she married the song and dance man William "Pa" Rainey, with whom she toured the South singing the blues and popular songs. She signed her first contract with Paramount Records in 1923 and recorded over one hundred songs by 1928, with titles such as "The Black Bottom," "Gone Daddy Blues," and "Trust No Man." A large woman who wore bright clothes, flashed a

The Bessie Smith Song Book (Milwaukee, Wis.: Frank Music Corporation, 1994), 148–51.

mouthful of gold teeth, and billed herself as "The Mother of the Blues," she served as a mentor to the equally ostentatious blues singer Bessie Smith (see Document 21). First recorded in 1924, "See See Rider" was one of Ma Rainey's most popular and lasting songs, in part because of its bold pronouncement of female independence. Rather than weeping when her lover cheats, she buys a long pistol, shoots her betrayer, and "catches the Cannon Ball," with every ounce of sexual innuendo enthusiastically intended.

See See Rider, see what you done done!
  Lord, Lord, Lord!
You made me love you, now your gal done come.
You made me love you, now your gal done come.

I'm goin' away, baby, I won't be back till fall.
  Lord, Lord, Lord!
Goin' away, baby, won't be back till fall.
If I find me a good man, I won't be back at all.

I'm gonna buy me a pistol just as long as I am tall.
  Lord, Lord, Lord!
Kill my man and catch the Cannon Ball.
If he won't have me, he won't have no gal at all.

See See Rider, where did you stay last night?
  Lord, Lord, Lord!
Your shoes ain't buttoned, clothes don't fit you right.
You didn't come home till the sun was shinin' bright.

21

BESSIE SMITH

Young Woman's Blues

1926

Bessie Smith began her singing career as a street entertainer in her native Chattanooga, Tennessee. In 1912, she joined a traveling show that featured Ma Rainey (see Document 20) and Rainey's husband. Benefiting from Ma Rainey's advice, Smith became one of the most popular blues singers in the southeast by 1920. She made her recording debut with Columbia Records in 1923 with "Gulf Coast Blues" and "Downhearted Blues," which sold more than 750,000 copies. In "Young Woman's Blues," Smith, "The Empress of the Blues"—who weighed 200 pounds, drank hard, fought hard, and loved both sexes—expresses her philosophy of female independence.

Woke up this mornin' when chickens was crowin' for days
And on the right side of my pilla my man had gone away
By the pilla he left a note reading I'm sorry Jane, you got my goat
No time to marry, no time to settle down
I'm a young woman and ain't done runnin' round
I'm a young woman and ain't done runnin' round.

Some people call me a hobo, some call me a bum
Nobody knows my name, nobody knows what I've done
I'm as good as any woman in your town
I ain't high yeller, I'm a deep killa brown
I ain't gonna marry, ain't gonna settle down
I'm gonna drink good moonshine and run these browns down.

See that long lonesome road
Lord, you know it's gotta end
I'm a good woman and I can get plenty men.

Bill Galiford et al., eds., *Just Blues Real Book* (Miami: Time, Warner Corporation, 2001), 325.

22

JOEL A. ROGERS

Jazz at Home

1925

Joel A. Rogers emigrated in 1906 from his native Jamaica to New York, where he inaugurated a distinguished career as a journalist and as an author of books on the history of race relations. Through his column "Your History" in the black newspaper The Pittsburgh Courier, *Rogers may have done more than any other figure of the Harlem Renaissance to popularize black history. "Your History" led to the publication of* The World's Greatest Men of African Descent *in 1931 and* The World's Greatest Men of Color 3000 B.C. to 1946 A.D. *in 1947. Rogers's light skin and Jamaican mulatto background may have contributed to his lifelong interest in race mixture throughout the ages, which culminated in a three-volume study,* Sex and Race: Negro-Caucasian in All Ages and Lands *(1942). In this article, which appeared in the Harlem issue of* The Survey Graphic *(see Document 11), he cites the role of jazz as an emotional "safety-valve" for modern civilization and as a "balm" for boredom arising from bureaucracy, the assembly line, and other sources of standardization. How does Rogers balance this general argument about the beginnings of jazz with the more specifically American and Afro-American circumstances surrounding its origin?*

Jazz is a marvel of paradox: too fundamentally human, at least as modern humanity goes, to be typically racial, too international to be characteristically national, too much abroad in the world to have a special home. And yet jazz in spite of it all is one part American and three parts American Negro, and was originally the nobody's child of the levee and the city slum. Transplanted exotic—a rather hardy one, we admit—of the mundane world capitals, sport of the sophisticated, it is really at home in its humble native soil wherever the modern unsophisticated Negro feels happy and sings and dances to his mood. It follows that jazz is more at home in Harlem than in Paris, though from the look and

---

Joel A. Rogers, "Jazz at Home," *The Survey Graphic*, 6 (March 1925), 665–67, 712.

sound of certain quarters of Paris one would hardly think so. It is just the epidemic contagiousness of jazz that makes it like the measles, sweep the block. But somebody had to have it first: that was the Negro.

What after all is this taking new thing, that, condemned in certain quarters, enthusiastically welcomed in others, had nonchalantly gone on until it ranks with the movie and the dollar as a foremost exponent of modern Americanism? Jazz isn't music merely, it is a spirit that can express itself in almost anything. The true spirit of jazz is a joyous revolt from convention, custom, authority, boredom, even sorrow—from everything that would confine the soul of man and hinder its riding free on the air. The Negroes who invented it called their songs the "Blues," and they weren't capable of satire or deception. Jazz was their explosive attempt to cast off the blues and be happy, carefree happy, even in the midst of sordidness and sorrow. And that is why it has been such a balm for modern ennui, and has become a safety valve for modern machine-ridden and convention-bound society. It is the revolt of the emotions against repression.

The story is told of the clever group of "Jazz-specialists" who, originating dear knows in what scattered places, had found themselves and the frills of the art in New York and had been drawn to the gay Bohemias of Paris. In a little cabaret of Montmartre they had just "entertained" into the wee small hours fascinated society and royalty; and, of course, had been paid royally for it. Then, the entertainment over and the guests away, the "entertainers" entertained themselves with their very best, which is always impromptu, for the sheer joy of it. That is jazz.

In its elementals, jazz has always existed. It is in the Indian war-dance, the Highland fling, the Irish jig, the Cossack dance, the Spanish fandango, the Brazilian *maxixe*, the dance of the whirling dervish, the hula hula of the South Seas, the *danse du vêntre* of the Orient, the *carmagnole* of the French Revolution, the strains of Gypsy music, and the ragtime of the Negro. Jazz proper, however, is something more than all these. It is a release of all the suppressed emotions at once, a blowing off of the lid, as it were. It is hilarity expressing itself through pandemonium; musical fireworks.

The direct predecessor of jazz is ragtime.[1] That both are atavistically African there is little doubt, but to what extent it is difficult to

[1]A piano-based musical style, most prominently associated with the African American piano master Scott Joplin (1868–1917), that alters, or "rags," the rhythms of existing songs.

determine. In its barbaric rhythm and exuberance there is something of the bamboula, a wild, abandoned dance of the West African and the Haytian Negro, so stirringly described by the anonymous author of *Untrodden Fields of Anthropology*, or of the *ganza* ceremony so brilliantly depicted in Maran's *Batouala*. But jazz time is faster and more complex than African music. With its cowbells, auto horns, calliopes, rattles, dinner gongs, kitchen utensils, cymbals, screams, crashes, clankings and monotonous rhythm it bears all the marks of a nerve-strung, strident, mechanized civilization. It is a thing of the jungles—modern man-made jungles.

The earliest jazz-makers were the itinerant piano players who would wander up and down the Mississippi from saloon to saloon, from dive to dive. Seated at the piano with a carefree air that a king might envy, their box-back coats flowing over the stool, their Stetsons pulled well over their eyes, and cigars at an angle of forty-five degrees, they would "whip the ivories" to marvellous chords and hidden racy, joyous meanings, evoking the intense delight of their hearers who would smother them at the close with huzzas and whiskey. Often wholly illiterate, these humble troubadours knowing nothing of written music or composition, but with minds like cameras, would listen to the rude improvisations of the dock laborers and the railroad gangs and reproduce them, reflecting perfectly the sentiments and the longings of these humble folk. The improvised bands at Negro dances in the South, or the little boys with their harmonicas and jews'-harps, each one putting his own individuality into the air, played also no inconsiderable part in its evolution. "Poverty," says J. A. Jackson of the *Billboard*, "compelled improvised instruments. Bones, tambourines, make-shift string instruments, tin can and hollow wood effects, all now utilized as musical novelties, were among early Negroes the product of necessity. When these were not available 'patting juba' prevailed. Present-day 'Charleston' is but a variation of this. Its early expression was the 'patting' for the buck dance."

The origin of the present jazz craze is interesting. More cities claim its birthplace than claimed Homer dead. New Orleans, San Francisco, Memphis, Chicago, all assert the honor is theirs. Jazz, as it is to-day, seems to have come into being this way, however: W. C. Handy, a Negro, having digested the airs of the itinerant musicians referred to, evolved the first classic, *Memphis Blues*. Then came Jasbo Brown, a reckless musician of a Negro cabaret in Chicago, who played this and other blues, blowing his own extravagant moods and risqué interpretations into them, while hilarious with gin. To give further meanings to his veiled allusions he would make the trombone "talk" by putting a derby hat and later a tin can at its mouth. The delighted patrons would shout, "More, Jasbo. More, Jas, more." And so the name originated.

As to the jazz dance itself: at this time Shelton Brooks, a Negro comedian, invented a new "strut," called "Walkin' the Dog." Jasbo's anarchic airs found in this strut a soul mate. Then as a result of their union came "The Texas Tommy," the highest point of brilliant, acrobatic execution and nifty footwork so far evolved in jazz dancing. The latest of these dances is the "Charleston," which has brought something really new to the dance step. The "Charleston" calls for activity of the whole body. One characteristic is a fantastic fling of the legs from the hip downwards. The dance ends in what is known as the "camel-walk"—in reality a gorilla-like shamble—and finishes with a peculiar hop like that of the Indian war dance. Imagine one suffering from a fit of rhythmic ague and you have the effect precisely.

The cleverest "Charleston" dancers perhaps are urchins of five and six who may be seen any time on the streets of Harlem, keeping time with their hands, and surrounded by admiring crowds. But put it on a well-set stage, danced by a bobbed-hair chorus, and you have an effect that reminds you of the abandon of the Furies. And so Broadway studies Harlem. Not all of the visitors of the twenty or more well-attended cabarets of Harlem are idle pleasure seekers or underworld devotees. Many are serious artists, actors and producers seeking something new, some suggestion to be taken, too often in pallid imitation, to Broadway's lights and stars.

This makes it difficult to say whether jazz is more characteristic of the Negro or of contemporary America. As was shown, it is of Negro origin plus the influence of the American environment. It is Negro-American. Jazz proper, however, is in idiom—rhythmic, musical and pantomimic—thoroughly American Negro; it is his spiritual picture on that lighter comedy side, just as the spirituals are the picture, on the tragedy side. The two are poles apart, but the former is by no means to be despised and it is just as characteristically the product of the peculiar and unique experience of the Negro in this country. The African Negro hasn't it, and the Caucasian never could have invented it. Once achieved, it is common property, and jazz has absorbed the national spirit, that tremendous spirit of go, the nervousness, lack of conventionality and boisterous good-nature characteristic of the American, white or black, as compared with the more rigid formal natures of the Englishman or German.

But there still remains something elusive about jazz that few, if any of the white artists, have been able to capture. The Negro is admittedly its best expositor. That elusive something, for lack of a better name, I'll call Negro rhythm. The average Negro, particularly of the lower classes, puts rhythm into whatever he does, whether it be shining shoes or carrying a basket on the head to market as the Jamaican women do. Some years ago while wandering in Cincinnati I happened upon a Negro revival meeting at its height. The majority present were women, a goodly few of whom were white. Under the influence of the "spirit" the sisters would come forward and strut—much of jazz enters where it would be least expected. The Negro women had the perfect jazz abandon, while the white ones moved lamely and woodenly. This same lack of spontaneity is evident to a degree in the cultivated and inhibited Negro.

In its playing technique, jazz is similarly original and spontaneous. The performance of the Negro musicians is much imitated, but seldom equalled. Lieutenant Europe, leader of the famous band of the "Fifteenth New York Regiment," said that the bandmaster of the Garde Republicaine, amazed at his jazz effects, could not believe without demonstration that his band had not used special instruments. Jazz has a virtuoso technique all its own: its best performers, singers and players lift it far above the level of mere "trick" or mechanical effects. Abbie Mitchell, Ethel Waters, and Florence Mills; the Blues singers, Clara, Mamie, and Bessie Smith; Eubie Blake, the pianist; "Buddy" Gilmore, the drummer; and "Bill" Robinson, the pantomimic dancer—to mention merely an illustrative few—are inimitable artists, with an inventive, improvising skill that defies imitation. And those who know their work most intimately trace its uniqueness without exception to the folk-roots of their artistry.

Musically jazz has a great future. It is rapidly being sublimated. In the more famous jazz orchestras like those of Will Marion Cook, Paul Whiteman, Sissle and Blake, Sam Stewart, Fletcher Henderson, Vincent Lopez and the Clef Club units, there are none of the vulgarities and crudities of the lowly origin or the only too prevalent cheap imitations. The pioneer work in the artistic development of jazz was done by Negro artists; it was the lead of the so-called "syncopated orchestras" of Tyers and Will Marion Cook, the former playing for the Castles of dancing fame, and the latter touring as a concertizing orchestra in the great American centers and abroad. Because of the difficulties of financial backing, these expert combinations have had to yield ground to white orchestras of the type of the Paul Whiteman and

Vincent Lopez, organizations that are now demonstrating the finer possibilities of jazz music. "Jazz," says Serge Koussevitzy, the new conductor of the Boston Symphony, "is an important contribution to modern musical literature. It has an epochal significance—it is not superficial, it is fundamental. Jazz comes from the soul, where all music has its beginning." And Leopold Stokowski[2] says more extendedly of it:

> Jazz has come to stay because it is an expression of the times, of the breathless, energetic, superactive times in which we are living, it is useless to fight against it. Already its new vigor, its new vitality is beginning to manifest itself. . . . America's contribution to the music of the past will have the same revivifying effect as the injection of new, and in the larger sense, vulgar blood into dying aristocracy. Music will then be vulgarized in the best sense of the word, and enter more and more into the daily lives of people. . . . The Negro musicians of America are playing a great part in this change. They have an open mind, and unbiased outlook. They are not hampered by conventions or traditions, and with their new ideas, their constant experiment, they are causing new blood to flow in the veins of music. The jazz players make their instruments do entirely new things, things finished musicians are taught to avoid. They are pathfinders into new realms.

And thus it has come about that serious modernistic music and musicians, most notably and avowedly in the work of the French modernists Auric, Satie and Darius Milhaud, have become the confessed debtors of American Negro jazz. With the same nonchalance and impudence with which it left the levee and the dive to stride like an upstart conqueror, almost overnight, into the grand salon, jazz now begins its conquest of musical Parnassus.

Whatever the ultimate result of the attempt to raise jazz from the mob-level upon which it originated, its true home is still its original cradle, the none too respectable cabaret. And here we have the seamy side to the story. Here we have some of the charm of Bohemia, but much more of the demoralization of vice. Its rash spirit is in Grey's popular song, *Runnin' Wild*:

> Runnin' wild; lost control
> Runnin' wild; mighty bold,
> Feelin' gay and reckless too

[2]Leopold Stokowski (1882–1977), musician and composer, founder of the New York City Symphony Orchestra and the American Symphony Orchestra.

Carefree all the time; never blue
Always goin' I don't know where
Always showin' that I don't care
Don' love nobody, it ain't worth while
All alone; runnin' wild.

Jazz reached the height of its vogue at a time when minds were reacting from the horrors and strain of war. Humanity welcomed it because in its fresh joyousness men found a temporary forgetfulness, infinitely less harmful than drugs or alcohol. It is partly for some such reasons that it dominates the amusement life of America to-day. No one can sensibly condone its excesses or minimize its social danger if uncontrolled; all culture is built upon inhibitions and control. But it is doubtful whether the "jazz-hounds" of high and low estate would use their time to better advantage. In all probability their tastes would find some equally morbid, mischievous vent. Jazz, it is needless to say, will remain a recreation for the industrious and a dissipater of energy for the frivolous, a tonic for the strong and a poison for the weak.

For the Negro himself, jazz is both more and less dangerous than for the white—less in that he is nervously more in tune with it; more, in that at his average level of economic development his amusement life is more open to the forces of social vice. The cabaret of better type provides a certain Bohemianism for the Negro intellectual, the artist and the well-to-do. But the average thing is too much the substitute for the saloon and the wayside inn. The tired longshoreman, the porter, the housemaid and the poor elevator boy in search of recreation, seeking in jazz the tonic for weary nerves and muscles, are only too apt to find the bootlegger, the gambler and the demi-monde who have come there for victims and to escape the eyes of the police.

Yet in spite of its present vices and vulgarizations, its sex informalities, its morally anarchic spirit, jazz has a popular mission to perform. Joy, after all, has a physical basis. Those who laugh and dance and sing are better off even in their vices than those who do not. Moreover, jazz with its mocking disregard for formality is a leveller and makes for democracy. The jazz spirit, being primitive, demands more frankness and sincerity. Just as it already has done in art and music, so eventually in human relations and social manners, it will no doubt have the effect of putting more reality in life by taking some of the needless artificiality out. . . . Naturalness finds the artificial in conduct ridiculous. "Cervantes smiled Spain's chivalry away," said Byron.[3] And

[3]Lord Byron (1788–1824), English romantic poet.

so this new spirit of joy and spontaneity may itself play the rôle of reformer. Where at present it vulgarizes, with more wholesome growth in the future, it may on the contrary truly democratize. At all events, jazz is rejuvenation, a recharging of the batteries of civilization with primitive new vigor. It has come to stay, and they are wise, who instead of protesting against it try to lift and divert it into nobler channels.

23

NELLA LARSEN

Passing

1929

Nella Larsen's complex racial background fed directly into her art. She was born in Chicago to a Danish mother and a black West Indian father. Two years after her father died, her mother married a Danish man. At the age of sixteen, Larsen traveled to Denmark for three years, but returned to the United States to attend historically black Fisk University in Tennessee. Lasting only a year at Fisk, she made a second trip to Denmark to attend the University of Copenhagen, where she stayed for two years. Returning once again to the United States, she attended nursing school and worked at hospitals in New York from 1912 until 1922, when she became a librarian at the Harlem Branch of the New York Public Library. Soon after, she began her writing career, which consisted mainly of two important novels, Quicksand *(1928) (see Document 25) and* Passing, *both of which explore the crossroads of gender, class, sexual identity, and racial identity—a combination that she knew intimately through personal experience.* Passing *tells the story of two friends from childhood, Clare Kendry and Irene Redfield, both of whom look like white women. Clare marries a racist white businessman, while the more conventional Irene marries a black doctor. When Irene decides temporarily to "pass" one day by going into a white hotel in Chicago, she sees Clare at the next table. Their conversation provokes guilt, fear, and loathing in Irene, who sees some of her own repressed desires represented in Clare's*

Nella Larsen, *Passing* (New York: Alfred A. Knopf, 1929), 3–9.

uncompromising and dangerous insistence on having it all. The novel revolves around the tensions created when the seductive and selfish Clare tries to reenter black society with Irene's help. In this scene, which resembles in some ways a story of two lovers, Irene weighs whether she should admit the disruptive, but alluring, Clare into her life.

It was the last letter in Irene Redfield's little pile of morning mail. After her other ordinary and clearly directed letters the long envelope of thin Italian paper with its almost illegible scrawl seemed out of place and alien. And there was, too, something mysterious and slightly furtive about it. A thin sly thing which bore no return address to betray the sender. Not that she hadn't immediately known who its sender was. Some two years ago she had one very like it in outward appearance. Furtive, but yet in some peculiar, determined way a little flaunting. Purple ink. Foreign paper of extraordinary size.

It had been, Irene noted, postmarked in New York the day before. Her brows came together in a tiny frown. The frown, however, was more from perplexity than from annoyance; though there was in her thoughts an element of both. She was wholly unable to comprehend such an attitude towards danger as she was sure the letter's contents would reveal; and she disliked the idea of opening and reading it.

This, she reflected, was of a piece with all that she knew of Clare Kendry. Stepping always on the edge of danger. Always aware, but not drawing back or turning aside. Certainly not because of any alarms or feeling of outrage on the part of others.

And for a swift moment Irene Redfield seemed to see a pale small girl sitting on a ragged blue sofa, sewing pieces of bright red cloth together, while her drunken father, a tall, powerfully built man, raged threateningly up and down the shabby room, bellowing curses and making spasmodic lunges at her which were not the less frightening because they were, for the most part, ineffectual. Sometimes he did manage to reach her. But only the fact that the child had edged herself and her poor sewing over to the farthermost corner of the sofa suggested that she was in any way perturbed by this menace to herself and her work.

Clare had known well enough that it was unsafe to take a portion of the dollar that was her weekly wage for the doing of many errands for the dressmaker who lived on the top floor of the building of which Bob Kendry was janitor. But that knowledge had not deterred her.

She wanted to go to her Sunday school's picnic, and she had made up her mind to wear a new dress. So, in spite of certain unpleasantness and possible danger, she had taken the money to buy the material for that pathetic little red frock.

There had been, even in those days, nothing sacrificial in Clare Kendry's idea of life, no allegiance beyond her own immediate desire. She was selfish, and cold, and hard. And yet she had, too, a strange capacity of transforming warmth and passion, verging sometimes almost on theatrical heroics.

Irene, who was a year or more older than Clare, remembered the day that Bob Kendry had been brought home dead, killed in a silly saloon-fight. Clare, who was at that time a scant fifteen years old, had just stood there with her lips pressed together, her thin arms folded across her narrow chest, staring down at the familiar pasty-white face of her parent with a sort of disdain in her slanting black eyes. For a very long time she had stood like that, silent and staring. Then, quite suddenly, she had given way to a torrent of weeping, swaying her thin body, tearing at her bright hair, and stamping her small feet. The outburst had ceased as suddenly as it had begun. She glanced quickly about the bare room, taking everyone in, even the two policemen, in a sharp look of flashing scorn. And, in the next instant, she had turned and vanished through the door.

Seen across the long stretch of years the thing had more the appearance of an outpouring of pent-up fury than of an overflow of grief for her dead father; though she had been, Irene admitted, fond enough of him in her own rather catlike way.

Catlike. Certainly that was the word which best described Clare Kendry, if any single word could describe her. Sometimes she was hard and apparently without feeling at all; sometimes she was affectionate and rashly impulsive. And there was about her an amazing soft malice, hidden well away until provoked. Then she was capable of scratching, and very effectively too. Or, driven to anger, she would fight with a ferocity and impetuousness that is disregarded or forgot any danger; superior strength, numbers, or other unfavourable circumstances. How savagely she had clawed those boys the day they had hooted her parent and sung a derisive rhyme, of their own composing, which pointed out certain eccentricities in his careening gait! And how deliberately she had—

Irene brought her thoughts back to the present, to the letter from Clare Kendry that she still held unopened in her hand. With a little feeling of apprehension, she very slowly cut the envelope, drew out the folded sheets, spread them, and began to read.

It was, she saw at once, what she had expected since learning from the postmark that Clare was in the city. An extravagantly phrased wish to see her again. Well, she needn't and wouldn't, Irene told herself, accede to that. Nor would she assist Clare to realize her foolish desire to return for a moment to that life which long ago, and of her own choice, she had left behind her.

She ran through the letter, puzzling out, as best she could, the carelessly formed words or making instinctive guesses at them.

". . . For I am lonely, so lonely . . . cannot help longing to be with you again, as I have never longed for anything before; and I have wanted many things in my life. . . . You can't know how in this pale life of mine I am all the time seeing the bright pictures of that other that I once thought I was glad to be free of. . . . It's like an ache, a pain that never ceases. . . ." Sheets upon thin sheets of it. And ending finally with, "and it's your fault 'Rene dear. At least partly. For I wouldn't now, perhaps, have this terrible, this wild desire if I hadn't seen you that time in Chicago. . . ."

Brilliant red patches flamed in Irene Redfield's warm olive cheeks.

"That time in Chicago." The words stood out from among the many paragraphs of other words, bringing with them a clear, sharp remembrance, in which even now, after two years, humiliation, resentment, and rage were mingled.

24

JESSIE FAUSET

Plum Bun

1929

An important influence on many Harlem Renaissance writers and a prolific novelist in her own right, Jessie Fauset was born in Camden County, New Jersey, the daughter of a minister. After graduating from Cornell University in 1905, she taught Latin and French at the all-black Dunbar High School in Washington, D.C. until 1919, when she became the literary editor of the NAACP journal, The Crisis. *Until she resigned from*

Jessie Fauset, *Plum Bun* (New York: Frederick A. Stokes, 1929), 77–81.

The Crisis *in 1926, she influenced the careers of many writers, including Jean Toomer, Countée Cullen, and Langston Hughes. Between 1924 and 1933, she wrote four novels, including* There Is Confusion *(1924), the first novel of the Harlem Renaissance (see Document 10), and* Plum Bun, *which most critics consider her best.* Plum Bun *tells the story of Angela Murray, an aspiring artist who decides to pass for white against the advice of her darker and more racially progressive sister, Virginia. After a botched romance with a white man and several other misadventures as an art student in New York, she eventually reunites with her sister. Accepting her racial heritage, she becomes an art student in Paris, where she finally finds love with Anthony Cross, an artist of mixed racial background. In this scene, which occurs early in the novel, Angela relates her reasons for passing to her dismayed sister.*

Angela, waking in the middle of the night and reviewing to herself the events of the day, said aloud: "This is the end," and fell asleep again.

The little back room was still Jinny's, but Angela, in order to give the third storey front to Hetty Daniels, had moved into the room which had once been her mother's. She and Virginia had placed the respective head-boards of their narrow, virginal beds against the dividing wall so that they could lie in bed and talk to each other through the communicating door-way, their voices making a circuit from speaker to listener in what Jinny called a hairpin curve.

Angela called in as soon as she heard her sister moving, "Jinny, listen. I'm going away."

Her sister, still half asleep, lay intensely quiet for another second, trying to pick up the continuity of this dream. Then her senses came to her.

"What'd you say, Angela?"

"I said I was going away. I'm going to leave Philadelphia, give up school teaching, break away from our loving friends and acquaintances, and bust up the whole shooting match."

"Haven't gone crazy, have you?"

"No, I think I'm just beginning to come to my senses. I'm sick, sick, sick of seeing what I want dangled right before my eyes and then of having it snatched away from me and all of it through no fault of my own."

"Darling, you know I haven't the faintest idea of what you're driving at."

"Well, I'll tell you." Out came the whole story, an accumulation of the slights, real and fancied, which her colour had engendered throughout her lifetime; though even then she did not tell of that first hurt through Mary Hastings. That would always linger in some remote, impenetrable fastness of her mind, for wounded trust was there as well as wounded pride and love. "And these two last happenings with Matthew and Mr. Shields are just too much; besides they've shown me the way."

"Shown you what way?"

Virginia had arisen and thrown an old rose kimono around her. She had inherited her father's thick and rather coarsely waving black hair, enhanced by her mother's softness. She was slender, yet rounded; her cheeks were flushed with sleep and excitement. Her eyes shone. As she sat in the brilliant wrap, cross-legged at the foot of her sister's narrow bed, she made the latter think of a striking dainty, colourful robin.

"Well you see as long as the Shields thought I was white they were willing to help me to all the glories of the promised land. And the doorman last night,—he couldn't tell what I was, but he could tell about Matthew, so he put him out; just as the Shields are getting ready in another way to put me out. But as long as they didn't know it didn't matter. Which means it isn't being coloured that makes the difference, it's letting it be known. Do you see?

"So I've thought and thought. I guess really I've had it in my mind for a long time, but last night it seemed to stand right out in my consciousness. Why should I shut myself off from all the things I want most,—clever people, people who do things, Art,—" her voice spelt it with a capital,—"travel and a lot of things which are in the world for everybody really but which only white people, as far as I can see, get their hands on. I mean scholarships and special funds, patronage. Oh Jinny, you don't know, I don't think you can understand the things I want to see and know. You're not like me—"

"I don't know why I'm not," said Jinny looking more like a robin than ever. Her bright eyes dwelt on her sister. "After all, the same blood flows in my veins and in the same proportion. Sure you're not laying too much stress on something only temporarily inconvenient?"

"But it isn't temporarily inconvenient; it's happening to me every day. And it isn't as though it were something that I could help. Look how Mr. Shields stressed the fact that I hadn't told him I was coloured. And see how it changed his attitude toward me; you can't think how different his manner was. Yet as long as he didn't know, there was nothing he wasn't willing and glad, glad to do for me. Now he might be willing but he'll not be glad though I need his assistance more than some white girl who will find a dozen people to help her just because she is white." Some faint disapproval in her sister's face halted her for a moment. "What's the matter? You certainly don't think I ought to say first thing: 'I'm Angela Murray. I know I look white but I'm coloured and expect to be treated accordingly!' Now do you?"

"No," said Jinny, "of course that's absurd. Only I don't think you ought to mind quite so hard when they do find out the facts. It seems sort of an insult to yourself. And then, too, it makes you lose a good chance to do something for—for all of us who can't look like you but who really have the same combination of blood that you have."

"Oh that's some more of your and Matthew Henson's philosophy. Now be practical, Jinny; after all I am both white and Negro and look white. Why shouldn't I declare for the one that will bring me the greatest happiness, prosperity and respect?"

"No reason in the world except that since in this country public opinion is against any infusion of black blood it would seem an awfully decent thing to put yourself, even in the face of appearances, on the side of black blood and say: 'Look here, this is what a mixture of black and white really means!' "

Angela was silent and Virginia, feeling suddenly very young, almost childish in the presence of this issue, took a turn about the room. She halted beside her sister.

"Just what is it you want to do, Angela? Evidently you have some plan."

She had. Her idea was to sell the house and to divide the proceeds. With her share of this and her half of the insurance she would go to New York or to Chicago, certainly to some place where she could by no chance be known, and launch out "into a freer, fuller life."

"And leave me!" said Jinny astonished. Somehow it had not dawned on her that the two would actually separate. She did not know what she had thought, but certainly not that. The tears ran down her cheeks.

Angela, unable to endure either her own pain or the sight of it in others, had all of a man's dislike for tears.

"Don't be absurd, Jinny! How could I live the way I want to if you're with me. We'd keep on loving each other and seeing one another from time to time, but we might just as well face the facts. Some of those girls in the art school used to ask me to their homes; it would have meant opportunity, a broader outlook, but I never dared accept because I knew I couldn't return the invitation."

Under that Jinny winced a little, but she spoke with spirit. "After that, Angela dear, I'm beginning to think that you *have* more white blood in your veins than I, and it was that extra amount which made it possible for you to make that remark." She trailed back to her room and when Hetty Daniels announced breakfast she found that a bad headache required a longer stay in bed.

25

NELLA LARSEN

Quicksand

1928

Nella Larsen's first novel, Quicksand, *tells the story of Helga Crane, a woman of mixed Danish and African American heritage who struggles to find a satisfactory sense of identity. Her quest begins in a black college in the South, proceeds to Harlem, and then moves to Denmark. Frustrated with repeated rejections, especially from her family, and unsatisfying relationships with suitors, she has a religious conversion and decides to marry the dark-skinned southerner Reverend Pleasant Green, who impregnates her five times. Here in the last scene of the novel, Helga, a talented but broken woman, contemplates her domestic imprisonment in the South.*

During the long process of getting well, between the dreamy intervals when she was beset by the insistent craving for sleep, Helga had had too much time to think. At first she had felt only an astonished anger at the quagmire in which she had engulfed herself. She had ruined her life. Made it impossible ever again to do the things that she wanted, have the things that she loved, mingle with the people she liked. She had, to put it as brutally as any one could, been a fool. The damnedest kind of a fool. And she had paid for it. Enough. More than enough.

Nella Larsen, *Quicksand* (New York: Negro Universities Press, 1969), 296–302.

Her mind, swaying back to the protection that religion had afforded her, almost she wished that it had not failed her. An illusion. Yes. But better, far better, than this terrible reality. Religion had, after all, its uses. It blunted the perceptions. Robbed life of its crudest truths. Especially it had its uses for the poor—and the blacks.

For the blacks. The Negroes.

And this, Helga decided, was what ailed the whole Negro race in America, this fatuous belief in the white man's God, this childlike trust in full compensation for all woes and privations in "kingdom come." Sary Jones's absolute conviction, "In de nex' worl' we's all recompense'," came back to her. And ten million souls were as sure of it as was Sary. How the white man's God must laugh at the great joke he had played on them! Bound them to slavery, then to poverty and insult, and made them bear it unresistingly, uncomplainingly almost, by sweet promises of mansions in the sky by and by.

"Pie in the sky," Helga said aloud derisively, forgetting for the moment Miss Hartley's brisk presence, and so was a little startled at hearing her voice from the adjoining room saying severely: "My goodness! No! I should say you can't have pie. It's too indigestible. Maybe when you're better—"

"That," assented Helga, "is what I said. Pie—by and by. That's the trouble."

The nurse looked concerned. Was this an approaching relapse? Coming to the bedside, she felt at her patient's pulse while giving her a searching look. No. "You'd better," she admonished, a slight edge to her tone, "try to get a little nap. You haven't had any sleep today, and you can't get too much of it. You've got to get strong, you know."

With this Helga was in full agreement. It seemed hundreds of years since she had been strong. And she would need strength. For in some way she was determined to get herself out of this bog into which she had strayed. Or—she would have to die. She couldn't endure it. Her suffocation and shrinking loathing were too great. Not to be borne. Again. For she had to admit that it wasn't new, this feeling of dissatisfaction, of asphyxiation. Something like it she had experienced before. In Naxos. In New York. In Copenhagen. This differed only in degree. And it was of the present and therefore seemingly more reasonable. The other revulsions were of the past, and now less explainable.

The thought of her husband roused in her a deep and contemptuous hatred. At his every approach she had forcibly to subdue a furious inclination to scream out in protest. Shame, too, swept over her at every thought of her marriage. Marriage. This sacred thing of which parsons and other Christian folk ranted so sanctimoniously, how immoral—according to their own standards—it could be! But Helga felt also a modicum of pity for him, as for one already abandoned. She meant to leave him. And it was, she had to concede, all of her own doing, this marriage. Nevertheless, she hated him.

The neighbors and churchfolk came in for their share of her all-embracing hatred. She hated their raucous laughter, their stupid acceptance of all things, and their unfailing trust in "de Lawd." And more than all the rest she hated the jangling Clementine Richards, with her provocative smirkings, because she had not succeeded in marrying the preacher and thus saving her, Helga, from that crowning idiocy.

Of the children Helga tried not to think. She wanted not to leave them—if that were possible. The recollection of her own childhood, lonely, unloved, rose too poignantly before her for her to consider calmly such a solution. Though she forced herself to believe that this was different. There was not the element of race, of white and black. They were all black together. And they would have their father. But to leave them would be a tearing agony, a rending of deepest fibers. She felt that through all the rest of her lifetime she would be hearing their cry of "Mummy, Mummy, Mummy," through sleepless nights. No. She couldn't desert them.

How, then, was she to escape from the oppression, the degradation, that her life had become? It was so difficult. It was terribly difficult. It was almost hopeless. So for a while—for the immediate present, she told herself—she put aside the making of any plan for her going. "I'm still," she reasoned, "too weak, too sick. By and by, when I'm really strong—"

It was so easy and so pleasant to think about freedom and cities, about clothes and books, about the sweet mingled smell of Houbigant and cigarettes in softly lighted rooms filled with inconsequential chatter and laughter and sophisticated tuneless music. It was so hard to think out a feasible way of retrieving all these agreeable, desired things. Just then. Later. When she got up. By and by. She must rest. Get strong. Sleep. Then, afterwards, she could work out some arrangement. So she dozed and dreamed in snatches of sleeping and waking, letting time run on. Away.

And hardly had she left her bed and become able to walk again without pain, hardly had the children returned from the homes of the neighbors, when she began to have her fifth child.

26

GEORGIA DOUGLASS JOHNSON

The Heart of a Woman

1918

Although she wrote plays and fiction, and authored "The Homely Philosophy," a column syndicated in twenty black newspapers from 1926 to 1932, Georgia Douglass Johnson made her greatest mark as a poet. But the artists of the Harlem Renaissance adored her also for her generosity in hosting Saturday night open houses at her Washington, D.C., home, which became a southern outpost of the 1920s black cultural movement where W. E. B. Du Bois, Jean Toomer, Alain Locke, Anne Spencer, and many others visited. In 1909, Johnson had moved with her husband to Washington from Atlanta, where she had grown up and attended Atlanta University. An accomplished musician, she also graduated from the Oberlin Conservatory of Music in Ohio. Johnson published three books of poetry, The Heart of a Woman *(1918),* Bronze: A Book of Verse *(1922), and* Autumn Love Cycle *(1928). In this poem from her collection by the same name, she reverses the conventional expectation of the period that a woman's heart ought to feel freest within the confines of the home.*

The heart of a woman goes forth with the dawn,
As a lone bird, soft winging, so restlessly on,
Afar o'er life's turrets and vales does it roam
In the wake of those echoes the heart calls home.

The heart of a woman falls back with the night,
And enters some alien cage in its plight,
And tries to forget it has dreamed of the stars
While it breaks, breaks, breaks on the sheltering bars.

Georgia Douglass Johnson, "The Heart of a Woman," *The Heart of a Woman and Other Poems* (New York: Cornhill Company, 1918), 1.

27

ANNE SPENCER

Lady, Lady and *Letter to My Sister*

1925 and 1928

A composer of complex and delicate verse, Anne Spencer often eschewed racial themes in her poetry. She lived not in Harlem but in Lynchburg, Virginia, where she ran the local NAACP chapter, hosted a well-attended literary salon, and sometimes incited controversy over her preference for wearing pants. In "Lady, Lady," which appeared in the Harlem issue of The Survey Graphic *(see Document 11), she points to the fire that still burns within the heart of an old washerwoman, and in "Letter to My Sister," she frankly and bitterly delineates a woman's predicament of powerlessness.*

Lady, Lady

Lady, Lady, I saw your face,
Dark as night withholding a star . . .
The chisel fell, or it might have been
You had borne so long the yoke of men.

Lady, Lady, I saw your hands,
Twisted, awry, like crumpled roots,
Bleached poor white in a sudsy tub,
Wrinkled and drawn from your rub-a-dub.

Lady, Lady, I saw your heart,
And altered there in its darksome place
Were the tongues of flame the ancients knew,
Where the good God sits to spangle through.

Anne Spencer, "Lady, Lady," *The Survey Graphic*, 6 (March 1925): 661. Anne Spencer, "Letter to My Sister," *The Norton Anthology of African American Literature*, ed. Henry Louis Gates and Nellie Y. McKay (New York: W. W. Norton, 1997), 949. "Letter to My Sister" first published as "Sybil Warns Her Sister" in *Ebony and Topaz: A Collectanea*, ed. Charles S. Johnson (New York: National Urban League, 1928), 94.

Letter to My Sister

It is dangerous for a woman to defy the gods;
To taunt them with the tongue's thin tip,
Or strut in the weakness of mere humanity,
Or draw a line daring them to cross;
The gods own the searing lightning,
The drowning waters, tormenting fears
And anger of red sins.

Oh, but worse still if you mince timidly—
Dodge this way or that, or kneel or pray,
Be kind, or sweat agony drops
Or lay your quick body over your feeble young;
If you have beauty or none, if celibate
Or vowed—the gods are Juggernaut,
Passing over . . . over . . .

This you may do:
Lock your heart, then, quietly,
And lest they peer within,
Light no lamp when dark comes down
Raise no shade for sun;
Breathless must your breath come through
If you'd die and dare deny
The gods their god-like fun.

3

Controversies in Art and Politics

28

GEORGE S. SCHUYLER

The Negro-Art Hokum

1926

In the summer of 1926, The Nation *published "The Negro-Art Hokum," by George S. Schuyler, satirist,* Pittsburgh Courier *columnist, and editor of the black socialist journal* The Messenger. *In biting language, Schuyler not only denounced but laughed at the idea of a separate black American culture. He dismissed the Harlem Renaissance as a trumped-up affair invented by racist whites and their black lackeys who gladly played racially stereotyped roles in exchange for money. This assertion flowed directly from his guiding assumption that cultural expression cannot occur along racial lines; it can only have a national basis. Do you agree with this assumption? Could Schuyler have done more to prove it?*

Negro art "made in America" is as non-existent as the widely advertised profundity of Cal Coolidge,[1] the "seven years of progress" of Mayor Hylan,[2] or the reported sophistication of New Yorkers. Negro art there has been, is, and will be among the numerous black nations of Africa; but to suggest the possibility of any such development among the ten million colored people in this republic is self-evident

[1]Calvin Coolidge (1872–1933), American president, 1923–1929.
[2]John F. Hylan (1868–1936), mayor of New York City, 1917–1925.

George S. Schuyler, "The Negro-Art Hokum," *The Nation*, 122 (June 1926): 662–63.

foolishness. Eager apostles from Greenwich Village, Harlem, and environs proclaimed a great renaissance of Negro art just around the corner waiting to be ushered on the scene by those whose hobby is taking races, nations, peoples, and movements under their wing. New art forms expressing the "peculiar" psychology of the Negro were about to flood the market. In short, the art of Homo Africanus was about to electrify the waiting world. Skeptics patiently waited. They still wait.

True, from dark-skinned sources have come those slave songs based on Protestant hymns and Biblical texts known as the spirituals, work songs and secular songs of sorrow and tough luck known as the blues, that outgrowth of ragtime known as jazz (in the development of which whites have assisted), and the Charleston, an eccentric dance invented by the gamins around the public market-place in Charleston, S. C. No one can or does deny this. But these are contributions of a caste in a certain section of the country. They are foreign to Northern Negroes, West Indian Negroes, and African Negroes. They are no more expressive or characteristic of the Negro race than the music and dancing of the Appalachian highlanders or the Dalmatian peasantry are expressive or characteristic of the Caucasian race. If one wishes to speak of the musical contributions of the peasantry of the South, very well. Any group under similar circumstances would have produced something similar. It is merely a coincidence that this peasant class happens to be of a darker hue than the other inhabitants of the land. One recalls the remarkable likeness of the minor strains of the Russian mujiks to those of the Southern Negro.

As for the literature, painting, and sculpture of Aframericans—such as there is—it is identical in kind with the literature, painting, and sculpture of white Americans: that is, it shows more or less evidence of European influence. In the field of drama little of any merit has been written by and about Negroes that could not have been written by whites. The dean of the Aframerican literati is W. E. B. Du Bois, a product of Harvard and German universities; the foremost Aframerican sculptor is Meta Warwick Fuller, a graduate of leading American art schools and former student of Rodin,[3] while the most noted Aframerican painter, Henry Ossawa Tanner,[4] is dean of American

[3]African American artist Meta Warwick Fuller (1877–1963) was proclaimed a "born sculptor" by the French artist Auguste Rodin (1840–1917) in her second year studying in Paris.

[4]Henry Ossawa Tanner (1859–1937), African American painter.

painters in Paris and has been decorated by the French Government. Now the work of these artists is no more "expressive of the Negro soul"—as the gushers put it—than are the scribblings of Octavus Cohen or Hugh Wiley.[5]

This, of course, is easily understood if one stops to realize that the Aframerican is merely a lampblacked Anglo-Saxon. If the European immigrant after two or three generations of exposure to our schools, politics, advertising, moral crusades, and restaurants becomes indistinguishable from the mass of Americans of the older stock (despite the influence of the foreign-language press), how much truer must it be of the sons of Ham who have been subjected to what the uplifters call Americanism for the last three hundred years. Aside from his color, which ranges from very dark brown to pink, your American Negro is just plain American. Negroes and whites from the same localities in this country talk, think, and act about the same. Because a few writers with a paucity of themes have seized upon imbecilities of the Negro rustics and clowns and palmed them off as authentic and characteristic Aframerican behavior, the common notion that the black American is so "different" from his white neighbor has gained wide currency. The mere mention of the word "Negro" conjures up in the average white American's mind a composite stereotype of Bert Williams, Aunt Jemima, Uncle Tom, Jack Johnson, Florian Slappey, and the various monstrosities scrawled by the cartoonists.[6] Your average Aframerican no more resembles this stereotype than the average American resembles a composite of Andy Gump, Jim Jeffries, and a cartoon by Rube Goldberg.[7]

Again, the Aframerican is subject to the same economic and social forces that mold the actions and thoughts of the white Americans. He is not living in a different world as some whites and a few Negroes would have us believe. When the jangling of his Connecticut alarm clock gets him out of his Grand Rapids bed to a breakfast similar to

[5]White humorists Octavus Roy Cohen (1891–1959) and Hugh Wiley (1884–1969) employed black stereotypes heavily in their stories and novels.

[6]Bert Williams (1876–1922), legendary African American comedian; Aunt Jemima, a smiling black female domestic depicted on the cover of Quaker Oats products; Jack Johnson (1878–1946), the first African American heavyweight boxing champion; Florian Slappey, a comical black character in the racist novels of Octavus Roy Cohen.

[7]Andy Gump, a comic book figure of the 1920s that caricatured the average American; Jim Jeffries (1875–1953), heavyweight boxing champion, 1899–1905, and famous loser to black champion Jack Johnson; Rube Goldberg (1883–1970), cartoonist famous for his drawings of machines that accomplished simple tasks in complicated ways.

that eaten by his white brother across the street; when he toils at the same or similar work in mills, mines, factories, and commerce alongside the descendants of Spartacus, Robin Hood, and Erik the Red; when he wears similar clothing and speaks the same language with the same degree of perfection; when he reads the same Bible and belongs to the Baptist, Methodist, Episcopal, or Catholic church; when his fraternal affiliations also include the Elks, Masons, and Knights of Pythias; when he gets the same or similar schooling, lives in the same kind of houses, owns the same makes of cars (or rides in them), and nightly sees the same Hollywood version of life on the screen; when he smokes the same brands of tobacco and avidly peruses the same puerile periodicals; in short, when he responds to the same political, social, moral, and economic stimuli in precisely the same manner as his white neighbor, it is sheer nonsense to talk about "racial differences" as between the American black man and the American white man. Glance over a Negro newspaper (it is printed in good Americanese) and you will find the usual quota of crime news, scandal, personals, and uplift to be found in the average white newspaper—which, by the way, is more widely read by the Negroes than is the Negro press. In order to satisfy the cravings of an inferiority complex engendered by the colorphobia of the mob, the readers of the Negro newspapers are given a slight dash of racialistic seasoning. In the homes of the black and white Americans of the same cultural and economic level one finds similar furniture, literature, and conversation. How, then, can the black American be expected to produce art and literature dissimilar to that of the white American?

Consider Coleridge-Taylor, Edward Wilmot Blyden, and Claude McKay, the Englishmen; Pushkin, the Russian; Bridgewater, the Pole; Antar, the Arabian; Latino, the Spaniard; Dumas, *père* and *fils*, the Frenchmen; and Paul Laurence Dunbar, Charles W. Chestnut, and James Weldon Johnson, the Americans.[8] All Negroes; yet their work shows an impress of nationality rather than race. They all reveal the

[8]Samuel Coleridge-Taylor (1875–1912), Afro-British composer; Edward Wilmot Blyden (1882–1912), Liberian educator and statesman; Alexander Pushkin (1799–1837), Russian poet; George Augustus Polgreen Bridgewater (1799–1860), concert violinist; 'Antarah ibn Shaddad (ca. 500), black Arab desert king and poet; Juan Latino (1516–1597), African-born poet and professor; Alexandre Dumas père (the father) (1802–1870), black French novelist and author of *The Three Musketeers* (1844); Alexandre Dumas fils (the son) (1824–1895), also a novelist and a playwright; Paul Laurence Dunbar (1872–1906), African American poet known for his dialect verse; Charles W. Chesnutt (1858–1932), African American novelist.

psychology and culture of their environment—their color is incidental. Why should Negro artists of America vary from the national artistic norm when Negro artists in other countries have not done so? If we can foresee what kind of white citizens will inhabit this neck of the woods in the next generation by studying the sort of education and environment the children are exposed to now, it should not be difficult to reason that the adults of today are what they are because of the education and environment they were exposed to a generation ago. And that education and environment were about the same for blacks and whites. One contemplates the popularity of the Negro-art hokum and murmurs, "How come?"

This nonsense is probably the last stand of the old myth palmed-off by Negrophobists for all these many years, and recently rehashed by the sainted Harding,[9] that there are "fundamental, eternal, and inescapable differences" between white and black Americans. That there are Negroes who will lend this myth a helping hand need occasion no surprise. It has been broadcast all over the world by the vociferous scions of slaveholders, "scientists" like Madison Grant and Lothrop Stoddard,[10] and the patriots who flood the treasury of the Ku Klux Klan; and is believed, even today, by the majority of free, white citizens. On this baseless premise, so flattering to the white mob, that the blackamoor is inferior and fundamentally different, is erected the postulate that he must needs be peculiar; and when he attempts to portray life through the medium of art, it must of necessity be a peculiar art. While such reasoning may seem conclusive to the majority of Americans, it must be rejected with a loud guffaw by intelligent people.

[9]Warren G. Harding (1865–1923), American president, 1920–1923. "Sainted" ironically refers to the praise he received upon his death despite the corruption that marred his presidency.

[10]Madison Grant (1865–1937) and Theodore Lothrop Stoddard (1883–1950) both authored popular book-length white-supremacist sociological and political studies.

29

LANGSTON HUGHES

The Negro Artist and the Racial Mountain

1926

When George Schuyler submitted "The Negro-Art Hokum" to The Nation, *the white managing editor Freda Kirchwey found it intriguing but a little too controversial. She thought it wise to send the article around among black intellectuals before publishing it. James Weldon Johnson suggested she send it to Langston Hughes, who agreed to write a response. Without directly addressing Schuyler, Hughes's "The Negro Artist and the Racial Mountain" made the case for black artistic independence with such grace that it achieved landmark status and gave further credence to the artistic integrity of Harlem Renaissance artists. In this historic essay, Hughes appears to take the high road of sincerity in contrast to Schuyler's excessive claims and tough language. Yet in accusing black artists of disloyalty for aspiring to "universal" rather than "racial" art, he makes tough assertions of his own. Does Hughes go too far in making this point?*

One of the most promising of the young Negro poets[1] said to me once, "I want to be a poet—not a Negro poet," meaning, I believe, "I want to write like a white poet"; meaning subconsciously, "I would like to be a white poet"; meaning behind that, "I would like to be white." And I was sorry the young man said that, for no great poet has ever been afraid of being himself. And I doubted then that, with his desire to run away spiritually from his race, this boy would never ever be a great poet. But this is the mountain standing in the way of any true Negro art in America—this urge within the race toward whiteness, the desire to pour racial individuality into the mold of American standardization, and to be as little Negro and as much American as possible.

[1]Here Hughes refers to Countée Cullen.

Langston Hughes, "The Negro Artist and the Racial Mountain," *The Nation*, 122 (June 1926): 692–94.

But let us look at the immediate background of this young poet. His family is of what I suppose one would call the Negro middle class: people who are by no means rich yet never uncomfortable nor hungry—smug, contented, respectable folk, members of the Baptist church. The father goes to work every morning. He is a chief steward at a large white club. The mother sometimes does fancy sewing or supervises parties for the rich families of the town. The children go to a mixed school. In the home they read white papers and magazines. And the mother often says "Don't be like niggers" when the children are bad. A frequent phrase from the father is, "Look how well a white man does things." And so the word white comes to be unconsciously a symbol of all the virtues. It holds for the children beauty, morality, and money. The whisper of "I want to be white" runs silently through their minds. This young poet's home is, I believe, a fairly typical home of the colored middle class. One sees immediately how difficult it would be for an artist born in such a home to interest himself in interpreting the beauty of his own people. He is never taught to see that beauty. He is taught rather not to see it, or if he does, to be ashamed of it when it is not according to Caucasian patterns.

For racial culture the home of a self-styled "high-class" Negro has nothing better to offer. Instead there will perhaps be more aping of things white than in a less cultured or less wealthy home. The father is perhaps a doctor, lawyer, landowner, or politician. The mother may be a social worker, or a teacher, or she may do nothing and have a maid. Father is often dark but he has usually married the lightest woman he could find. The family attend a fashionable church where few really colored faces are to be found. And they themselves draw a color line. In the North they go to white theaters and white movies. And in the South they have at least two cars and a house "like white folks." Nordic manners, Nordic faces, Nordic hair, Nordic art (if any), and an Episcopal heaven. A very high mountain indeed for the would-be racial artist to climb in order to discover himself and his people.

But then there are the low-down folks, the so-called common element, and they are the majority—may the Lord be praised! The people who have their nip of gin on Saturday nights and are not too important to themselves or the community, or too well fed, or too learned to watch the lazy world go round. They live on Seventh Street in Washington or State Street in Chicago and they do not particularly care whether they are like white folks or anybody else. Their joy runs, bang! into ecstasy. Their religion soars to a shout. Work maybe a little today, rest a little tomorrow. Play awhile. Sing awhile. O, let's dance!

These common people are not afraid of spirituals, as for a long time their more intellectual brethren were, and jazz is their child. They furnish a wealth of colorful, distinctive material for any artist because they still hold their own individuality in the face of American standardizations. And perhaps these common people will give to the world its truly great Negro artist, the one who is not afraid to be himself. Whereas the better-class Negro would tell the artist what to do, the people at least let him alone when he does appear. And they are not ashamed of him—if they know he exists at all. And they accept what beauty is their own without question.

Certainly there is, for the American Negro artist who can escape the restrictions the more advanced among his own group would put upon him, a great field of unused material ready for his art. Without going outside his race, and even among the better classes with their "white" culture and conscious American manners, but still Negro enough to be different, there is sufficient matter to furnish a black artist with a lifetime of creative work. And when he chooses to touch on the relations between Negroes and whites in this country with their innumerable overtones and undertones, surely, and especially for literature and the drama, there is an inexaustible supply of themes at hand. To these the Negro artist can give his racial individuality, his heritage of rhythm and warmth, and his incongruous humor that so often, as in the Blues, becomes ironic laughter mixed with tears. But let us look again at the mountain.

A prominent Negro clubwoman in Philadelphia paid eleven dollars to hear Raquel Meller[2] sing Andalusian popular songs. But she told me a few weeks before she would not think of going to hear "that woman," Clara Smith,[3] a great black artist, sing Negro folksongs. And many an upper-class Negro church, even now, would not dream of employing a spiritual in its services. The drab melodies in white folks' hymnbooks are much to be preferred. "We want to worship the Lord correctly and quietly. We don't believe in 'shouting.' Let's be dull like the Nordics," they say, in effect.

The road for the serious black artist, then, who would produce a racial art is most certainly rocky and the mountain is high. Until recently he received almost no encouragement for his work from either

[2]Raquel Meller, stage name for Francisca Marqués López (1888–1962), Spanish actress and singer famous for singing popular Spanish songs.

[3]Clara Smith (1894–1935), blues singer of the 1920s, billed as "Queen of the Moaners."

white or colored people. The fine novels of Chestnutt go out of print with neither race noticing their passing. The quaint charm and humor of Dunbar's dialect verse brought to him, in his day, largely the same kind of encouragement one would give a sideshow freak (A colored man writing poetry! How odd!) or a clown (How amusing!).

The present vogue in things Negro, although it may do as much harm as good for the budding colored artist, has at least done this: it has brought him forcibly to the attention of his own people among whom for so long, unless the other race had noticed him beforehand, he was a prophet with little honor. I understand that Charles Gilpin[4] acted for years in Negro theaters without any special acclaim from his own, but when Broadway gave him eight curtain calls, Negroes, too, began to beat a tin pan in his honor. I know a young colored writer, a manual worker by day, who had been writing well for the colored magazines some years, but it was not until he recently broke into the white publications and his first book was accepted by a prominent New York publisher that the "best" Negroes in his city took the trouble to discover that he lived there. Then almost immediately they decided to give a grand dinner for him. But the society ladies were careful to whisper to his mother that perhaps she'd better not come. They were not sure she would have an evening gown.

The Negro artist works against an undertow of sharp criticism and misunderstanding from his own group and unintentional bribes from the whites. "O, be respectable, write about nice people, show how good we are," say the Negroes. "Be stereotyped, don't go too far, don't shatter our illusions abut you, don't amuse us too seriously. We will pay you," say the whites. Both would have told Jean Toomer not to write "Cane." [See Document 7.] The colored people did not praise it. The white people did not buy it. Most of the colored people who did read "Cane" hate it. They are afraid of it. Although the critics gave it good reviews the public remained indifferent. Yet (excepting the work of DuBois) "Cane" contains the finest prose written by a Negro in America. And like the singing of Robeson,[5] it is truly racial.

But in spite of the Nordicized Negro intelligentsia and the desires of some white editors we have an honest American Negro literature already with us. Now I await the rise of the Negro theater. Our folk

[4]Charles Gilpin (1878–1930), African American actor best known for his brilliant performance in the leading role of Eugene O'Neill's play *The Emperor Jones* (1920).

[5]Paul Robeson (1898–1976), African American actor, singer, and civil rights activist, known for his renditions of African American spirituals.

music, having achieved world-wide fame, offers itself to the genius of the great individual American Negro composer who is to come. And within the next decade I expect to see the work of a growing school of colored artists who paint and model the beauty of dark faces and create with new technique the expressions of their own soul-world. And the Negro dancers who will dance like flame and the singers who will continue to carry our songs to all who listen—they will be with us in even greater numbers tomorrow.

Most of my own poems are racial in theme and treatment, derived from the life I know. In many of them I try to grasp and hold some of the meanings and rhythms of jazz. I am sincere as I know how to be in these poems and yet after every reading I answer questions like these from my own people: Do you think Negroes should always write about Negroes? I wish you wouldn't read some of your poems to white folks. How do you find anything interesting in a place like a cabaret? Why do you write about black people? You aren't black. What makes you do so many jazz poems?

But jazz to me is one of the inherent expressions of Negro life in America: the eternal tom-tom beating in the Negro soul—the tom-tom of revolt against weariness in a white world, a world of subway trains, and work, work, work; the tom-tom of joy and laughter, and pain swallowed in a smile. Yet the Philadelphia clubwoman is ashamed to say that her race created it and she does not like me to write about it. The old subconscious "white is best" runs through her mind. Years of study under white teachers, a lifetime of white books, pictures, and papers, and white manners, morals, and Puritan standards made her dislike the spirituals. And now she turns up her nose at jazz and all its manifestations—likewise almost everything else distinctly racial. She doesn't care for the Winold Reiss portraits of Negroes because they are "too Negro." She does not want a true picture of herself from anybody. She wants the artist to flatter her, to make the white world believe that all Negroes are as smug and as near white in soul as she wants to be. But, to my mind, it is the duty of the younger Negro artist, if he accepts any duties at all from outsiders, to change through the force of his art that old whispering "I want to be white," hidden in the aspirations of his people, to "Why should I want to be white? I am a Negro—and beautiful!"

So I am ashamed for the black poet who says, "I want to be a poet, not a Negro poet," as though his own racial world were not as interesting as any other world. I am ashamed, too, for the colored artist who runs from the painting of Negro faces to the painting of sunsets after the manner of the academicians because he fears the strange unwhiteness of his own features. An artist must be free to choose what he does, certainly, but he must also never be afraid to do what he might choose.

Let the blare of Negro jazz bands and the bellowing voice of Bessie Smith singing Blues penetrate the closed ears of the colored near-intellectuals until they listen and perhaps understand. Let Paul Robeson singing Water Boy, and Rudolph Fisher writing about the streets of Harlem, and Jean Toomer holding the heart of Georgia in his hands, and Aaron Douglas drawing strange black fantasies cause the smug Negro middle class to turn from their white, respectable, ordinary books and papers to catch a glimmer of their own beauty. We younger Negro artists who create now intend to express our individual dark-skinned selves without fear or shame. If white people are pleased we are glad. If they are not, it doesn't matter. We know we are beautiful. And ugly too. The tom-tom cries and the tom-tom laughs. If colored people are pleased we are glad. If they are not, their displeasure doesn't matter either. We build our temples for tomorrow, strong as we know how, and we stand on top of the mountain, free within ourselves.

30

WALLACE THURMAN, Editor

Fire!!

Cover Illustration by Aaron Douglas

1926

The journal Fire!!, *edited by the youthful, brilliant, and endlessly frustrated Wallace Thurman, rejected everything conventional in the Harlem Renaissance. By 1926, Thurman and a circle of associated young artists—including Richard Bruce Nugent, Zora Neale Hurston, Gwendolyn Bennett, and Langston Hughes—became convinced that civil rights journals such as* The Crisis *and* Opportunity *had forced black art down*

Aaron Douglas, cover art, *Fire!!*, 1 (November 1926). Wallace Thurman, "Cordelia the Crude," *Fire!!*, 1 (November 1926): 5.

Special Collections, University of Virginia Library.

a narrow path calculated to make political progress and gain mainstream white acceptance, but unsuited to the requirements of open and free artistic development. Some black leaders, such as W. E. B. Du Bois, the editor of The Crisis, *wanted to de-emphasize the depiction of black lower-class urban life, especially when it involved pimps, prostitutes, gamblers, and other unsavory figures. Yet these subjects attracted Thurman and his circle, in part because they implicitly resisted models of conventional decency and order that mainstream society praised. Reflecting the radical artistic tone of* Fire!!, *Aaron Douglass's artwork on the cover of the volume puts forth Africa as a symbol of rebellious inspiration in defiance of both the American mainstream and the "best foot forward" school of Du Bois. Viewed one way, Douglass's drawing depicts a sphinx, but a slight shift in perspective reveals the outlines of a regal African profile. Wallace Thurman's "Cordelia the Crude" reflects another dimension of the culturally rebellious energy of* Fire!! *through the frank depiction of a young Harlem prostitute. Do you find Thurman's portrait of the young prostitute convincing or exaggerated? Why?*

WALLACE THURMAN

Cordelia the Crude

Physically, if not mentally, Cordelia was a potential prostitute, meaning that although she had not yet realized the moral import of her wanton promiscuity nor become mercenary, she had, nevertheless, become quite blasé and bountiful in the matter of bestowing sexual favors upon persuasive and likely young men. Yet, despite her seeming lack of discrimination, Cordelia was quite particular about the type of male to whom she submitted, for numbers do not necessarily denote a lack of taste, and Cordelia had discovered after several months of active observation that one could find the qualities one admires or reacts positively to in a varied hodge-podge of outwardly different individuals.

The scene of Cordelia's activities was The Roosevelt Motion Picture Theatre on Seventh Avenue near 145th Street. Thrice weekly the program changed, and thrice weekly Cordelia would plunk down the necessary twenty-five cents evening admission fee, and saunter gaily into the foul-smelling depths of her favorite cinema shrine. The Roosevelt Theatre presented all of the latest pictures, also, twice weekly, treated its audiences to a vaudeville bill, then too, one could always have the most delightful physical contacts . . . hmm. . . .

Cordelia had not consciously chosen this locale nor had there been any conscious effort upon her part to take advantage of the extra opportunities afforded for physical pleasure. It had just happened that the Roosevelt Theatre was more close to her home than any other neighborhood picture palace, and it had also just happened that Cordelia had become almost immediately initiated into the ways of a Harlem theatre chippie soon after her discovery of the theatre itself.

It is the custom of certain men and boys who frequent these places to idle up and down the aisle until some female is seen sitting alone, to slouch down into a seat beside her, to touch her foot or else press her leg in such a way that it can be construed as accidental if necessary, and then, if the female is wise or else shows signs of willingness to become wise, to make more obvious approaches until, if successful, the approached female will soon be chatting with her baiter about the picture being shown, lolling in his arms, and helping to formulate plans for an after-theatre rendezvous. Cordelia had, you see, shown a willingness to become wise upon her second visit to The Roosevelt. In a short while she had even learned how to squelch the bloated, lewd faced Jews and eager middle aged Negroes who might approach as well as how to inveigle the likeable little yellow or brown half men, embryo avenue sweetbacks, with their well modeled heads, stickily plastered hair, flaming cravats, silken or broadcloth shirts, dirty underwear, low cut vests, form fitting coats, bell-bottom trousers and shiny shoes with metal cornered heels clicking with a brave, brazen rhythm upon the bare concrete floor as their owners angled and searched for prey.

Cordelia, sixteen years old, matronly mature, was an undisciplined, half literate product of rustic South Carolina, and had come to Harlem very much against her will with her parents and her six brothers and sisters. Against her will because she had not been at all anxious to leave the lackadaisical life of the little corn pone settlement where she had been born, to go trooping into the unknown vastness of New York, for she had been in love, passionately in love with one John Stokes who raised pigs, and who, like his father before him, found the raising of pigs so profitable that he could not even consider leaving Lintonville. Cordelia had blankly informed her parents that she would not go with them when they decided to be lured to New York by an older son who had remained there after the demobilization of the war time troops. She had even threatened to run away with John until they should be gone, but of course John could not leave his pigs, and John's mother was not very keen on having Cordelia for a daughter-in-law—those Joneses have bad mixed blood in 'em—so Cordelia had had to join the Gotham bound caravan and leave her lover to his succulent porkers.

However, the mere moving to Harlem had not doused the rebellious flame. Upon arriving Cordelia had not only refused to go to school and refused to hold even the most easily held job, but had also victoriously defied her harassed parents so frequently when it came to matters of discipline that she soon found herself with a mesmerizing lack of home restraint, for the stress of trying to maintain themselves and their family in the new environment was far too much of a task for Mr. and Mrs. Jones to attend to facilely and at the same time try to control a recalcitrant child. So, when Cordelia had refused either to work or to attend school, Mrs. Jones herself had gone out for day's work, leaving Cordelia at home to take care of their five room railroad flat, the front room of which was rented out to a couple "living together," and to see that the younger children, all of whom were of school age, made their four trips daily between home and the nearby public school—as well as see that they had their greasy, if slim, food rations and an occasional change of clothing. Thus Cordelia's days were full—and so were her nights. The only difference being that the days belonged to the folks at home while the nights (since the folks were too tired or too sleepy to know or care when she came in or went out) belonged to her and to—well—whosoever will, let them come.

Cordelia had been playing this hectic, entrancing game for six months and was widely known among a certain group of young men and girls on the avenue as a fus' class chippie when she and I happened to enter the theatre simultaneously. She had clumped down the aisle before me, her open galoshes swishing noisily, her two arms busy wriggling themselves free from the torn sleeve lining of a shoddy imitation fur coat that one of her mother's wash clients had sent to her. She was of medium height and build, with overly developed legs and bust, and had a clear, keen light brown complexion. Her too slick, too naturally bobbed hair, mussed by the removing of a tight, black turban was of an undecided nature, i.e., it was undecided whether to be kinky or to be kind, and her body, as she sauntered along in the partial light had such a conscious sway of invitation that unthinkingly I followed, slid into the same row of seats and sat down beside her.

Naturally she had noticed my pursuit, and thinking that I was eager to play the game, let me know immediately that she was wise, and not the least bit averse to spooning with me during the evening's performance. Interested, and, I might as well confess, intrigued physically, I too became wise, and played up to her with all the fervor, or so I thought, of an old timer, but Cordelia soon remarked that I was different from mos' of des' sheiks, and when pressed for an explanation brazenly told me in a slightly scandalized and patronizing tone that I had not even felt her legs. . . !

At one o'clock in the morning we strolled through the snowy bleakness of one hundred and forty-fourth street between Lenox and Fifth Avenues to the walk-up tenement flat in which she lived, and after stamping the snow from our feet, pushed through the double outside doors, and followed the dismal hallway to the rear of the building where we began the tedious climbing of the crooked, creaking, inconveniently narrow stairway. Cordelia had informed me earlier in the evening that she lived on the top floor—four flights up east side rear—and on our way we rested at each floor and at each half way landing, rested long enough to mingle the snowy dampness of our respective coats, and to hug clumsily while our lips met in an animal kiss.

Finally only another half flight remained, and instead of proceeding as was usual after our amourous demonstration I abruptly drew away from her, opened my overcoat, plunged my hand into my pants pocket, and drew out two crumpled one dollar bills which I handed to her, and then, while she stared at me foolishly, I muttered good-night, confusedly pecked her on her cold brown cheek, and darted down into the creaking darkness.

Six months later I was taking two friends of mine, lately from the provinces, to a Saturday night house-rent party in a well known whore house on one hundred and thirty-fourth street near Lenox Avenue. The place as we entered seemed to be a chaotic riot of raucous noise and clashing color all rhythmically merging in the red, smoke filled room. And there I saw Cordelia savagely careening in a drunken abortion of the Charleston and surrounded by a perspiring circle of hand-clapping enthusiasts. Finally fatigued, she whirled into an abrupt finish, and stopped so that she stared discreetly into my face, but, being dizzy from the calisthenic turns and the cauterizing liquor she doubted that her eyes recognized someone out of the past, and, visibly trying to sober herself, languidly began to dance a slow drag with a lean hipped pimply faced yellow man who had walked between her and me. At last he released her, and seeing that she was about to leave the room I rushed forward calling Cordelia?—as if I was not yet sure who it was. Stopping in the doorway, she turned to see who had called, and finally recognizing me said simply, without the least trace of emotion—'Lo kid. . . .

And without another word turned her back and walked into the hall to where she joined four girls standing there. Still eager to speak, I followed and heard one of the girls ask: Who's the dicty kid? . . .

And Cordelia answered: The guy who gimme ma' firs' two bucks. . . .

31

W. E. B. DU BOIS

Criteria of Negro Art

1926

As part of his attempt in the mid-1920s to guide the Harlem Renaissance toward a more explicit concern with civil rights and with black control of artistic institutions, W. E. B. Du Bois published "Criteria of Negro Art," his address to the 1926 NAACP convention, in The Crisis. *His argument set into motion a wide debate on the issue of art versus propaganda in intellectual journals and throughout the black press. In 1928, Du Bois published the novel* Dark Princess*—where the darker races unite under an Indian princess to fight against European domination—to exemplify what he meant by politically effective black art. Do you agree with Du Bois that black art has an important role to play in race politics? Do you think that it should explicitly promote civil rights? What do you think of black art that refuses this role?*

I do not doubt but there are some in this audience who are a little disturbed at the subject of this meeting, and particularly at the subject I have chosen. Such people are thinking something like this: "How is it that an organization like this, a group of radicals trying to bring new things into the world, a fighting organization which has come up out of the blood and dust of battle, struggling for the right of black men to be ordinary human beings—how is it that an organization of this kind can turn aside to talk about Art? After all, what have we who are slaves and black to do with Art?"

W. E. B. Du Bois, "Criteria of Negro Art," *The Crisis*, 32 (October 1926): 290–97.

Or perhaps there are others who feel a certain relief and are saying, "After all it is rather satisfactory after all this talk about rights and fighting to sit and dream of something which leaves a nice taste in the mouth."

Let me tell you that neither of these groups is right. The thing we are talking about tonight is part of the great fight we are carrying on and it represents a forward and an upward look—a pushing onward. You and I have been breasting hills; we have been climbing upward; there has been progress and we can see it day by day looking back along blood-filled paths. But as you go through the valleys and over the foothills, so long as you are climbing, the direction,—north, south, east or west,—is of less importânce. But when gradually the vista widens and you begin to see the world at your feet and the far horizon, then it is time to know more precisely whither you are going and what you really want.

What do we want? What is the thing we are after? As it was phrased last night it had a certain truth: We want to be Americans, full-fledged Americans, with all the rights of other American citizens. But is that all? Do we want simply to be Americans? Once in a while through all of us there flashes some clairvoyance, some clear idea, of what America really is. We who are dark can see America in a way that white Americans can not. And seeing our country thus, are we satisfied with its present goals and ideals?

In the high school where I studied we learned most of Scott's "Lady of the Lake"[1] by heart. In after life once it was my privilege to see the lake. It was Sunday. It was quiet. You could glimpse the deer wandering in unbroken forests; you could hear the soft ripple of romance on the waters. Around me fell the cadence of that poetry of my youth. I fell asleep full of the enchantment of the Scottish border. A new day broke and with it came a sudden rush of excursionists. They were mostly Americans and they were loud and strident. They poured upon the little pleasure boat,—men with their hats a little on one side and drooping cigars in the wet corners of their mouths; women who shared their conversation with the world. They all tried to get everywhere first. They pushed other people out of the way. They made all sorts of incoherent noises and gestures so that the quiet home folk and the visitors from other lands silently and half-wonderingly gave way before them. They struck a note not evil but wrong. They carried,

[1]A poem published in 1810 by the Scottish poet Sir Walter Scott (1871–1932).

perhaps, a sense of strength and accomplishment, but their hearts had no conception of the beauty which pervaded this holy place.

If you tonight suddenly should become full-fledged Americans; if your color faded, or the color line here in Chicago was miraculously forgotten; suppose, too, you became at the same time rich and powerful;—what is it that you would want? What would you immediately seek? Would you buy the most powerful of motor cars and outrace Cook County? Would you buy the most elaborate estate on the North Shore? Would you be a Rotarian or a Lion or a What-not of the very last degree? Would you wear the most striking clothes, give the richest dinners and buy the longest press notices?

Even as you visualize such ideals you know in your hearts that these are not the things you really want. You realize this sooner than the average white American because, pushed aside as we have been in America, there has come to us not only a certain distaste for the tawdry and flamboyant but a vision of what the world could be if it were really a beautiful world; if we had the true spirit; if we had the Seeing Eye, the Cunning Hand, the Feeling Heart; if we had, to be sure, not perfect happiness, but plenty of good hard work, the inevitable suffering that always comes with life; sacrifice and waiting, all that—but, nevertheless, lived in a world where men know, where men create, where they realize themselves and where they enjoy life. It is that sort of a world we want to create for ourselves and for all America.

After all, who shall describe Beauty? What is it? I remember tonight four beautiful things: The Cathedral at Cologne, a forest in stone, set in light and changing shadow, echoing with sunlight and solemn song; a village of the Veys in West Africa, a little thing of mauve and purple, quiet, lying content and shining in the sun; a black and velvet room where on a throne rests, in old and yellowing marble, the broken curves of the Venus of Milo; a single phrase of music in the Southern South—utter melody, haunting and appealing, suddenly arising out of night and eternity, beneath the moon.

Such is Beauty. Its variety is infinite, its possibility is endless. In normal life all may have it and have it yet again. The world is full of it; and yet today the mass of human beings are choked away from it, and their lives distorted and made ugly. This is not only wrong, it is silly. Who shall right this well-nigh universal failing? Who shall let this world be beautiful? Who shall restore to men the glory of sunsets and the peace of quiet sleep?

We black folk may help for we have within us as a race new stirrings; stirrings of the beginning of a new appreciation of joy, of a new desire to create, of a new will to be; as though in this morning of group life we had awakened from some sleep that at once dimly mourns the past and dreams a splendid future; and there has come the conviction that the Youth that is here today, the Negro Youth, is a different kind of Youth, because in some new way it bears this mighty prophecy on its breast, with a new realization of itself, with new determination for all mankind.

What has this Beauty to do with the world? What has Beauty to do with Truth and Goodness—with the facts of the world and the right actions of men? "Nothing," the artists rush to answer. They may be right. I am but an humble disciple of art and cannot presume to say. I am one who tells the truth and exposes evil and seeks with Beauty and for Beauty to set the world right. That somehow, somewhere eternal and perfect Beauty sits above Truth and Right I can conceive, but here and now and in the world in which I work they are for me unseparated and inseparable.

This is brought to us peculiarly when as artists we face our own past as a people. There has come to us—and it has come especially through the man we are going to honor tonight[2]—a realization of that past, of which for long years we have been ashamed, for which we have apologized. We thought nothing could come out of that past which we wanted to remember; which we wanted to hand down to our children. Suddenly, this same past is taking on form, color and reality, and in a half shamefaced way we are beginning to be proud of it. We are remembering that the romance of the world did not die and lie forgotten in the Middle Age; that if you want romance to deal with you must have it here and now and in your own hands.

I once knew a man and woman. They had two children, a daughter who was white and a daughter who was brown; the daughter who was white married a white man; and when her wedding was preparing the daughter who was brown prepared to go and celebrate. But the mother said, "No!" and the brown daughter went into her room and turned on the gas and died. Do you want Greek tragedy swifter than that?

Or again, here is a little southern town and you are in the public square. On one side of the square is the office of a colored lawyer and

[2]Carter G. Woodson (1875–1950), early pioneer of black history known as "The Father of Negro History." Woodson founded the Association for Negro Life and History.

on all the other sides are men who do not like colored lawyers. A white woman goes into the black man's office and points to the white-filled square and says, "I want five hundred dollars now and if I do not get it I am going to scream."

Have you heard the story of the conquest of German East Africa? Listen to the untold tale: There were 40,000 black men and 4,000 white men who talked German. There were 20,000 black men and 12,000 white men who talked English. There were 10,000 black men and 400 white men who talked French. In Africa then where the Mountains of the Moon raised their white and snow-capped heads into the mouth of the tropic sun, where Nile and Congo rise and the Great Lakes swim, these men fought; they struggled on mountain, hill and valley, in river, lake and swamp, until in masses they sickened, crawled and died; until the 4,000 white Germans had become mostly bleached bones; until nearly all the 12,000 white Englishmen had returned to South Africa, and the 400 Frenchmen to Belgium and Heaven; all except a mere handful of the white men died; but thousands of black men from East, West and South Africa, from Nigeria and the Valley of the Nile, and from the West Indies still struggled, fought and died. For four years they fought and won and lost German East Africa; and all you hear about it is that England and Belgium conquered German Africa for the allies!

Such is the true and stirring stuff of which Romance is born and from this stuff come the stirrings of men who are beginning to remember that this kind of material is theirs; and this vital life of their own kind is beckoning them on.

The question comes next as to the interpretation of these new stirrings, of this new spirit: Of what is the colored artist capable? We have had on the part of both colored and white people singular unanimity of judgment in the past. Colored people have said: "This work must be inferior because it comes from colored people." White people have said: "It is inferior because it is done by colored people." But today there is coming to both the realization that the work of the black man is not always inferior. Interesting stories come to us. A professor in the University of Chicago read to a class that had studied literature a passage of poetry and asked them to guess the author. They guessed a goodly company from Shelley and Robert Browning down to Tennyson and Masefield.[3] The author was Countee Cullen. Or again the

[3]Percy Bysshe Shelley (1792–1822), Robert Browning (1812–1889), Alfred, Lord Tennyson (1809–1892), and John Masefield (1878–1967) were all English poets.

English critic John Drinkwater went down to a Southern seminary, one of the sort which "finishes" young white women of the South. The students sat with their wooden faces while he tried to get some response out of them. Finally he said, "Name me some of your Southern poets." They hesitated. He said finally, "I'll start out with your best: Paul Laurence Dunbar"!

With the growing recognition of Negro artists in spite of the severe handicaps, one comforting thing is occurring to both white and black. They are whispering, "Here is a way out. Here is the real solution of the color problem. The recognition accorded Cullen, Hughes, Fauset, White and others shows there is no real color line. Keep quiet! Don't complain! Work! All will be well!"

I will not say that already this chorus amounts to a conspiracy. Perhaps I am naturally too suspicious. But I will say that there are today a surprising number of white people who are getting great satisfaction out of these younger Negro writers because they think it is going to stop agitation of the Negro question. They say, "What is the use of your fighting and complaining; do the great thing and the reward is there." And many colored people are all too eager to follow this advice; especially those who are weary of the eternal struggle along the color line, who are afraid to fight and to whom the money of philanthropists and the alluring publicity are subtle and deadly bribes. They say, "What is the use of fighting? Why not show simply what we deserve and let the reward come to us?"

And it is right here that the National Association for the Advancement of Colored People comes upon the field, comes with its great call to a new battle, a new fight and new things to fight before the old things are wholly won: and to say that the Beauty of Truth and Freedom which shall some day be our heritage and the heritage of all civilized men is not in our hands yet and that we ourselves must not fail to realize.

There is in New York tonight a black woman molding clay by herself in a little bare room, because there is not a single school of sculpture in New York where she is welcome. Surely there are doors she might burst through, but when God makes a sculptor He does not always make the pushing sort of person who beats his way through doors thrust in his face. This girl is working her hands off to get out of this country so that she can get some sort of training.

There was Richard Brown. If he had been white he would have been alive today instead of dead of neglect. Many helped him when he asked but he was not the kind of boy that always asks. He was simply one who made colors sing.

There is a colored woman in Chicago who is a great musician. She thought she would like to study at Fontainebleau this summer where Walter Damrosch[4] and a score of leaders of Art have an American school of music. But the application blank of this school says: "I am a white American and I apply for admission to the school."

We can go on the stage; we can be just as funny as white Americans wish us to be; we can play all the sordid parts that America likes to assign to Negroes; but for anything else there is still small place for us.

And so I might go on. But let me sum up with this: Suppose the only Negro who survived some centuries hence was the Negro painted by white Americans in the novels and essays they have written. What would people in a hundred years say of black Americans? Now turn it around. Suppose you were to write a story and put in it the kind of people you know and like and imagine. You might get it published and you might not. And the "might not" is still far bigger than the "might." The white publishers catering to white folk would say, "It is not interesting"—to white folk, naturally not. They want Uncle Toms, Topsies, good "darkies" and clowns. I have in my office a story with all the earmarks of truth. A young man says that he started out to write and had his stories accepted. Then he began to write about the things he knew best about, that is, about his own people. He submitted a story to a magazine which said, "We are sorry, but we cannot take it." "I sat down and revised my story, changing the color of the characters and the locale and sent it under an assumed name with a change of address and it was accepted by the same magazine that had refused it, the editor promising to take anything else I might send in providing it was good enough."

We have, to, be sure, a few recognized and successful Negro artists; but they are not all those fit to survive or even a good minority. They are but the remnants of that ability and genius among us whom the accidents of education and opportunity have raised on the tidal waves of chance. We black folk are not altogether peculiar in this. After all, in the world at large, it is only the accident, the remnant, that gets the chance to make the most of itself; but if this is true of the white world it is infinitely more true of the colored world. It is not simply the great clear tenor of Roland Hayes[5] that opened the ears of America. We

[4]Walter Damrosch (1862–1950), conductor, popularizer of classical music, and a pioneer in the performance of music on the radio.

[5]Roland Hayes (1887–1977), African American singer of international fame. In 1925 Hayes was depicted on the cover of the Harlem issue of *The Survey Graphic* (see Document 11).

have had many voices of all kinds as fine as his and America was and is as deaf as she was for years to him. Then a foreign land heard Hayes and put its imprint on him and immediately America with all its imitative snobbery woke up. We approved Hayes because London, Paris and Berlin approved him and not simply because he was a great singer.

Thus it is the bounden duty of black America to begin this great work of the creation of Beauty, of the preservation of Beauty, of the realization of Beauty, and we must use in this work all the methods that men have used before. And what have been the tools of the artist in times gone by? First of all, he has used the Truth—not for the sake of truth, not as a scientist seeking truth, but as one upon whom Truth eternally thrusts itself as the highest handmaid of imagination, as the one great vehicle of universal understanding. Again artists have used Goodness—goodness in all its aspects of justice, honor and right—not for sake of an ethical sanction but as the one true method of gaining sympathy and human interest.

The apostle of Beauty thus becomes the apostle of Truth and Right not by choice but by inner and outer compulsion. Free he is but his freedom is ever bounded by Truth and Justice; and slavery only dogs him when he is denied the right to tell the Truth or recognize an ideal of Justice.

Thus all Art is propaganda and ever must be, despite the wailing of the purists. I stand in utter shamelessness and say that whatever art I have for writing has been used always for propaganda for gaining the right of black folk to love and enjoy. I do not care a damn for any art that is not used for propaganda. But I do care when propaganda is confined to one side while the other is stripped and silent.

In New York we have two plays: "White Cargo" and "Congo." In "White Cargo" there is a fallen woman. She is black. In "Congo" the fallen woman is white. In "White Cargo" the black woman goes down further and further and in "Congo" the white woman begins with degradation but in the end is one of the angels of the Lord.

You know the current magazine story: A young white man goes down to Central America and the most beautiful colored woman there falls in love with him. She crawls across the whole isthmus to get to him. The white man says nobly, "No." He goes back to his white sweetheart in New York.

In such cases, it is not the positive propaganda of people who believe white blood divine, infallible and holy to which I object. It is the denial of a similar right of propaganda to those who believe black blood human, lovable and inspired with new ideals for the world.

White artists themselves suffer from this narrowing of their field. They cry for freedom in dealing with Negroes because they have so little freedom in dealing with whites. DuBose Heywood [*sic*] writes "Porgy"[6] and writes beautifully of the black Charleston underworld. But why does he do this? Because he cannot do a similar thing for the white people of Charleston, or they would drum him out of town. The only chance he had to tell the truth of pitiful human degradation was to tell it of colored people. I should not be surprised if Octavius Roy Cohen had approached the *Saturday Evening Post* and asked permission to write about a different kind of colored folk than the monstrosities he has created; but if he has, the *Post* has replied, "No. You are getting paid to write about the kind of colored people you are writing about."

In other words, the white public today demands from its artists, literary and pictorial, racial pre-judgment which deliberately distorts Truth and Justice, as far as colored races are concerned, and it will pay for no other.

On the other hand, the young and slowly growing black public still wants its prophets almost equally unfree. We are bound by all sorts of customs that have come down as second-hand soul clothes of white patrons. We are ashamed of sex and we lower our eyes when people will talk of it. Our religion holds us in superstition. Our worst side has been so shamelessly emphasized that we are denying we have or ever had a worst side. In all sorts of ways we are hemmed in and our new young artists have got to fight their way to freedom.

The ultimate judge has got to be you and you have got to build yourselves up into that wide judgment, that catholicity of temper which is going to enable the artist to have his widest chance for freedom. We can afford the Truth. White folk today cannot. As it is now we are handing everything over to a white jury. If a colored man wants to publish a book, he has got to get a white publisher and a white newspaper to say it is great: and then you and I say so. We must come to the place where the work of art when it appears is reviewed and acclaimed by our own free and unfettered judgment. And we are going to have a real and valuable and eternal judgment only as we make ourselves free of mind, proud of body and just of soul to all men.

[6]DuBose Heyward (1885–1940), white author of *Porgy* (New York: George H. Doran Co., 1925).

And then do you know what will be said? It is already saying. Just as soon as true Art emerges; just as soon as the black artist appears, someone touches the race on the shoulder and says "He did that because he was an American, not because he was a Negro; he was born here; he was trained here; he is not a Negro—what is a Negro anyhow? He is just human; it is the kind of thing you ought to expect."

I do not doubt that the ultimate art coming from black folk is going to be just as beautiful, and beautiful largely in the same ways, as the art that comes from white folk, or yellow, or red; but the point today is that until the art of the black folk compells recognition they will not be rated as human. And when through art they compell recognition then let the world discover if it will that their art is as new as it is old and as old as new.

I had a classmate once who did three beautiful things and died. One of them was a story of a folk who found fire and then went wandering in the gloom of night seeking again the stars they had once known and lost; suddenly out of blackness they looked up and there loomed the heavens; and what was it that they said? They raised a mighty cry: "It is the stars, it is the ancient stars, it is the young and everlasting stars!"

32

ALAIN LOCKE

Art or Propaganda

1928

In response to Du Bois's "Criteria of Negro Art" (see Document 31) and to the other advocates of his position, Alain Locke published his case against propaganda in the first and only issue of Harlem, *Wallace Thurman's vain hope for a successful follow-up to* Fire!! *(see Document 30). Although he makes a strong case for art, Locke does attempt to balance his position with ideas from the opposition. How does this help his argument?*

Alain Locke, "Art or Propaganda," *Harlem: A Forum of Negro Life*, 1 (November 1928): 12–13.

Artistically it is the one fundamental question for us today—Art or Propaganda. Which? Is this more the generation of the prophet or that of the poet; shall our intellectual and cultural leadership preach and exhort or sing? I believe we are at that interesting moment when the prophet becomes the poet and when prophecy becomes the expressive song, the chant of fulfillment. We have had too many Jeremiahs, major and minor;—and too much of the drab wilderness. My chief objection to propaganda, apart from its besetting sin of monotony and disproportion, is that it perpetuates the position of group inferiority even in crying out against it. For it leaves and speaks under the shadow of dominant majority whom it harangues, cajoles, threatens or supplicates. It is too extroverted for balance or poise or inner dignity and self-respect. Art in the best sense is rooted in self-expression and whether naive or sophisticated is self-contained. In our spiritual growth genius and talent must more and more choose the role of group expression, or even at times the role of free individualistic expression,—in a word must choose art and put aside propaganda.

The literature and art of the younger generation already reflects this shift of psychology, this regeneration of spirit. David should be its patron saint; it should confront the Phillistines with its five smooth pebbles fearlessly.[1] There is more strength in a confident camp than in a threatened enemy. The sense of inferiority must be innerly compensated, self-conviction must supplant self-justification and in the dignity of this attitude a convinced minority must confront a condescending majority. Art cannot completely accomplish this, but I believe it can lead the way.

Our espousal of art thus becomes no mere idle acceptance of "art for art's sake," or cultivation of the last decadences of the over-civilized, but rather a deep realization of the fundamental purpose of art and of its function as a tap root of vigorous, flourishing living. Not all of our younger writers are deep enough in the sub-soil of their native materials,—too many are pot-plants seeking a forced growth according to the exotic tastes of a pampered and decadent public. It is the art of the people that needs to be cultivated, not the art of the coteries. Propaganda itself is preferable to shallow, truckling imitation.

[1]Refers to the biblical story (I Samuel 17) in which David, the eventual king of Israel, slays the Philistine giant, Goliath, with a single throw from his slingshot. The passage also plays on another meaning of "Philistine," indifferent or hostile to artistic values.

Negro things may reasonably be a fad for others; for us they must be a religion. Beauty, however, is its best priest and psalms will be more effective than sermons.

To date we have had little sustained art unsubsidized by propaganda; we must admit this debt to these foster agencies. The three journals[2] which have been vehicles of most of our artistic expressions have been the avowed organs of social movements and organized social programs. All our purely artistic publications have been sporadic. There is all the greater need then for a sustained vehicle of free and purely artistic expression. If *Harlem* should happily fill this need, it will perform an honorable and constructive service. I hope it may, but should it not, the need remains and the path toward it will at least be advanced a little.

We need, I suppose in addition to art some substitute for propaganda. What shall that be? Surely we must take some cognizance of the fact that we live at the centre of a social problem. Propaganda at least nurtured some form of serious social discussion, and social discussion was necessary, is still necessary. On this side: the difficulty and shortcoming of propaganda is its partisanship. It is one-sided and often pre-judging. Should we not then have a journal of free discussion, open to all sides of the problem and to all camps of belief? Difficult, that,—but intriguing. Even if it has to begin on the note of dissent and criticism and assume Menckenian[3] scepticism to escape the commonplaces of conformity. Yet, I hope we shall not remain at this negative pole. Can we not cultivate truly free and tolerant discussion, almost Socratically minded for the sake of truth? After Beauty, let Truth come into the Renaissance picture,—a later cue, but a welcome one. This may be premature, but one hopes not,—for eventually it must come and if we can accomplish that, instead of having to hang our prophets, we can silence them or change their lamentations to song with a Great Fulfillment.

[2]*The Crisis*, *Opportunity*, and *The Messenger*.

[3]Refers to H. L. Mencken (1880–1956), satirist, cultural critic, and editor of the intellectual journal *The American Mercury*.

33

RICHARD WRIGHT

Blueprint for Negro Writing

March 1937

Published in the second and last issue of New Challenge, *Richard Wright's "Blueprint for Negro Writing" is one of the great manifestos in the history of black literature. Originally from Mississippi, Richard Wright moved to Chicago in 1927, where he became affiliated with the Communist Party. Moving to New York in 1937, he became the Harlem editor of the communist journal* The Daily Worker *and published two books that changed the course of black American literature—the short-story collection* Uncle Tom's Children *(1938) and* Native Son *(1940)—which many critics regard as signaling the end of the Harlem Renaissance and the beginning of a new era of tough urban realism. In his attempt to guide black literature toward a more explicitly political purpose in "Blueprint for Negro Writing," Wright follows Du Bois and other cultural critics of the Harlem Renaissance in insisting that black literature ought to play a more explicit role in promoting black emancipation.*

---

1. The Role of Negro Writing: Two Definitions

Generally speaking, Negro writing in the past has been confined to humble novels, poems, and plays, prim and decorous ambassadors who went a-begging to white America. They entered the Court of American Public Opinion dressed in the knee-pants of servility, curtsying to show that the Negro was not inferior, that he was human, and that he had a life comparable to that of other people. For the most part these artistic ambassadors were received as though they were French poodles who do clever tricks.

White America never offered these Negro writers any serious criticism. The mere fact that a Negro could write was astonishing. Nor was there any deep concern on the part of white America with the role

---

Richard Wright, "Blueprint for Negro Writing," *New Challenge*, 2 (March 1937): 53–65.

Negro writing should play in American culture; and the role it did play grew out of accident rather than intent or design. Either it crept in through the kitchen in the form of jokes; or it was the fruits of that foul soil which was the result of a liaison between inferiority-complexed Negro "geniuses" and burnt-out white Bohemians with money.

On the other hand, these often technically brilliant performances by Negro writers were looked upon by the majority of literate Negroes as something to be proud of. At best, Negro writing has been something external to the lives of educated Negroes themselves. That the productions of their writers should have been something of a guide in their daily living is a matter which seems never to have been raised seriously.

Under these conditions Negro writing assumed two general aspects: 1) It became a sort of conspicuous ornamentation, the hallmark of "achievement." 2) It became the voice of the educated Negro pleading with white America for justice.

Rarely was the best of this writing addressed to the Negro himself, his needs, his sufferings, his aspirations. Through misdirection, Negro writers have been far better to others than they have been to themselves. And the mere recognition of this places the whole question of Negro writing in a new light and raises a doubt as to the validity of its present direction.

2. The Minority Outlook

Somewhere in his writings Lenin[1] makes the observation that oppressed minorities often reflect the techniques of the bourgeoisie more brilliantly than some sections of the bourgeoisie themselves. The psychological importance of this becomes meaningful when it is recalled that oppressed minorities, and especially the petty bourgeois sections of oppressed minorities, strive to assimilate the virtues of the bourgeoisie in the assumption that by doing so they can lift themselves into a higher social sphere. But not only among the oppressed petty bourgeoisie does this occur. The workers of a minority people, chafing under exploitation, forge organizational forms of struggle to better their lot. Lacking the handicaps of false ambition and property, they have access to a wide social vision and a deep social consciousness. They display a greater freedom and initiative in pushing their

[1]Vladimir Ilyich Lenin (1870–1924), Communist and leader of the Russian Revolution.

claims upon civilization than even do the petty bourgeoisie. Their organizations show greater strength, adaptability, and efficiency than any other group or class in society.

That Negro workers, propelled by the harsh conditions of their lives, have demonstrated this consciousness and mobility for economic and political action there can be no doubt. But has this consciousness been reflected in the work of Negro writers to the same degree as it has in the Negro workers' struggle to free Herndon[2] and the Scottsboro Boys,[3] in the drive toward unionism, in the fight against lynching? Have they as creative writers taken advantage of their unique minority position?

The answer decidedly is *no*. Negro writers have lagged sadly, and as time passes the gap widens between them and their people.

How can this hiatus be bridged? How can the enervating effects of this long standing split be eliminated?

In presenting questions of this sort an attitude of self-consciousness and self-criticism is far more likely to be a fruitful point of departure than a mere recounting of past achievements. An emphasis upon tendency and experiment, a view of society as something becoming rather than as something fixed and admired is the one which points the way for Negro writers to stand shoulder to shoulder with Negro workers in mood and outlook.

3. A Whole Culture

There is, however, a culture of the Negro which is his and has been addressed to him; a culture which has, for good or ill, helped to clarify his consciousness and create emotional attitudes which are conducive to action. This culture has stemmed mainly from two sources: 1) the Negro church; 2) and the folklore of the Negro people.

It was through the portals of the church that the American Negro first entered the shrine of western culture. Living under slave condi-

[2]Angelo Herndon (1913–), a black Communist activist sentenced in 1933 to twenty years in prison for leading an antidiscrimination march in Georgia and thus violating a one-hundred-year-old slave law against inciting insurrection. The Supreme Court released him on appeal in 1937.

[3]The Scottsboro boys, nine African American teenagers accused in 1931 of raping two white women on a train near Scottsboro, Alabama. The Communist Party won a contentious public battle with the NAACP to represent them in court, but by the late 1930s, the NAACP had taken over the lengthy litigation that prevented the boys from facing execution and eventually resulted in their release.

tions of life, bereft of his African heritage, the Negroes' struggle for religion on the plantations between 1820–60 assumed the form of a struggle for human rights. It remained a relatively revolutionary struggle until religion began to serve as an antidote for suffering and denial. But even today there are millions of American Negroes whose only sense of a whole universe, whose only relation to society and man, and whose only guide to personal dignity comes through the archaic morphology of Christian salvation.

It was, however, in a folklore moulded out of rigorous and inhuman conditions of life that the Negro achieved his most indigenous and complete expression. Blues, spirituals, and folk tales recounted from mouth to mouth; the whispered words of a black mother to her black daughter on the ways of men; the confidential wisdom of a black father to his black son; the swapping of sex experiences on street corners from boy to boy in the deepest vernacular; work songs sung under blazing suns—all these formed the channels through which the racial wisdom flowed.

One would have thought that Negro writers in the last century of striving at expression would have continued and deepened this folk tradition, would have tried to create a more intimate and yet a more profoundly social system of artistic communication between them and their people. But the illusion that they could escape through individual achievement the harsh lot of their race swung Negro writers away from any such path. Two separate cultures sprang up: one for the Negro masses, unwritten and unrecognized; and the other for the sons and daughters of a rising Negro bourgeoisie, parasitic and mannered.

Today the question is: Shall Negro writing be for the Negro masses, moulding the lives and consciousness of those masses toward new goals, or shall it continue begging the question of the Negroes' humanity? . . .

6. Social Consciousness and Responsibility

The Negro writer who seeks to function within his race as a purposeful agent has a serious responsibility. In order to do justice to his subject matter, in order to depict Negro life in all of its manifold and intricate relationships, a deep, informed, and complex consciousness is necessary; a consciousness which draws for its strength upon the fluid lore of a great people, and moulds this lore with the concepts that move and direct the forces of history today.

With the gradual decline of the moral authority of the Negro church, and with the increasing irresolution which is paralyzing Negro middle class leadership, a new role is devolving upon the Negro writer. He is being called upon to do no less than create values by which his race is to struggle, live and die.

By his ability to fuse and make articulate the experiences of men, because his writing possesses the potential cunning to steal into the inmost recesses of the human heart, because he can create the myths and symbols that inspire a faith in life, he may expect either to be consigned to oblivion, or to be recognized for the valued agent he is.

This raises the question of the personality of the writer. It means that in the lives of Negro writers must be found those materials and experiences which will create a meaningful picture of the world today. Many young writers have grown to believe that a Marxist analysis of society[4] presents such a picture. It creates a picture which, when placed before the eyes of the writer, should unify his personality, organize his emotions, buttress him with a tense and obdurate will to change the world.

And, in turn, this changed world will dialectically change the writer. Hence, it is through a Marxist conception of reality and society that the maximum degree of freedom in thought and feeling can be gained for the Negro writer. Further, this dramatic Marxist vision, when consciously grasped, endows the writer with a sense of dignity which no other vision can give. Ultimately, it restores to the writer his lost heritage, that is, his role as a creator of the world in which he lives, and as a creator of himself.

Yet, for the Negro writer, Marxism is but the starting point. No theory of life can take the place of life. After Marxism has laid bare the skeleton of society, there remains the task of the writer to plant flesh upon those bones out of his will to live. He may, with disgust and revulsion, say *no* and depict the horrors of capitalism encroaching upon the human being. Or he may, with hope and passion, say *yes* and depict the faint stirrings of a new and emerging life. But in whatever social voice he chooses to speak, whether positive or negative, there should always be heard or *over*-heard his faith, his necessity, his judgement.

His vision need not be simple or rendered in primer-like terms; for the life of the Negro people is not simple. The presentation of their

[4]Marxist analysis regards economic class as the primary cause of political movements, culture, and other aspects of society.

lives should be simple, yes; but all the complexity, the strangeness, the magic wonder of life that plays like a bright sheen over the most sordid existence, should be there. To borrow a phrase from the Russians, it should have a *complex simplicity*. Eliot, Stein, Joyce, Proust, Hemingway, and Anderson; Gorky, Barbusse, Nexo, and Jack London no less than the folklore of the Negro himself should form the heritage of the Negro writer.[5] Every iota of gain in human thought and sensibility should be ready grist for his mill, no matter how far-fetched they may seem in their immediate implications. . . .

9. Autonomy of Craft

For the Negro writer to depict this new reality requires a greater discipline and consciousness than was necessary for the so-called Harlem school of expression. Not only is the subject matter dealt with far more meaningful and complex, but the new role of the writer is qualitatively different. The Negro writers' new position demands a sharper definition of the status of his craft, and a sharper emphasis upon its functional autonomy.

Negro writers should seek through the medium of their craft to play as meaningful a role in the affairs of men as do other professionals. But if their writing is demanded to perform the social office of other professions, then the autonomy of craft is lost and writing detrimentally fused with other interests. The limitations of the craft constitute some of its greatest virtues. If the sensory vehicle of imaginative writing is required to carry too great a load of didactic material, the artistic sense is submerged.

The relationship between reality and the artistic image is not always direct and simple. The imaginative conception of a historical period will not be a carbon copy of reality. Image and emotion possess a logic of their own. A vulgarized simplicity constitutes the greatest danger in tracing the reciprocal interplay between the writer and his environment.

Writing has its professional autonomy; it should complement other professions, but it should not supplant them or be swamped by them.

[5]T. S. Eliot (1888–1965), American-born British poet and critic; Gertrude Stein (1874–1946), American writer; James Joyce (1882–1941), Irish novelist; Marcel Proust (1871–1922), French novelist; Ernest Hemingway (1899–1961), American novelist; Sherwood Anderson (1876–1941), American writer; Maxim Gorky (1868–1936), Russian novelist and political activist; Henri Barbusse (1873–1935), French novelist; Martin Andersen Nexo (1869–1954), Danish novelist; Jack London (1876–1916), American novelist.

34

ZORA NEALE HURSTON

Their Eyes Were Watching God

1937

Widely regarded as the best novel of the Harlem Renaissance, and as Zora Neale Hurston's masterpiece, Their Eyes Were Watching God *may also qualify as the last product of the period. It tells the story of Janie Starks, whose maturation from unself-conscious girlhood to womanly self-possession proceeds through three relationships with progressively younger men: first with a spiritually dead sharecropper, and then with the domineering mayor of an all-black town, and last with a jobless roustabout who proves to be the love of her life. The first two men die, but she has to shoot the third herself when rabies causes him to threaten her life. The ability to tell her painful story in artful words provides the ultimate sign of Janie's coming of age. In this scene, which opens the novel, Janie returns to her hometown as a complete woman, self-possessed in every respect—body, mind, and soul. Yet she does not fit the town's ideal of female acceptability. What textual evidence can you cite for this? What do the townspeople find objectionable about Janie? What do they find mysterious? Why will Janie relate her tale only to Pheoby, her "kissin' friend"?*

Ships at a distance have every man's wish on board. For some they come in with the tide. For others they sail forever on the horizon, never out of sight, never landing until the Watcher turns his eyes away in resignation, his dreams mocked to death by Time. That is the life of men.

Now, women forget all those things they don't want to remember, and remember everything they don't want to forget. The dream is the truth. Then they act and do things accordingly.

So the beginning of this was a woman and she had come back from burying the dead. Not the dead of sick and ailing with friends at the

---

Zora Neale Hurston, *Their Eyes Were Watching God* (Philadelphia: J. B. Lippincott, 1937), 9–19.

pillow and the feet. She had come back from the sodden and the bloated; the sudden dead, their eyes flung wide open in judgment.

The people all saw her come because it was sundown. The sun was gone, but he had left his footprints in the sky. It was the time for sitting on porches beside the road. It was the time to hear things and talk. These sitters had been tongueless, earless, eyeless conveniences all day long. Mules and other brutes had occupied their skins. But now, the sun and the bossman were gone, so the skins felt powerful and human. They became lords of sounds and lesser things. They passed nations through their mouths. They sat in judgment.

Seeing the woman as she was made them remember the envy they had stored up from other times. So they chewed up the back parts of their minds and swallowed with relish. They made burning statements with questions, and killing tools out of laughs. It was mass cruelty. A mood come alive. Words walking without masters; walking altogether like harmony in a song.

"What she doin' coming back here in dem overhalls? Can't she find no dress to put on?— Where's dat blue satin dress she left here in?— Where all dat money her husband took and died and left her?— What dat ole forty year ole 'oman doin' vid her hair swingin' down her back lak some young gal?— Where she left dat young lad of a boy she went off here wid?— Thought she was going to marry?— Where he left *her*?— What he done wid all her money?— Betcha he off wid some gal so young she ain't even got no hairs—why she don't stay in her class?—"

When she got to where they were she turned her face on the bander log and spoke. They scrambled a noisy "good evenin'" and left their mouths setting open and their ears full of hope. Her speech was pleasant enough, but she kept walking straight on to her gate. The porch couldn't talk for looking.

The men noticed her firm buttocks like she had grape fruits in her hip pockets; the great rope of black hair swinging to her waist and unraveling in the wind like a plume; then her pugnacious breasts trying to bore holes in her shirt. They, the men, were saving with the mind what they lost with the eye. The women took the faded shirt and muddy overalls and laid them away for remembrance. It was a weapon against her strength and if it turned out of no significance, still it was a hope that she might fall to their level some day.

But nobody moved, nobody spoke, nobody even thought to swallow spit until after her gate slammed behind her.

Pearl Stone opened her mouth and laughed real hard because she didn't know what else to do. She fell all over Mrs. Sumpkins while she laughed. Mrs. Sumpkins snorted violently and sucked her teeth.

"Humph! Y'all let her worry yuh. You ain't like me. Ah ain't got her to study 'bout. If she ain't got manners enough to stop and let folks know how she been makin' out, let her g'wan!"

"She ain't even worth talkin' after," Lulu Moss drawled through her nose. "She sits high, but she looks low. Dat's wat Ah say 'bout dese ole women runnin' after young boys."

Pheoby Watson hitched her rocking chair forward before she spoke. "Well, nobody don't know if it's anything to tell or not. Me, Ah'm her best friend, and *Ah* don't know."

"Maybe us don't know into things lak you do, but we all know how she went 'way from here and us sho seen her come back. 'Tain't no use in your tryin' to cloak no ole woman lak Janie Starks, Pheoby, friend or no friend."

"At dat she ain't so ole as some of y'all dat's talking."

"She's way past forty to my knowledge, Pheoby."

"No more'n forty at de outside."

"She's 'way too old for a boy like Tea Cake."

"Tea Cake ain't been no boy for some time. He's round thirty his ownself."

"Don't keer what it was, she could stop and say a few words with us. She act like we done done something to her," Pearl Stone complained. "She de one been doin' wrong."

"You mean, you mad 'cause she didn't stop and tell us all her business. Anyhow, what you ever know her to do so bad as y'all make out? The worst thing Ah ever knowed her to do was taking a few years offa her age and dat ain't never harmed nobody. Y'all makes me tired. De way you talkin' you'd think de folks in dis town didn't do nothin' in de bed 'cept praise de Lawd. You have to 'scuse me, 'cause Ah'm bound to take her some supper." Pheoby stood up sharply.

"Don't mind us," Lulu smiled, "just go right ahead, us can mind yo' house for you till you git back. Mah supper is done. You bettah go see how she feel. You kin let de rest of us know."

"Lawd," Pearl agreed, "Ah done scorched up dat lil meat and bread too long to talk about. Ah kin stay 'way from home long as Ah please. Mah husband ain't fussy."

"Oh, er, Pheoby, if youse ready to go, Ah could walk over dere wid you," Mrs. Sumpkins volunteered. "It's sort of duskin' down dark. De booger man might ketch yuh."

"Naw, Ah thank yuh. Nothin' couldn't ketch me dese few steps Ah'm goin'. Anyhow mah husband tell me say no first class booger would have me. If she got anything to tell yuh, you'll hear it."

Pheoby hurried on off with a covered bowl in her hands. She left the porch pelting her back with unasked questions. They hoped the answers were cruel and strange. When she arrived at the place, Pheoby Watson didn't go in by the front gate and down the palm walk to the front door. She walked around the fence corner and went in the intimate gate with her heaping plate of mulatto rice. Janie must be round that side.

She found her sitting on the steps of the back porch with the lamps all filled and the chimneys cleaned.

"Hello, Janie, how you comin'?"

"Aw, pretty good, Ah'm tryin' to soak some uh de tiredness and de dirt outa mah feet." She laughed a little.

"Ah see you is. Gal, you sho looks *good.* You looks like youse yo' own daughter." They both laughed. "Even wid dem overhalls on, you shows yo' womanhood."

"G'wan! G'wan! You must think Ah brought yuh somethin'. When Ah ain't brought home a thing but mahself."

"Dat's a gracious plenty. Yo' friends wouldn't want nothin' better."

"Ah takes dat flattery offa you, Pheoby, 'cause Ah know it's from de heart." Janie extended her hand. "Good Lawd, Pheoby! ain't you never goin' tuh gimme dat lil rations you brought me? Ah ain't had a thing on mah stomach today exceptin' mah hand." They both laughed easily. "Give it here and have a seat."

"Ah knowed you'd be hongry. No time to be huntin' stove wood after dark. Mah mulatto rice ain't so good dis time. Not enough bacon grease, but Ah reckon it'll kill hongry."

"Ah'll tell you in a minute," Janie said, lifting the cover. "Gal, it's *too* good! you switches a mean fanny round in a kitchen."

"Aw, dat ain't much to eat, Janie. But Ah'm liable to have something sho nuff good tomorrow, 'cause you done come."

Janie ate heartily and said nothing. The varicolored cloud dust that the sun had stirred up in the sky was settling by slow degrees.

"Here, Pheoby, take yo' ole plate. Ah ain't got a bit of use for a empty dish. Dat grub sho come in handy."

Pheoby laughed at her friend's rough joke. "Youse just as crazy as you ever was."

"Hand me dat wash-rag on dat chair by you, honey. Lemme scrub mah feet." She took the cloth and rubbed vigorously. Laughter came to her from the big road.

"Well, Ah see Mouth-Almighty is still sittin' in de same place. And Ah reckon they got *me* up in they mouth now."

"Yes indeed. You know if you pass some people and don't speak tuh suit 'em dey got tuh go way back in yo' life and see whut you ever done. They know mo' 'bout yuh than you do yo' self. An envious heart makes a treacherous ear. They done 'heard' 'bout you just what they hope done happened."

"If God don't think no mo' 'bout 'em then Ah do, they's a lost ball in de high grass.

"Ah hears what they say 'cause they just will collect round mah porch 'cause it's on de big road. Mah husband git so sick of 'em sometime he makes 'em all git for home."

"Sam is right too. They just wearin' out yo' sittin' chairs."

"Yeah, Sam say most of 'em goes to church so they'll be sure to rise in Judgment. Dat's de day dat every secret is s'posed to be made known. They wants to be there and hear it *all.*"

"Sam is *too* crazy! You can't stop laughin' when youse round him."

"Uuh hunh. He says he aims to be there hisself so he can find out who stole his corn-cob pipe."

"Pheoby, dat Sam of your'n just won't quit! Crazy thing!"

"Most of dese zigaboos is so het up over yo' business till they liable to hurry theyself to Judgment to find out about you if they don't soon know. You better make haste and tell 'em 'bout you and Tea Cake gittin' married, and if he taken all yo' money and went off wid some young gal, and where at he is now and where at is all yo' clothes dat you got to come back here in overhalls."

"Ah don't mean to bother wid tellin' 'em nothin', Pheoby. 'Tain't worth de trouble. You can tell 'em what Ah say if you wants to. Dat's just de same as me 'cause mah tongue is in mah friend's mouf."

"If you so desire Ah'll tell 'em what you tell me to tell 'em."

"To start off wid, people like dem wastes up too much time puttin' they mouf on things they don't know nothin' about. Now they got to look into me loving Tea Cake and see whether it was done right or not! They don't know if life is a mess of corn-meal dumplings, and if love is a bed-quilt!"

"So long as they get a name to gnaw on they don't care whose it is, and what about, 'specially if they can make it sound like evil."

"If they wants to see and know, why they don't come kiss and be kissed? Ah could then sit down and tell 'em things. Ah been a delegate to de big 'ssociation of life. Yessuh! De Grand Lodge, de big convention of livin' is just where Ah been dis year and a half y'all ain't seen me."

They sat there in the fresh young darkness close together. Pheoby eager to feel and do through Janie, but hating to show her zest for fear it might be thought mere curiosity. Janie full of that oldest human longing—self revelation. Pheoby held her tongue for a long time, but she couldn't help moving her feet. So Janie spoke.

"They don't need to worry about me and my overhalls long as Ah still got nine hundred dollars in de bank. Tea Cake got me into wearing 'em—following behind him. Tea Cake ain't wasted up no money of mine, and he ain't left me for no young gal, neither. He give me every consolation in de world. He'd tell 'em so too, if he was here. If he wasn't gone."

Pheoby dilated all over with eagerness, "Tea Cake gone?"

"Yeah, Pheoby, Tea Cake is gone. And dat's de only reason you see me back here—cause Ah ain't got nothing to make me happy no more where Ah was at Down in the Everglades there, down on the muck."

"It's hard for me to understand what you mean, de way you tell it. And then again Ah'm hard of understandin' at times."

"Naw, 'tain't nothin' lak you might think. So 'tain't no use in me telling you somethin' unless Ah give you de understandin' to go 'long wid it. Unless you see de fur, a mink skin ain't no different from a coon hide. Looka heah, Pheoby, is Sam waitin' on you for his supper?"

"It's all ready and waitin'. If he ain't got sense enough to eat it, dat's his hard luck."

"Well then, we can set right where we is and talk. Ah got the house all opened up to let dis breeze get a little catchin'.

"Pheoby, we been kissin'-friends for twenty years, so Ah depend on you for a good thought. And Ah'm talking to you from dat standpoint."

Time makes everything old so the kissing, young darkness became a monstropolous old thing while Janie talked.

35

ALAIN LOCKE

The Negro: "New" or Newer?

1939

In this article from Opportunity *magazine, Alain Locke explains why he regards the new literary generation of the 1930s as "newer" rather than "new"—as a child of the Harlem Renaissance rather than a revolutionary departure. Thus, he offers a vision of continuity to oppose the view of Richard Wright in "Blueprint for Negro Writing" (see Document 33) and others who believed that emerging generation of writers in the 1930s had made a radical break with the past.*

It is now fifteen years, nearly a half a generation, since the literary advent of the "New Negro." In such an interval a new generation of creative talent should have come to the fore and presumably those talents who in 1924–25 were young and new should today be approaching maturity or have arrived at it. Normally too, at the rate of contemporary cultural advance, a new ideology with a changed world outlook and social orientation should have evolved. And the question back of all this needs to be raised, has it so developed or hasn't it, and do we confront today on the cultural front another Negro, either a newer Negro or a maturer "New Negro"?

A critic's business is not solely with the single file reviewing-stand view of endless squads of books in momentary dress parade but with the route and leadership of cultural advance, in short, with the march of ideas. There is no doubt in the panoramic retrospect of the years 1924 to 1938 about certain positive achievements:—a wider range of Negro self-expression in more of the arts, an increasing maturity and objectivity of approach on the part of the Negro artist to his subject-matter, a greater diversity of styles and artistic creeds, a healthier and firmer trend toward self-criticism, and perhaps most important of all, a deepening channel toward the mainstream of American literature and art as white and Negro artists share in ever-increasing collaboration

---

Alain Locke, "The Negro: 'New' or Newer?", *Opportunity*, 17 (January 1939): 4–6.

the growing interest in Negro life and subject-matter. These are encouraging and praiseworthy gains, all of which were confidently predicted under the convenient but dangerous caption of "The New Negro."

But a caption's convenience is part of its danger; so is its brevity. In addition, in the case in question, there was inevitable indefiniteness as to what was meant by the "New Negro." Just that question must be answered, however, before we can judge whether today's Negro represents a matured phase of the movement of the 20's, or is, as many of the youngest Negroes think and contend, a counter-movement, for which incidentally they have a feeling but no name. These "bright young people" to the contrary, it is my conviction that the former is true and that the "New Negro" movement is just coming into its own after a frothy adolescence and a first-generation course which was more like a careen than a career. Using the nautical figure to drive home the metaphor, we may say that there was at first too little ballast in the boat for the heavy head of sail that was set. Moreover, the talents of that period (and some of them still) were far from skillful mariners; artistically and sociologically they sailed many a crooked course, mistaking their directions for the lack of steadying common-sense and true group loyalty as a compass. But all that was inevitable in part; and was, as we shall later see, anticipated and predicted.

But the primary source of confusion perhaps was due to a deliberate decision not to define the "New Negro" dogmatically, but only to characterize his general traits and attitudes. And so, partly because of this indefiniteness, the phrase became a slogan for cheap race demagogues who wouldn't know a "cultural movement" if they could see one, a handy megaphone for petty exhibitionists who were only posing as "racialists" when in fact they were the rankest kind of egotists, and a gilded fetish for race idolaters who at heart were still sentimentalists seeking consolation for inferiority. But even as it was, certain greater evils were avoided—a growing race consciousness was not cramped down to a formula, and a movement with a popular ground swell and a folk significance was not tied to a partisan art creed or any one phase of culture politics.

The most deliberate aspect of the New Negro formulation—and it is to be hoped, its crowning wisdom—was just this repudiation of any and all one-formula solutions of the race question, (its own immediate emphases included), and the proposed substitution of a solidarity of group feeling for unity within a variety of artistic creeds and social programs. To quote: "The Negro today wishes to be known for what he is, even in his faults and shortcomings, and scorns a craven and precarious survival at the price of seeming to be what he is not. He thus resents being spoken of as a social ward or minor, even by his own, and to being regarded a chronic patient for the sociological clinic, the sick man of American Democracy. For the same reasons, *he himself is through with those social nostrums and panaceas, the so-called 'solutions' of his 'problem', with which he and the country have been so liberally dosed in the past. Religion, freedom, education, money—in turn he has ardently hoped for and peculiarly trusted these things; he still believes in them, but not in blind trust that they alone will solve his life-problem.*"

How then even the *enfants terribles* of today's youth movement could see "cultural expression" as a substitute formula proposed by the "New Negro" credo I cannot understand, except on the ground that they did not read carefully what had been carefully written. Nor would a careful reading have been auspicious for their own one-formula diagnosis of "economic exploitation" and solution by "class action." Not only was there no foolish illusion that "racial prejudice would soon disappear before the altars of truth, art and intellectual achievement," as has been asserted, but a philosophy of cultural isolation from the folk ("masses") and of cultural separatism were expressly repudiated. It was the bright young talents of the 20's who themselves went cosmopolite when they were advised to go racial, who went exhibitionist instead of going documentarian, who got jazz-mad and cabaret-crazy instead of getting folk-wise and sociologically sober. Lest this, too, seem sheer rationalizing hind-sight, let a few direct quotations from *The New Negro* testify to the contrary. Even more, the same excerpts will show that a social Reformation was called for as the sequel and proper goal of a cultural Renaissance, and that the present trends of second generation "New Negro" literature which we are now passing in review were predicted and reasonably anticipated. For reasons of space, quotations must be broken and for reasons of emphasis, some are italicized:

> . . . This cannot be—even if it were desirable. The racialism of the Negro is no limitation or reservation with respect to American life; it is only a constructive effort to build the obstructions in the stream of his progress into an efficient dam of social energy and power. Democracy itself is obstructed and stagnated to the extent that any of its channels are closed. Indeed they cannot be selectively closed. So the choice is not between one way for the Negro and another for the rest, but between American institutions frustrated on the one

hand and American ideals progressively fulfilled and realized on the other." (p. 12).[1]

The generation of the late 30's is nearer such a cultural course and closer to such social insight than the tangential generation of the late 20's. Artistic exploitation is just as possible from the inside as from the outside, and if our writers and artists are becoming sounder in their conception of the social role of themselves and their art, as indeed they are, it is all the more welcome after considerable delay and error. If, also, they no longer see cultural racialism as cultural separatism, which it never was or was meant to be, then, too, an illusory dilemma has lost its paralyzing spell. And so, we have only to march forward instead of to counter-march; only to broaden the phalanx and flatten out the opposition salients that threaten divided ranks. Today we pivot on a sociological front with our novelists, dramatists and social analysts in deployed formation. But for vision and morale we have to thank the spiritual surge and aesthetic inspiration of the first generation artists of the renaissance decade.

[1]Alain Locke, *The New Negro*, ed. Alain Locke (New York: Albert and Charles Boni, 1925), 12.

A Brief Chronology of the Harlem Renaissance (1914–1939)

1914 World War I begins in Europe.

1915 The first wave of black migration from the South to the North begins. Booker T. Washington dies.

1916 Marcus Garvey founds the Universal Negro Improvement Association.

1917 East St. Louis riot and the "Silent March" mark a new era of racial violence and protest. Claude McKay publishes "The Harlem Dancer."

1918 The 369th Regiment receives the Croix de Guerre. World War I ends. W. E. B. Du Bois publishes "Returning Soldiers."

1919 Race riots across the United States collectively referred to as the "Red Summer." Claude McKay publishes "If We Must Die." Prohibition Amendment Pacified.

1920 In "Red Scare," Attorney General A. Mitchell Palmer arrests suspected communist sympathizers. Marcus Garvey holds the First International Convention of the Negro Peoples of the World in Madison Square Garden.

1921 Flournoy Miller and Aubrey Lyles's *Shuffle Along* opens on Broadway to record audiences.

1922 Claude McKay publishes the poetry collection *Harlem Shadows.* James Weldon Johnson publishes *The Book of American Negro Poetry* (republished in an expanded edition in 1931).

1923 Jean Toomer publishes *Cane.*

1924 Jessie Fauset publishes *There Is Confusion.* The Civic Club dinner brings together major artists and publishers.

1925 Special Harlem issue of *The Survey Graphic* appears, edited by Alain Locke. Countée Cullen publishes *Color.* Alain Locke edits *The New Negro.*

1926 Langston Hughes publishes *The Weary Blues*. George S. Schuyler publishes "The Negro-Art Hokum." Langston Hughes publishes "The Negro Artist and the Racial Mountain." Carl Van Vechten publishes *Nigger Heaven*. Wallace Thurman edits the first and only edition of the journal *Fire!!* W. E. B. Du Bois publishes "Criteria of Negro Art."

1927 Langston Hughes publishes the poetry collection *Fine Clothes to the Jew*. Countée Cullen publishes the poetry collections *Copper Sun* and *Ballad of a Brown Girl* and his edited collection *Caroling Dusk*. Marcus Garvey is deported.

1928 Nella Larsen publishes the novel *Quicksand*. Claude McKay publishes the novel *Home to Harlem*. Alan Locke publishes "Art or Propaganda" in the first and only issue of the journal *Harlem*.

1929 Jessie Fauset publishes the novel *Plum Bun*. Nella Larsen publishes the novel *Passing*. The stock market crash begins the Great Depression.

1930 James Weldon Johnson publishes the social history *Black Manhattan*.

1932 Sterling Brown publishes the poetry collection *Southern Road*.

1934 Dorothy West starts the journal *Challenge*. Wallace Thurman and Rudolph Fisher die. Zora Neale Hurston publishes *Mules and Men*.

1935 The Harlem Riot signals a new kind of black anger precipitated by the Depression.

1937 Dorothy West's journal *Challenge* becomes *New Challenge* and Richard Wright joins West as co-editor. Claude McKay publishes *A Long Way from Home*. Richard Wright publishes "Blueprint for Negro Writing" in the second and last issue of *New Challenge*. Zora Neale Hurston publishes *Their Eyes Were Watching God*.

1939 Alain Locke publishes "The Negro: 'New' or Newer," in *Opportunity*.

Questions for Consideration

1. What was the Harlem Renaissance? What relationship does it have to larger conceptions of the American experience?
2. What role did the black migration to the North play in shaping the racial politics of the World War I era?
3. How many conceptions of the New Negro can you identify? Who were their chief exponents? How did the concept change from the beginning to the end of the Harlem Renaissance?
4. Compare Jean Toomer's artistic approach to depicting the language of rural black folk to that of Zora Neale Hurston? To that of Sterling Brown? Why did these artists find folk culture valuable?
5. What was the significance of Africa both as a place and as an idea in the Harlem Renaissance?
6. What attracted Harlem Renaissance artists to Europe?
7. What role did gender play in the Harlem Renaissance?
8. Did white patrons of black art play a positive role in the Harlem Renaissance? Explain.
9. What influence did jazz and the blues have on the literature of the Harlem Renaissance? How do you see its role in Langston Hughes's poetry, in particular?
10. How does the theme of "passing" in Nella Larsen's *Passing* and Jessie Fauset's *Plum Bun* reveal the contradictions inherent in American racial standards? Do you see these contradictions reflected in any of the other works in this volume? If so, how?
11. Claude McKay, Wallace Thurman, Richard Bruce Nugent, and Carl Van Vechten each supported in his own way the frank and realistic representation of black life in literature, even when this involved the depiction of black underworld figures such as pimps, prostitutes, and gamblers. Others, such as W. E. B. Du Bois, regarded such representations as cheap and exploitative. Which side had the better case in this dispute? Why?

12. Judging from the selections from his work in this volume, how would you describe Alain Locke's viewpoint on the significance of black art? What do you think he would say about George Schuyler's "The Negro-Art Hokum"? About Langston Hughes's "The Negro Artist and the Racial Mountain"?
13. Compare Richard Wright's position in "Blueprint for Negro Writing" to that of W. E. B. Du Bois's in "Criteria of Negro Art." Do you see any similarities with Wallace Thurman's attempt at realistic portrayal of black lower-class life in *Fire!!*?
14. In "The Negro: 'New' or Newer?" Alain Locke argues for a strong social conscience in the literature of the Harlem Renaissance. What evidence can you find to support his view?
15. Choose a poem, an illustration, or a story that you love from this volume. Why does it move you? In comparison to other works of the Harlem Renaissance, how do you understand its significance?

Selected Bibliography

Anderson, Paul Allen. *Deep River: Music and Memory in Harlem Renaissance Thought*. Durham, N.C.: Duke University Press, 2001.

Douglas, Ann. *Terrible Honesty: Mongrel Manhattan in the 1920s*. New York: Farrar, Straus and Giroux, 1995.

Edwards, Brent Hayes. *The Practice of Diaspora: Literature, Translation, and the Rise of Black Internationalism*. Cambridge, Mass.: Harvard University Press, 2003.

Huggins, Nathan Irvin. *Harlem Renaissance*. New York: Oxford University Press, 1971.

Hull, Gloria T. *Color, Sex, and Poetry: Three Women Writers of the Harlem Renaissance*. Bloomington: Indiana University Press, 1987.

Hutchinson, George. *The Harlem Renaissance in Black and White*. Cambridge, Mass.: Harvard University Press, 1995.

Krasner, David. *A Beautiful Pageant: African American Theatre, Drama, and Performance in the Harlem Renaissance, 1910–1927*. New York: Palgrave Macmillan, 2002.

Lewis, David Levering. *When Harlem Was in Vogue*. New York: Oxford University Press, 1989.

Nadel, Martha Jane. *Enter the New Negroes: Images of Race in American Culture*. Cambridge, Mass.: Harvard University Press, 2004.

Schwartz, A. B. Christa. *Gay Voices of the Harlem Renaissance*. Bloomington: Indiana University Press, 2003.

Singh, Amritjit. *The Novels of the Harlem Renaissance: Twelve Black Writers, 1923–1933*. University Park: University of Pennsylvania Press, 1976.

Spencer, Jon Michael. *The New Negroes and Their Music: The Success of the Harlem Renaissance*. Knoxville: The University of Tennessee Press, 1997.

Wall, Cheryl A. *Women of the Harlem Renaissance*. Bloomington: Indiana University Press, 1995.

Watson, Steven. *The Harlem Renaissance: Hub of African-American Culture, 1920–1930*. New York: Pantheon, 1995.

Wintz, Cary D., ed. *The Harlem Renaissance, 1920–1940*. 7 vols. New York: Garland Publishing, 1996.

Acknowledgments (continued from p. iv)

Document 1: Courtesy of the Crisis Publishing Co., Inc., the publisher of the magazine of the National Association for the Advancement of Colored People, for the use of this material first published in the May 1919 issue of *The Crisis.*

Document 2: From the Asa Philip Randolph Institute.

Document 3: Reprinted with the permission of Scribner, an imprint of Simon & Schuster Adult Publishing Group, from *The Philosophy and Opinions of Marcus Garvey* by Amy Jacques-Garvey. Copyright © 1923, 1925 by Amy Jacques-Garvey. All rights reserved.

Document 4: Excerpt from *Black Manhattan* is reprinted here by permission of Dr. Sondra Kathryn Wilson, literary executor of the Estate of Grace and James Weldon Johnson.

Document 6: Courtesy of the Library Representative for the Works of Claude McKay, Schomburg Center for Research in Black Culture, The New York Public Library, Astor, Lenox and Tilden Foundations.

Document 7: "Becky," "Karintha," "Reapers," "November Cotton Flower," from *Cane* by Jean Toomer. Copyright 1923 by Boni & Liveright, renewed 1951 by Jean Toomer. Used by permission of Liveright Publishing Corporation.

Document 8: Reprinted by permission of GRM Associates, Agents of the Estate of Countée Cullen. "To John Keats, Poet, at Spring Time" © 1925 from *Color* by Countée Cullen, © 1925. "Yet I Do Marvel" © 1924 from *Color* by Countée Cullen, © 1925. "From the Dark Tower" © 1924 from *Copper Sun*, by Countée Cullen, © 1927. "Harlem Wine" © 1925 from *Copper Sun* by Countée Cullen, © 1927.

Document 9: "The Negro Speaks of Rivers," copyright © 1994 by The Estate of Langston Hughes, "The Weary Blues," copyright © 1994 by The Estate of Langston Hughes, "Dream Variations," copyright © 1994 by The Estate of Langston Hughes, "Harlem Night Club," edited by Arnold Rampersad with David Roessel, Associate Editor, "I, Too," from *The Collected Poems of Langston Hughes* by Langston Hughes, edited with David Roessel, Associate Editor, copyright © 1994 by The Estate of Langston Hughes. Used by the permission of Alfred A. Knopf, a division of Random House, Inc.

Document 10: Courtesy of the Library Representative for the Works of Gwendolyn B. Bennett, Schomburg Center for Research in Black Culture, The New York Public Library, Astor, Lenox and Tilden Foundations.

Document 11: The Alain Locke Papers, Moorland-Spingarn Research Center, Howard University.

Document 12: Reprinted with the permission of Scribner, an imprint of Simon & Schuster Adult Publishing Group, from *The New Negro* by Alain Locke. Copyright © 1925 by The Macmillan Company. All rights reserved.

Document 13: Courtesy of the Library Representative for the Works of Claude McKay, Schomburg Center for Research in Black Culture, The New York Public Library, Astor, Lenox and Tilden Foundations.

Document 14: "Song for a Dark Girl," "Jazz Band in a Parisian Cabaret," from *The Collected Poems of Langston Hughes* by Langston Hughes, edited with David Roessel, Associate Editor, copyright © 1994 by The Estate of Langston Hughes. Used by the permission of Alfred A. Knopf, a division of Random House, Inc.

Document 15: Reprinted by permission of GRM Associates, Agents of the Estate of Countée Cullen. "Heritage" © 1925 from *Color* by Countée Cullen, © 1925.

Document 16: Courtesy of the Library Representative for the Works of Gwendolyn B. Bennett, Schomburg Center for Research in Black Culture, The New York Public Library, Astor, Lenox and Tilden Foundations.

Document 18: Reprinted by permission of HarperCollins Publishers.

Document 19: All lines from "Southern Road" from *The Collected Poems of Sterling A. Brown*, edited by Michael S. Harper. Copyright 1932 by Harcourt, Brace, & Co.; renewed © 1960 by Sterling A. Brown. Originally appeared in *Southern Road.* Reprinted by permission of HarperCollins Publishers. All lines from "Odyssey of Big Boy" from *The Collected Poems of Sterling A. Brown*, edited by Michael S. Harper. Copyright © 1980 by Sterling A. Brown. This poem originally appeared in *Southern Road* by Sterling A. Brown. Copyright 1932 by Harcourt, Brace, & Co. Copyright renewed by 1960 by Sterling Brown. Reprinted by permission of HarperCollins Publishers. All lines from "Ma Rainey" from *The Collected Poems of Sterling A. Brown*, edited by Michael S. Harper. Copyright 1932 by Harcourt, Brace, & Co. Copyright renewed by 1960 by Sterling A. Brown. Reprinted by permission of HarperCollins Publishers. All lines from "Strong Men" from *The Collected Poems of Sterling A. Brown*, edited by Michael S. Harper. Copyright 1932 by Harcourt, Brace, & Co.; renewed © 1960 by Sterling A. Brown. Originally appeared in *Southern Road.* Reprinted by permission of HarperCollins Publishers.

Document 20: "See, See Rider" by Ma Rainey © 1943, renewed 1971 by Leeds Music Corp. All rights administered by Universal Music Corp./ASCAP. Used by permission. All rights reserved.

Document 21: "Young Woman's Blues," by Bessie Smith. © 1927 (Renewed), 1974 Frank Music Corp. All Rights Reserved.

Document 27: J. Lee Greene, *Time's Unfading Garden: Anne Spencer's Life and Poetry.* Baton Rouge: LSU Press, 1976.

Document 28: "The Negro-Art Hokum," by George Schuyler. Reprinted with permission from the June 23, 2006, issue of *The Nation*. For subscription information, call 1-800-333-8536. Portions of each week's *Nation* magazine can be accessed at www.thenation.com.

Document 29: "The Negro Artist and the Racial Mountain," by Langston Hughes. Reprinted with permission from the June 23, 2006, issue of *The Nation.* For subscription information, call 1-800-333-8536. Portions of each week's *Nation* magazine can be accessed at www.thenation.com.

Document 31: Courtesy of the Crisis Publishing Co., Inc., the publisher of the magazine of the National Association for the Advancement of Colored People, for the use of this material first published in the October 1926 issue of *The Crisis.*

Document 32: The Alain Locke Papers, Moorland-Spingarn Research Center, Howard University.

Document 33: Copyright © 1934 Richard Wright. Reprinted by permission of John Hawkins & Associates, Inc.

Document 34: Reprinted by permission of HarperCollins Publishers.

Document 35: The Alain Locke Papers, Moorland-Spingarn Research Center, Howard University.

Index